Illinois

Indiana

★ CINCINNATI

THE OHIO RIVER

THE WABASH RIVER

Vevay
Warsaw
L & D
Markland
L & D

McAlpin
L & D

Rocky Point

★ LOUISVILLE

Mount Vernon
Evansville
Rockport
John T. Myers L & D
Cincinnati Island
Cannelton
L & D
Newburgh L & D
Henderson

Kentucky

Golconda
Smithland L & D

The Leap

Barkley L & D
Green Turtle Bay
Grand
Rivers
Kentucky
L & D ←   ← Murray

THE CUMBERLAND RIVER

Paris
Paris Landing
Cambden
★ NASHVILLE

Cuba Landing
Clifton
Tennessee

Savannah
Aqua Yacht Harbor → ← Pickwick Landing L & D

Mississippi River

ly & Debbie's Transport
★ IUKA

THE TENNESSEE RIVER

THE TOMBIGBEE RIVER

Mississippi   Alabama

RIVER
QUEENS

To Peter
With great thanksgiving &

RIVER
QUEENS

Appreciation for his kind

Saucy boat, stout mates,
spotted dog, America

Hospitality

A. Watson

ALEXANDER WATSON

ORANGE *frazer* PRESS
Wilmington, Ohio

Published for the author by:
Orange Frazer Press
P.O. Box 214
Wilmington, OH 45177
Telephone: 937.382.3196 for price
and shipping information.
Website: www.orangefrazer.com

Front cover photograph from original silver gelatin print by Jody Crown.
Back cover photograph courtesy of Rhoda Carpenter.

Book and cover design: Alyson Rua and Orange Frazer Press

Library of Congress Control Number: 2018948763

First Printing

To Mary Anne Sanders who sat me down in Penny Hoskin's kitchen and said, "You must write."

Found screwed to the deckhouse bulkhead aboard the *King and I*: "Amended Collision Rules: When in Danger or in Doubt; Run in Circles, Scream, and Shout."

ACKNOWLEDGMENTS

Rochelle Melander drew breath and answered patiently when I asked, "What's a platform?" She has lit the way ever since. Friends steadfastly asked, "How's the book?" Harrison Watson and Barbara Kuether waded fiercely into first drafts and managed, by some miracle, to say something encouraging. John Baskin, my editor, taught me how to write, the first lesson being: "You write a line. Then another. And the two have to have something to do with each other." The talent at Orange Frazer Press—Alyson, Sarah, and Marcy—turned my stammering and flailing into a finished book. Doris Faye, Dale Harris, and the people along the river.

CONTENTS

FOREWORD
by Melissa Fay Greene

I cannot figure out why a book about two middle-aged white guys in the antiques-and-renovations business in Dallas, who find a decrepit sixty-year-old wooden yacht on the verge of sinking to the bottom of a Texas lake, pay good money for her, name her *Betty Jane*, restore her, move aboard with their rescue Dalmatian, and then putter off across the middle of the United States from Oklahoma to Ohio without really knowing what they're doing is keeping me up nights.

I think it's because Alexander Watson captures people's natures and voices like little kids catch and trap fireflies at the shore before *Betty Jane*'s big launch. Because Dale says to his disconcerted mother, who'd naturally hoped he'd find a blue-blooded woman to marry: "Mama, home is where Alexander is." Because the river folks they meet, trying to make out the situation, offer jokes like, "You got the ugliest wife I ever saw." And because one guy sums them up: "God, what it must be like to be y'all. I mean, being like y'all an' going' deep into country full of men like me... An' what for?... Cuz yer stupid? No, y'all've answered the river's call. Takes guts."

Alexander and Dale, tracing the Arkansas, Tennessee, and Ohio Rivers, show up with their boat at docks and yacht clubs and let strangers size them up. "Most had never met a homosexual before," Alexander writes. "Certainly not two together." Soon the strangers' eyes flit to the beautiful boat, restored by craftsmen, and the differences vanish.

Of course river-lovers, boat-lovers, restoration-lovers, houseboat-dwellers, and Mark Twain fans must have this book. Other than loving *Life on the Mississippi*, I don't have much in common with it myself. But I love it. I can't put it down.

—MELISSA FAY GREENE, author of *Praying for Sheetrock, The Temple Bombing* and other books, as well as two-time finalist for the National Book Award

PREFACE
The Start of Something Big

S he arrived at her usual hour, shortly after six, in a blast
of cold air and a flurry of peasant skirt, paisley shawl,
bangles and beads and always that topaz ring which some
man from South America had given her. She never would
quite say. Her make-up was stale, her hair disheveled. Habit
sent Mother directly to her boudoir to freshen up after work.
It was her time to unwind with a drink and a cigarette before
starting dinner. But that night, she fell into the reproduction
Louis Seize chair, the only dining chairs I ever knew, the only
one she ever sat in, and waited.

"Your brother, John, has shot himself with his grandfather's pearl-handled pistol," she said when, finally, I looked
up from my book. "He is dead."

Grief crushed her antique tortoise shell glasses in a
clenched fist. Blood dripped onto the period Aubusson carpet, unusual in its design of solitary primrose blossoms regu-
larly spotted on a light brown field.

I was fifteen years old.

I finished high school, went away to college, and returned
to take up the family business—a manufacturers' representative agency that supplied the finest antiques and antique

reproduction furniture to clients for whom cost was not a factor. In those thirteen years which separated my brother's funeral from my mother's death, I learned that my family expected great things of me, would not tell me what they were, and if my brother's suicide were any example, would not forgive disappointment. His name was never spoken again. Consequently, I always bet the long shot. The first was Mother's business itself.

I sat alone at one end of the table. Huddled together at the other were Mother's accountant, Mother's lawyer, and Mother's financial planner. Bellies—the province of successful careers, happy marriages, and remarkable offspring—folded over their belts; Mont Blanc pens peeked from behind their designer lapels; and entourages, with briefcases and satchels ready, stood at their beck and call.

"There's nothing here," the lawyer said, a twinkle of gloat in his eye. "Beach it."

My inheritance was bankrupt, ravaged of all assets, all future profits already pledged to leverage an insupportable lifestyle of glamour and alcohol. Mother's vibrant élan had been the stock-in-trade that kept creditors at bay. In death, her debts became immediately due and payable.

I was twenty-eight.

Fortunately, I had nothing to lose, record-keeping was not a strength of the artistic temperament, and my domestic partner of three years, Dale Harris, knew how to read a balance sheet. We recovered Mother's legacy only to sell it. It had become a prison, its glass doors no less infuriating than steel bars and razor wire.

I was thirty-two.

My suits hung limp in the closet, my polished shoes collected dust under the bed while I, in overalls and straw hat, rode around in an unairconditioned pickup named Buttercup; it had been yellow once, the itinerant shop of an undocumented laborer. The sides were torn, the tailgate ill-fitting, the truck box securely welded in against thievery. An iron headboard served as a headache rack and a rescued Dalmatian dog, Doris Faye, watched over my tools. I was a handyman, repairing everything from crack houses to high-rise condominiums in Dallas's Oak Lawn, a predominately gay subdivision in transition from sodomic depravity to posh gentrification.

"Is this what you intend to do with your life?" Grandmother asked in disgust.

I was thirty-five.

Eventually, Dale and I invested in a rental of our own. It was a duplex on a busy thoroughfare. The brick veneer was falling off, the garage was falling down, the upstairs was vacant, the downstairs renter did not pay, and our offer—one third below asking price—was rejected out of hand. Two weeks later, the realtor called to say, "You pay all closing costs and it is yours." A ten percent down payment—dimes, nickels, and pennies, mostly—financed a mortgage that paid all fees, commissions, and put the cost of a new roof in escrow. We were landlords by five p. m. when the air conditioning blew up.

Subsequent property purchases plumbed the depths of sound judgement until Dale, at one point, threw up his hands in surrender and said, "It's your money." They were two frame and clapboarded houses side-by-side on a corner, leaning in opposite directions with derelict cars parked under a dead hackberry tree in the front yard. Charity alone qualified their apartments as squalor.

The sweat of our brow and miserly cash transformed the two into our signature addresses, neighborhood landmarks. Deeply tanned real estate agents in open cars called to their clients, riding stony-faced in the back seat, "*A dollar!* Those boys bought those houses for *a dollar!*" Then all the deals were done, all the renovations complete, and all vacancies filled as developers razed properties like ours, replacing them one-by-one with cheek-by-jowl, zero-lot line, vertical town-homes that featured stainless steel appliances, granite coun-tertops, off-street covered parking, and balconied views of the next door neighbor's daily routine.

I was forty.

The winter sun pressed low and orange on the horizon. Dale and I had come out of a forgettable movie that left our appetite for escapism unsatisfied. I suggested we go to the 2001 Dallas Winter Boat Show, an attraction for its novelty. Neither of us had ever been to a boat show, nor did we know anything about boats. We talked it over, Dale and I, back and forth across the cab, without conviction, in a moment indis-tinguishable from all others, and completely unaware that we were discussing a bet—of all that we would have on a thing we did not yet know existed.

And there, in such an unassuming moment, our life together would change more radically than we could have ever imagined.

RIVER
QUEENS

CHAPTER ONE
Upon a Winter's Night

D ale and I must choose. Foul weather moving across the Texas plain between Fort Worth and Wichita Falls, faster, more severe than predicted, blows away a warm, sunny morning. Temperatures plummet, the sky darkens, and rain begins to freeze. One hundred miles south are the safety and warmth of our Dallas apartment. Equidistant to the north are the brunt of the storm, Lake Texoma, and a boat.

We are not boaters. We are landlords, out here on other business and decided upon an excursion, a side trip, to the Texas-Oklahoma border in order to satisfy a curiosity. What we know comes from a photograph, pinned to a for-sale board at the 2001 Dallas Winter Boat Show and captioned, "1955. Chris-Craft. Connie. 45 feet. $30K." What we believe is that somewhere in that fuzzy image is something we've never seen before. Even so, we are not buying a boat. We've called several times along icing farm-to-market roads to cancel our appointment, but the man who is to meet us insists, "No, no. Long as you're on your way you might as well c'mon. I'll be waiting."

We arrive at a marina abandoned except for a small incandescent glow in the window of the clubhouse. It is a hulking structure, a throw-back from headier days: twin gazebos perfectly at home on the Texas Gulf coast but garishly out of place, overstated, and grotesque these nearly four hundred miles inland. Nonetheless, it was the jewel in Lake Texoma's crown property, Loe's Highport. Politicians, athletes, and rock stars mixed and mingled beneath sweeping verandas which overlook the harbor. That was before.

"The federal government could convict a ham sandwich if it wanted to," the scion, DeWitte Loe, junior, insisted shortly after serving his time.

Now, the marina is just Highport, in receivership and waiting for a buyer, like a certain boat moored its harbor.

Our tap on the door calls a man from the recess of offices. His figure fractures and reassembles in the facets of a leaded glass entry beneath a huge brass chandelier. He steps out on the veranda, clasps the thin lapels of his brown pinstripe suit across his chest with one hand and awkwardly extends the other. He introduces himself as Joe McBride, head of accounts. He is middle-aged, bookish, shy, uncomfortable around strangers—the man left to watch over the place while everyone else staffs the Dallas show. "Hellava day to be looking at boats," he says, leading us over to a marina vehicle.

Joe keeps the truck from sliding off the sleet-slick blacktop while engaging Dale, seated in the front, with inquiries about Dale's church music, my remodeling business, and our combined investment in real estate. My mood sours. I wonder if we are not wasting everyone's time. Boathouse after boathouse, little more than corrugated roofs reaching across black water, pass by my window as we weave in and out on a shoreline road. Suddenly, the truck stops, seemingly in the middle of nowhere, and Joe says, "Well, here we are."

———— ◆ ————

I wipe the breath condensed on my window with a sleeve and look out. I see nothing. Standing in the congealed rain, I see nothing. At the bottom of the cliff is a boathouse so old, badly repaired and extended that it writhes and crinkles on the surface like a withered leaf. It is not open on four sides like the others. It is almost fully enclosed and covered with rust. Doors, like a paddock, open onto a cantilevered catwalk that flexes and groans with our stride, dipping perilously close to the surface if we stand too close together. Joe fumbles with keys, icy drip off the roof runs down my neck, and the voice of my late mother quashes my budding rebellion.

Hush. Hush. Hush, I hear her say.

She always recognized my habit of clenching my teeth before saying something uncharitable.

This man has waited all day to show you this boat. At least, you owe him the courtesy to look it. You might even be grateful. At the very least.

Divorced with three boys to raise, Mother pioneered a furniture showroom of eighteenth-century French style to a Dallas market stuck in Sheraton and Duncan Phyfe. She cultivated a reputation for the finest antique and reproduction pieces at the most extravagant prices. *That is,* she would say to the sticker-shocked consumer, *if craftsmanship matters at all.*

She taught me about fine furniture and fine finishes, detail, and sacrificing good judgment for the sake of art. The rescue of her showroom, her legacy, from bankruptcy was Dale's and my first shared project.

Joe fails to find the correct key, so we backtrack, trying each door along the way until one opens—not all tenants are careful about security. We duck in and discover where the harbingers of summer fun come to die. These former pride-and-joys of young, active, successful owners who once held life by a string are now reminders that grandpa is not as much fun as teen-aged boys and that mother does not get around as well as she used to. Parents try to keep up the old routines after the children are gone, but out of sight and forgotten, these boats slowly, almost imperceptibly sink. They are our first impressions of boating.

Joe takes out his pad and jots down rules violations—leaking batteries, improper fuel storage, and gear gone to varmint and vermin. Dale and I hurdle debris left behind. When we arrive at the next-to-last slip and stand upright to catch our breath, our eyes catch the first glimpse of *The King and I*. The boat-like shape buried in the grainy photo becomes real. I hear Mother again: *True beauty, the kind that comes from men and women applying lifetimes of experience and practice to create for the comfort and enjoyment of others, must be preserved in order to honor the Creator.*

It was her exhortation to some oil-rich nobody to look at the purchase of an antique Bessarabian carpet or authentic Chippendale four-poster bed as a civic duty rather than a selfish indulgence.

Don't you think so?

The rise of the prow out of the water, the arc, the grace as it comes up to form the dolphin nose—Chris-Craft's signature 1950s detail—draws us as if bewitched. We take in the oval windows, the bullnosed edges, and the backwards-canted stern. A boat like this comes charging out of the Kennedy compound at Hyannisport, not floating in some forgotten boathouse in Texas.

If not, it is lost forever, right? We'd be nothing but marauders, Mother always said, absently adjusting a floral arrangement or delicately picking a stray tobacco leaf off the tip of her tongue. She would then excuse herself from the sales floor to leave the decorator and client alone to decide if the price of acquisition were worth denying a beloved child its college education.

Joe catches up.

"This boat floats real good right here in this slip," he says, before stepping inside, turning on a light, and inviting us in. "There are two deep steps. And watch your head."

The tiniest hint of Jean Patou's *Joy* perfume, Mother's scent, pushes through the nearly overpowering stench of mold and cigarettes closed up for over two years.

"Now this here is the deckhouse, also called the salon or saloon, whichever," Joe says. "And we're standing over the engine room."

He reaches down to lift one of three hatches embedded in the floor and reveals a spaghetti of wires that bars any investigation of the engine room below.

"It's too dark to see anything, anyway," Dale says. "But there are the mains."

"Chevy 350s, I suspect," Joe says.

"And the oldest generator I've ever seen."

Three steps down and forward is the galley/dinette. Crew's quarters are in the bow. Three steps down and aft is the stateroom; embroidered linens and duvets matching the curtains make up twin beds separated by a passage to the stern. The *en suite* is behind a mirrored door. Makeup, neatly laid on the counter, implies that Mrs. has just stepped away.

"Perky King—she's the widow and the seller and all," Joe explains, "well, when John King—that's her husband— died, she lost all interest in boating. They were regulars down here. Been part of the marina since John and DeWitte, junior, used to jump off the roof of this very boathouse when they was kids.

"Anyway," he says as we peer into closets and peek into drawers. "Perky got osteoporosis and was too frail to get on board any more, John figured that down here he could drink and smoke all he wanted to. He had heart disease and emphysema, I think. He'd take this boat out on the lake and go back home, stinking of booze and cigarettes. That stuff there killed John King." Joe points to the half-empty bottle of bourbon and the overfull ashtray stuck to the dinette table by spilled Coke. "But Perky blames the boat."

He turns off the lights and closes the hatches that Dale and I have carelessly left on and open. We gawk at polished mahogany frames around windows blacked out by night. Every edge is rounded off. Every joint is flush and smooth with care taken to match the grain wherever possible.

"It's like my uncles' farms in Wisconsin," Dale whispers. "They still use the barns their great-grandfathers built with nothing more than mortises, tenons, and pegs."

"It's the biggest chest of drawers I've ever seen," I say.

"Yep, she's a classic," Joe says. "Don't go real fast, though."

We drive back to the clubhouse wondering what we have just seen. It is not the assembly of ready-cast fiberglass components we saw at the boat show. It is a suite of rooms filled with custom furnishings, every piece purposely designed for its use. Tables have lips, doors have latches, every drawer is notched to keep it from flying open on the high seas. Joe pulls up next to the truck where we, not expecting to be gone almost two hours, have left our dog, Doris Faye, to half freeze.

"Well, whaddya think?" Joe asks, brimming with the excitement of having successfully shown his first boat.

"I think Alexander and I are going to have to talk about this."

But we don't. We are consumed by our individual thoughts. I try to remember what we've just seen. I question whether a boat is really something we want to take on or if I am caught up in its novelty as an antique. The highway signs remind me of the ninety miles we will have to drive each way. I hear Grandmother ask, *Is this what you intend to do with your life?*

CHAPTER TWO
Coming Aboard

Six days pass before we are able to broach the subject. A boat is a luxury, impractical and expensive from beginning to end. Talk of expectation, desire, and risk extend well beyond our usual debates of tax deduction and return on investment. We agree to call the broker who arranged for us to see *The King and I*. He suggests that we meet him at the show, still in progress, for a crash course in buying a boat.

"What do you know about wooden boats?" Jim Arney asks.

Jim has Robert Redford's rugged good looks, the easy manner of a natural salesman, and no intention of selling us a wooden yacht.

"Nothing."

"Then you don't want to do that," he says, shaking his head.

"Fine," I say. "But why not?"

"Because a woodie is never anyone's first boat. They are usually not anyone's boat *ever*. Woodies are a come-on."

We reiterate our interest in *The King and I*.

"Look, fellahs, a guy's first boat is the small ski boat that he buys just after he buys his first car. He fixes it up, runs it on the lake, trades it in on a bigger boat. A long line of boats

follows him through life until, at last, he arrives at the cruiser.
The kids are gone; he is approaching retirement. He and the
missus are going to cruise the Great Circle Loop or move to
Florida or just have a sort of lake house floating on the water."

"What does 'Connie' mean?" I ask.

Jim's patience begins to fray as more qualified buyers fill
the hall.

"It's short for Constellation. It's a Chris-Craft mark like
Buick Skylark or Ford Fairmont."

"How much do you think we should offer?" Dale asks.

Jim wipes his forehead and shrugs.

"I don't know. Eighteen K. How's that?"

"Okay. Call us back when Mrs. King goes to fifteen." I
press my card into his hand with no expectation of hearing
from him again, but Jim calls after the show is over. Mrs.
King has agreed to our price, and we want another look.

———— ◆ ————

The King and I is not the bridled Valkyrie that we remember. It is an old wooden tub, spitting water out its side.
The nose cone is stove in, the starboard flank is crushed,
the canvas over the fly bridge is in tatters. The whitewashed
decks are gray under the same grime that covers everything
else in the boathouse. The generator does not spin. Her engines won't start.

"Now, fellahs," says Jim, seizing the opportunity, if
you'll just tell me how much you want to spend, I can get
you in a boat today."

I say, "I'm not interested in another boat."

Dale says, "I am not buying a boat that doesn't go. Too
much is at stake. A problem anywhere in the drive train from

the fuel pump to the transmissions will not show up unless we can spin the propellers."

Jim says, "We could call service and they'll tell you what you need to do and it's gonna be a lot."

Yacht brokerage is the most recent spin-off from the Loe's break-up. The once complementary departments of sales and service that used to work hand-in-hand to generate revenue for both now suspect one of perverting the efforts of the other.

"Now, what about another boat which I know will run?"

"Or, we could just look and see what's wrong," Dale says.

The ignition system's condensers and points are fried, something we can easily fix. We drive into town for parts and, on the way back, pick up Jim and the keys.

"Okay," Dale calls up from the engine room, "Give 'er a spin."

"Port or starboard?" Jim asks.

"Doesn't matter."

Jim pumps the throttles, turning one key and then the other, but the engines do not start. I shoot ether into the carburetor.

Jim cranks and the engine roars to life, *Va-Room*, but dies just as fast from lack of fuel.

Dale is all smiles, saying, "Let's do the other one."

Jim turns the key, the starter spins, and the second engine fires but dies immediately like the first.

"Great," Dale says, excitedly. "Now let's see if we can draw some fuel and keep these babies running."

Jim pumps the throttles until Dale yells, "Stop! I smell gas!"

"Good," says Jim, enthusiastic for the first time. He turns the key. The engine runs rough but does not cause Dale any concern.

"Alexander," Jim calls down, "run to the back and see what the discharge is like."

"What?"

"Go to the back and tell me how much water is coming out."

I look at Dale and shrug before climbing out on the dock to see water running out the tailpipes in waves.

"Is it supposed to do that?" I ask skeptically.

"Yeah," Jim says. "They're wet exhausts. Water drawn out of the lake cools the engines before mixing with exhaust gases and pushing out the tailpipe. Do we have good flow?"

"I guess."

Jim starts the second engine, and the three of us stand at the back of the boat to gloat over our success. Jim's demeanor has changed. Now, he sees *The King and I* as saleable, us as qualified buyers, and himself as our advocate. On our way out of the marina, he asks, "You've talked to Clay Burns, haven't you?"

"No," Dale and I answer together. "Who's Clay Burns?"

"Clay Burns is Highport's one and only boatwright." Jim hands us one of his cards with Clay's home number scribbled on the back. "Call him. Call him at home. No, he won't mind. Ask him anything you want to know about that boat."

———— ◆ ————

Clay Burns is stout, wears a snow white flattop, and has a jowly German face. He busts through the boathouse door like he owns the place. The bilge pump discharges as if greeting an old friend. Clay looks at his watch.

"This here old bowt. She's a fine old bowt," he says, before blowing out a deep breath. "But, fellahs, I cain't tell you to buy a wood bowt or not. A wood bowt is a somthin' you live with, not somethin' you own. But I can tell you that I took the best care of 'er as John King would allow. He and Perky didn't have no bowt at the time. They thought they'd sold their last one, but DEE-witte took this 'un in on trade and said, 'sed, Clay what am I going to do with this bowt? Ain't no one is going to want a twenty-five-year-old wooden bowt 'thout no engines. Not in 1980.' I said, 'Give 'er to John King.' And that's what he done. John King always loved old cars and always had wood bowts, and DEE-witte missed not seeing his college roommate around the marina."

He stops to recollect.

"Didn't say nothing 'bout it neither. Just sent John a bill for slip rent. John called him up and said, 'DEE-witte, how can I have slip rent when I don't even have a BOWT?"

Clay laughs before he can get the punchline out.

"DEE-witte said, 'Do now.' An' just hung up the phone. 'Course John weren't gonna take care of no gift bowt like it was his bought'n one. But it was enough for 'em two men at the time."

Dale and I stand silently as Clay pretends to revisit work he has done. He sights his cheek down the deck and lovingly pats the splintered plank where John came in too fast, too drunk one night, but he is checking *us* out. He knows who we are. Two guys don't go snooping around an old wooden boat in a place as tight-knit as Texomaland without getting some notice. And he knows what he thinks of us.

I know what I think about him, too. All his fingers are intact. A woodworker with all his fingers is either inexperienced or expert. Clay, at his age, must be extraordinary.

The bilge pump fires. Clay looks at his watch, timing the interval between discharges. He looks out across the sail-

boats tied up in open slips at the end of the cove. The breeze
pings the riggings against the masts. He clasps his hands beneath his paunch, interlaces his fingers, and pauses. His tone
changes from storytelling to sobering advice.

"You see 'em 'glass boats?" he asks, waving toward the
end of the slip. "They're cheaper, easier to take care of. If you
can butter toast, you can fix 'em damn things. But fellahs,
one day they die. They all die. The sun eats 'em up, an' there
ain't nothin' you can do about it 'cept go buy another and
watch it die, too."

He beats on *The King and I* bow rail with clenched fist.

"You take care of this boat an' there ain't no reason why
she won't outlive both you fellahs...*twice,*" he says, wiping
the schmutz off his hand.

He pauses.

"But you're up to it. I dare say you are up to it. And when
you're done, you'll have what all the money in the world cannot buy. But, son, I don't envy you. No, sir. It's gonna take
more that either one of you got by yourselves. And maybe
more than what you got together. We'll have to see."

His eye traces the contours of her cabins and fly bridge.
He smiles more to himself than us and says, "Yessir, this boat
floats real good right here in this slip."

"What does that mean?" I insist, having now heard it on
three separate occasions, first from Joe, then Jim, and now Clay.

Clay squints like a gnome.

"It means that a wooden boat ain't no educated gasoline shot into no Jell-O mold. She is made out of trees by
men who spent their lives coaxin' each plank to lie down flat
and true against each rib. It means she needs attention like
your dog or your girl or your child, and when she don't get
it, she'll go down." Anger flushes his cheeks. "People say,

'Floats right here in this slip', 'cause they don't know nothing. They think that wood boats just sink or break apart in the sling for no reason. That's bull. They fail 'cause somebody quit lovin' 'em."

An awkward silence descends on the boathouse. Clay regains his composure. "I say it 'cause if someone don't love this boat soon, she's going down."

The bilge pump fires; Clay checks his watch. The time between discharges indicates how tight the hull is—more leakage, more discharges.

"Well, fellahs, I've got to get home before it gets dark or my wife will worry. My eyes aren't as sharp at night as they used to be. Nice meetin' y'. Call me if you got any more questions, hear?"

He catches himself as he turns to leave.

"An' fellahs, all boats are work. Don't let anyone tell you different. It just a matter of kind and purpose."

———◆———

Before the sale can close, we need insurance which requires a survey, an inspection of the boat on the hard, which is dry land in boat talk. The last vestige of DeWitte Loe's showmanship displays itself in hauling *The King and I* out of the water. The entire service staff gathers around the liftwell. Machinists leave their tools, mechanics leave their benches, and painters leave brushes to dry. Department heads bark orders at Hispanic coulees—*quienes no haban inglés*—until, at last, an executive whirligigs his finger over his head, and the boat, cradled in the slings of a crane called a Travelift, rises out of the water and hangs suspended over the boatyard. When the crane shuts down, the crowd dissipates, leaving

Dale and me alone with Dennis Gibbs, the surveyor, and his assistant, Drew.

They sound the length and width of each plank with a ball-peen hammer, carefully cataloging, with photograph and notation, any suspected defect. They check every on-board system and component, again citing anything that may be amiss. At the end of a long day, Dennis draws us aside and says, "What you have here, gentlemen, is a hull, a remarkable hull for being wood, an exceptional hull for its age. The rest is junk."

His written survey, with copies sent to Arney and the insurance company, itemizes his initial assessment in minute detail, from burnt-out light bulbs to severe frame damage to broken hose clamps. Dale and I console ourselves that it was a long shot and that we are better men for having tried. Then the phone rings.

"Forty-two defects," Mr. Parks says, foregoing the usual pleasantries.

Karl Parks is the underwriter at Heritage Marine in Mystic, Connecticut, one of the few companies that will insure a forty-six-year-old wooden craft owned by two men who have absolutely no experience.

"Forty-two," Mr. Parks repeats. "Plus," he says, reading the surveyor's special note, "'the bottom sanded, painted, and the deteriorated planks replaced.'"

"Yessir," Dale answers.

"Well, let's see," Parks says, prioritizing the necessary repairs in accordance to risk. "The first are the obvious fire hazards; those must be remedied within twenty-four hours of possession. The second are the risks of sinking from inoperable valves and leaky hoses; those must be repaired within thirty days of possession. The hull work can wait until you haul out in the fall. She'll be what we call dockside operational until all these faults are rectified, which means that if she moves without a tow, I don't want to hear about it, understood?"

"Yessir."

"Our contract and premium advice go out this afternoon. Do you have any questions?"

"No, sir," Dale answers.

"Then that takes care of it. Thank you for your call, Mr. Harris. Please keep us apprised of your progress and do let us know when you close so we can begin coverage. Thanks for using Heritage and good luck."

"Shit," Dale says after hanging up the phone.

"What?"

"We're insured."

I call Jim. Renegotiation after an inspection is my standard real estate practice. I open with "Eight grand."

"I'm not even going to call them with that," Jim scoffs.

I raise my voice, "Have you read the survey? Have the Boy Scouts read the survey?"

Mrs. King had lost confidence in our ability to close the deal and, halfway to closing, donated the boat to the Boy Scouts of America.

"They don't need to. They've got your contract."

"Call 'em," I insist.

Phone calls back and forth end in a stalemate at $14,500.

"They are not going to haul that piece of shit over land to another lake and let a bunch of kids scramble all over it in an effort to do what?"

"They've given a receipt for $30,000 to Mrs. King. They believe that the asset is worth thirty grand."

"The boat isn't worth crap," I say. "You haven't had an offer in two years."

"Fourteen-five. They won't budge."

"Okay, let me talk to Dale."

I cup the receiver.

"Jim says he has several parties interested in that boat and that the Boy Scouts won't move."

"Every broker has 'several parties interested.' What's their counter?"

"Fourteen-five," I answer.

"Take it or leave it?"

"I dunno."

I ask Jim.

"Take it or leave it?"

"Right-o," Jim says, venting his frustration.

"Okay."

I cover the phone.

"Yeah. That's it."

Silence.

"Well?" Dale asks.

"Well. I'm not happy with the price."

"You are *never* happy with any price, *ever.*"

"I know, but—"

"But nothing, kiddo. The ante at this table is 14,500 U.S. dollars. Do you want in? Yes or no?"

Mother's ghost intervenes.

You'll only regret the chances you let slip by in life. Not the failures.

"Yes," I answer Dale.

"Then tell Mr. Arney we'll bring a cashier's check up to the marina tomorrow. Ask him how he wants it styled. And remember to thank him for all his help."

On Memorial Day Weekend, 2001, *The King and I* is ours. Dale fixes our first meal on board while I sit alone on the dock, thinking, *What have we done?*

CHAPTER THREE
From Start to Finish

What we have done is buy what the industry euphemistically calls a project boat. We have bitten off more than we can chew, taken on more than we can handle, overreached; but we start anyway. While the rest of Highport celebrates opening day of a new boating season, we haul the remnants of Perky and John's life to the dumpster in trash bags, attend to Mr. Parks's list, and cut wires out of the engine room. I, younger and more nimble, squeeze myself under the deckhouse floor. Dale, son of an electrical engineer, is at the rudimentary connection block located behind the helm.

"It's a black wire with a white stripe," he calls down, describing the first of hundreds we will have to cut.

"There's no light down here. They are all black wires. If they have a faint white stripe, I can't see it." I pick a wire at random and ask, "That one?" before setting the dykes on it.

"Wiggle it."

"I am."

"I can't see it."

"Now?" I ask.

"What?"

"Can you feel it...NOW?"

"Are you wiggling it?"

"Yes."

"No. I can't feel it."

I wiggle more vigorously.

"Now?" I ask.

"N-n-n...YES."

"Is that the one?"

"What?" he asks.

"THIS ONE?"

"I think so."

"You want me to cut it?" I ask.

"What?"

"Do. You. Want. Me. To. Cut. It."

"Wiggle it again."

"That one?"

"Yes...NO...wait a minute."

"Now?" I ask.

"Yes."

"Sure?"

"Okay."

Snip.

If we are lucky, something goes dark, identifying the circuit we have disabled. Sometimes Dale says, "Oh, shit. Not *that* one. Sorry," which means I have to tug, splice, tape, and guess again. Sometimes he says, "Okay, let's pull that one out," and we move along to the next wire—"It's a black wire with a faint white stripe."

The work is difficult, but by the end of July we have moved on to ripping out the plumbing. Clay Burns, as is his habit, comes by to check on us. I lodge a complaint the moment he arrives.

"Goddammed fuckin' hoses, Clay Burns."

"Yeah, yeah, I know," he says, pulling a comb across his flattop.

"Those that aren't so brittle they crumble when you look at them are so gooey they smear this black shit all over everywhere and you can't get a grip."

"Yeah. But you gotta get 'em off."

"Then the damned clamps are rusted on."

"Yeah. Old boats are like that."

"We're drinking out of an Igloo and eating out of an ice chest."

"Got all your electrical out?"

"Damned fucking uncomfortable. That's what we are. Covered in sweat and grime, frustrated, and sick and fuckin' tired."

"Are y'all ready to kill each other yet?" Clay asks timidly.

"NO," Dale and I answer incredulously. We're having a ball.

"Good," he says with a wink. "You still got a chance, and I got something to talk to y'all about."

We climb out on the dock.

"Fellahs, next year is my last year working on boats. I'm sick of boats. I'm taking my wife and my fifth wheel up Colorado way where there ain't no boats and I'm gonna retire there, and then, I'm gonna die there. Ain't no prettier country and ain't no point in my taking everything I know to the grave. You might as well learn whatever you can."

———— ◆ ————

The boatyard used to be open to "Authorized personnel only"—an ambiguous designation, seemingly based more on excluding do-it-yourselfers like Dale and me than any actual qualification. Under new policies, the boatyard is available to anyone who can show proof of insurance, naming Highport as beneficiary. Our boat insurance policy will indemnify Highport from any loss, damage, or injury Dale and I may cause or suffer while working in the yard. Now, we can work beside Clay and absorb all he knows whereas before we could not.

We will not, however, be welcomed as honored guests or respected as valued customers. We will be regarded as squatters, taking up revenue-producing space and robbing idle hands of work. The new manager is Lily. His razor-creased slacks and polished shoes circle *The King and I* before arriving at my feet.

"What are you doing?" he asks.

I stick out my head from underneath the boat, remove my goggles and my respirator out of respect, and answer, "Sanding."

"You have to have an OSHA-approved dust recovery system in order to discharge toxins into the atmosphere. It's EPA."

It is harassment. No one said a thing about a dust-capturing system, but by some miracle, I manage to keep my cool.

"Where do *you* sand boats?" I ask.

"We have a sanding well."

"May I see it?"

"Certainly," Lily answers, inviting me with grand gesture to follow him to where a young, shirtless, Hispanic male, wearing a bandana instead of a respirator and sunglasses instead of eye protection, toils feverishly beneath a fifty-foot fiberglass sailboat. A hose connects his sander to a Shop-Vac that shoots a v-shaped plume of abraded glass high into the air. Some of which glitters in the sun on its way back to earth; the rest gets blown across the lake by the wind.

"See?" says Lily.

"Yes," I say.

"Well?"

"Well, Mr. Lily, if it would satisfy you, OSHA, and the EPA for me to stop, go to Home Depot, buy a Shop-Vac, remove the filter, and shoot my dust even higher into the atmosphere than it would fall of its own accord, then I will. But I think you just want to make trouble in the hopes that I will walk away and leave the work for your men to do."

I turn to go back to my boat. When Lily catches up, I stop.

"You see, this boat is supposed to be a fun experience, a sort of hobby for me and Dale. We've never owned a boat before and are interested in doing the restoration ourselves. You understand, of course. We also hope to learn a lot from Mr. Burns. We have complied with all of Highport's rules; however, if for reasons of your own, we are not allowed, then as I see it, you have a choice to make."

"Me?" he says with astonishment.

"Yes, sir. You have to decide if you want a classic motor yacht or not. I will be glad to sign the boat over to you for unpaid expenses, as is my option according to the slip agreement. Dale and I will collect our tools, get in our truck with our dog, and drive back to Dallas feeling richer for the experience. Or, you can leave me in peace to do the work I came to do. What's your pleasure?"

"Well, I didn't mean—," Lily says as we make our way back to our boat.

"What you meant or did not mean, Mr. Lily, is of no bearing at this late date. Just tell me what you want to do."

We have returned to *The King and I* where Dale, in the bilge wrestling with through-hull fittings, recognizes my politesse as forced and appears on the stern ready to do damage control.

"What's up?" asks the past master of diversion.

"Mr. Lily is considering a transaction."

"Now, now, I've got rules. I can't have just anyone come into *my* yard and start telling *me* how it is going to be. *I* run this place."

"Mr. Lily, I am offering you a deal. Are you accepting or not?"

Dale asks brightly, "I wonder if there is a fresh pot of coffee? Do y'all think there is any fresh coffee?"

"What?" Mr. Lily asks.

"I bet we can work this out over a hot cup of coffee, been a long morning already, hasn't it? How about Alexander and I discuss the situation while you ask one of the girls to put the pot on?"

Lily leaves.

"*What is the matter with you?*" whispers an infuriated and bewildered Dale Harris.

As I explain, his impatience turns to amusement, then smirks, giggles, and finally outright laughter.

"What's so goddammed funny?"

"Darling, Mr. Lily is a manager."

"So?"

"Managers manage."

"So?"

"Lily can make no such decision. The dear man has no power. You've cornered him, poor thing. He doesn't make the rules; he enforces them. Even if he were to call your bluff—"

"No bluff."

"Regardless, he would have to explain to receivables, how instead of cash for billable hours, he took in a rotten good-for-nothing tub that they just unloaded on a couple of unsuspecting faggots. Now, how would that go over, d'you think?"

"I'm following the goddammed rules."

"You are *stretching* the goddamned rules. It is part of your charm, but 'Authorized personnel only in the yard.'"

"Where does it say that?" I ask. "Besides, I'm 'authorized'."

"Yes, dear, by sleight of hand."

"Still."

"Still. You do take everything so personally, and the man's just doing his job. If you ever had a real job—"

"I had a real job."

"Working for your mother was never real."

"Coffee's ready," a secretary calls out the office door.

"Thank you," Dale answers back, "Now, let's go get a cup of coffee and retract your offer to Mr. Lily."

"I am not apologizing."

"Did you hear me say 'apologize'? I said, 'retract'. They are two different words. One starts with an 'a', the other—"

"All right. All right."

———— ◆ ————

Over the month, we soak up everything we can from Clay and return *The King and I*, now *Betty Jane,* to the water as Highport ceases to be a resource. The workshops are idle; the stores are empty; the talent is gone.

Breathing new life into something left for dead is reward enough, but the greater satisfaction comes from Dale and me working more closely together than we ever have. Our skill sets do not overlap which allows us to segregate responsibility according to aptitude. In rental units, Dale works in the office while I work in the field. On the boat, he—preferring a plan, a course of action, and the correct way of doing anything—is the better electrician and mechanic. I—more comfortable with variation and irregularity—am the better plumber, carpenter, painter.

But a complete restoration of a vintage craft is too hard, too mind-numbingly tedious, too frustrating to afford such separation. We tag-team. The one who has the greater expertise is the first. The second passes tools, provides emotional support, and asks the simplest, most obvious questions at times of abject failure like, "Is the power on?", "Is the valve open?", "What do the instructions say?", and "How about a sandwich?"

In the process, the boat comes back together. Lights light and pumps whir. Decks—stripped, stained, and varnished—gleam. Chrome shines. And the engines send that distinctive Chris-Craft burble out across the water.

In the process, Dale and I have to reconcile personal shortcomings with ourselves and each other. We have to forgive impatience and fatigue. We must relive pasts of neglect and abuse which taught us that we do not know what we were doing, never will, have no business trying, and accept that none of that is true. We celebrate the slightest victory and overlook the massive failures until on Memorial Day 2003, exactly two years from purchase, she is ready for her maiden voyage.

Invitations go out, and as Highport receives the annual onslaught of holiday-makers eager to resume summer fun after the winter hiatus, we are expecting our first guests. The people who listened to our trials, lauded our successes, fetched parts, and tirelessly put ham sandwiches and Diet Cokes into our hands arrive along with the licensed captain whom Mr. Parks requires to be on board until we can show proficiency in basic seamanship.

"Damn the torpedoes! Full speed ahead! We'll outrun the goddamned thing," the captain says as we pull out of the harbor into the kind of pop-up thunderstorm that is famous on Texoma.

Halfway down the lake, a shrill whine cuts through the laughter and gossip. It is the high-temperature alarm, indicating that the transmissions are over-heated and threaten to ignite the engine room—in a thunderstorm, with a dozen of our closest friends on board, all landlubbers.

Highport installed the transmissions incorrectly. In order to push the boat forward, the transmissions engage the reverse gear—a gear designed for in-port maneuvering. Excessive wear and friction over distances or at high speed cause the transmissions to get too hot. John, who never went very far or very fast, possibly never knew about the error because DeWitte also installed dumb plugs where the high-temperature sensors should have gone. Dale replaced those plugs with proper sensors connected to alarms, which now shriek and avert disaster. It is the defect that Dale, without knowing, suspected to be lurking somewhere in the drive train; and why he insisted that the engines start before survey.

Over the next few years, Lake Texoma gets smaller with each subsequent foray. We explore tributaries that reach deep into the adjoining states, discover remote coves, and picnic on sandy beaches, but our eyes look upon the dam with growing contempt, our minds imagining what may lie beyond.

CHAPTER FOUR
Beyond the Dam

Applegate Cove Marina, self-styled as "Oklahoma's Outlet to the Sea," is five hours from Dallas, three hours from Lake Texoma, and a world away from Highport, if by scale alone. There are no Hispanic yard hands, no service managers, no heads of accounts; no waterside restaurants or bars; no boathouses reaching out for open water. There is a modest frame house by the entrance where live the couple who look after the place, Alon and Rhoda Carpenter. Dale and I have stopped by on our way home from an organist convention in Tulsa, Oklahoma, to make inquires.

"You'll have to ask him," Rhoda Carpenter says. Her white tee-shirt stuffs into skin-tight jeans. "He and Kenn just tied this thing up last night. And he pulled out before dawn on a transport. Didn't even stop for breakfast, poor thing. There's the old one right there."

She points to the old gas dock, somewhat-floating with two pumps and a cashier's hut.

"This one'll be much better. More space for beer and stuff I can sell."

The new dock is a shiny white pre-fab floating box. Two fuel pumps face the river on one side. A deck for tables, chairs, and a barbecue juts out of the other. Overhead doors on both ends catch the breeze.

"'Least 'til Alon gets the air conditioning fixed. And he'll have to install the sanitary pump-out station. He wants to put it down here. But I don't want it here. I want to put the cash register here."

We ask about transport.

"You'll have to ask him," she repeats distractedly. "He'll be back next week."

Rhoda gloats over her new store.

"Them guys pushed this thing all the way up from Pine Bluff. How he found it I'll never know. That's Alon. Anyway, he says to Kenn, 'Let's go get that thing. They're not gonna use it.' Kenn thought Alon was plumb crazy pushing this thing the length of the river. But Alon said, 'We'll put me in one boat, you 'n' t'other and just push the damn thing up here. Won't Rhoda be surprised?'

"I was, too," she says, laughing at her husband's folly. "I'm going to have a glass counter full of candy bars and fishing lures. The ice cream cooler goes at the far end. Beer cases'll line up on one wall and a low bench'll run down opposite. I'm gonna leave the center open and a stack of plastic chairs in the corner. That way ev'rybody'll have a place to sit in the ev'nin's."

We try again to interest her with the business we came to do.

"Look," she says, resting her hand on Dale's wrist. "I'm sure there won't be a problem, but I cannot speak for him."

Dale asks if we can look around.

"Please do, and if I can answer any questions you have about the marina, I'll be right here. But Alon does the hauling."

Applegate has the bare essentials of what we will need: a Travelift, a boat yard, a work shed, a covered slip for *Betty Jane*, a shower house, and a place to park our car long term. Engine work and transport are up to Alon. The boat-hauling business goes strong until right before Christmas. We make an appointment for immediately after the new year. The lush-and-green-with-huge-shade-trees Applegate in summertime that we remember is, now in January, a scene from *Doctor Zhivago*. Icicles hang long and thick from the front porch of the caretaker's house where a grinning giant of a man stands in his bare feet to greet us.

"C'min. C'min. C'min wher't's warm," Alon Carpenter says, laying burly arms on our shoulders and guiding us into the living room where a fire blazes at one end. Rhoda is in the kitchen taking just-baked Toll House cookies out of the oven. She invites us to sit down on the part of the sectional sofa that her husband—a former roughneck from the West Texas oilfields, with receding brown hair and clear brown eyes—does not.

"Rhoda says you guys want to bring a boat up here."

"Yes," Dale answers.

"What kind of a boat?"

"It is a fifty-three-year-old Chris-Craft. Corsair. Forty-five feet."

"How much does she weigh?"

"Thirteen tons wet."

"Had 'er long?"

"About seven years," Dale answers.

"Fixed up?"

"Yes," we answer together.

"Floats?"

"With the help of an occasional bilge pump," Dale says with a wry smile.

"Then what's the problem?" Alon asks, shrugging.

"She's wood," I say.

Alon leans forward and says, "I know that. If she's three years older than I am and as you say, 'thirteen tons wet,' then she has to soak up something from somewhere somehow so I figure she ain't 'glass, aluminum, or steel." He winks. The spaces between his teeth make him look like a kid. "Am I right?"

"Yessir," I answer, feeling a little foolish.

"So? what's the problem?" he repeats.

"I guess there isn't one," I admit.

"Not unless there's something you're not telling me."

"Well, there is," Dale says. "The problem is that we don't know if she'll make it over the hard. And if she doesn't get here damaged beyond repair, we'll need a place where we can work on her."

"First of all, boats don't fall apart on my trailer. Do they, hon?" Alon says, calling out to his wife in the kitchen.

"No, honey, they don't," she answers, bringing in a tray with coffee and cookies.

"Second, if she does, you're the only ones who're going to fix 'er 'cause I ain't got a boatwright this side of Clay Burns who I hear is long gone some years back to Colorado to die. Third, I ain't got no mahogany neither. But—" He holds up a finger. "I do have an excellent painter. Robert works part-time and you'll have to lemme have that much. You're squatting in my yard, after all."

Fine, I think. *Finally I have a place where I can work at leisure without a service manager breathing down my back.*

"Fine," I answer out loud, "but I do the prep. The hull leaks under the galley sink. I need to fix that. I've got some trim to replace and I want to do the sanding."

Nodding as I talk, Alon agrees. "Fine."

"Cream?" Rhoda asks.

"No, thanks," I answer, taking the mug from her hand. Dale continues his list.

"There's a leak in the starboard pan gasket, the transmissions run backward, and we'll need new props."

"Whoa, whoa, whoa. The trannies run backwards?" asks Alon, leaning back and resting his feet on the coffee table until Rhoda takes a swat.

"I got my shoes off," Alon complains.

"I don't care," she whispers, "not in front of company." She smiles and holds out a plate to us.

"Cookie?" she asks.

"Transmissions run backwards," Dale explains. "It's how DeWitte installed them."

"DEE-witte LOE?" Alon asks, shaking his head. A knowing grin breaks across his face, but he says nothing except, "Well, you'll have to get that fixed. River ain't goin' to let you get away with that. Lockmasters ain't gonna be too keen neither."

"Right," Dale says. "Can you do it?"

Mechanics are Alon's strength and making do is a way of life out here beyond cellphone coverage.

"In fact, I've gotta pair of trannies in the shop that came off that...that..." Alon snaps his fingers in the air trying to remember. "Oh, hell, hon..." he turns to the woman sitting next to him, "What was the name of that b—"

"*Eye Candy*," Rhoda answers, getting up to get cigarettes and an ashtray. "Y'all want me to brew another pot? And eat up those cookies. With the kids gone, they're just going to make us fat."

"*Eye Candy*," Alon repeats, "That's right. Now, you wanna hear about a restoration. That was a wooden Trojan about fifty feet long what had sat in the dirt for years up there on the hill. Not only was it rotten, it had bugs."

Rhoda sits back down and mouths, "Bugs," beneath her page-boy salt-and-pepper haircut.

Alon continues the tangent, "Anyway, that man—What was his name, hon?"

"Earl," Rhoda says while packing unopened cigarettes against the heel of her hand. She is used to filling the gaps in her husband's memory.

"Yeah. Earl. Anyway, he bought that boat without really telling his wife and pretty soon they'd sold everything and lived on that hulk until he got it floating. Real nice inside, too."

"Trannies," Rhoda says.

She passes a lit cigarette to him and exhales the smoke.

"Yeah. Like I was saying, those casings're laying up in the shop. Robert can re-gear them and pop 'em into your boat. Cheaper 'n' buying brandee new from the factory an' b'sides we need the work."

Brandee new?

"Anything else?" Alon asks.

"Don't think so," Dale and I answer together.

"Well, fine, I'll call you at first thaw," Alon promises, getting up to show us out. "That way, we can get you what you need done and be on the way just after the spring floods."

Spring floods?

———◆———

It will be the third week in May before Alon's call comes. He wants to transport on the Monday before Memorial Day weekend and move the haul-out point to another marina.

Dale and I get ready, off-loading or securing anything that can get damaged in transit. We vacate the slip, host family and friends to *Betty Jane's* good-bye cruise, and fall dead asleep in our bunks for a couple of hours before the sound of a semi-tractor trailer grinding its way down to the water wakes us up. Alon, wincing in pain, alights from the cab. A colostomy bag bulges from above his belt. He stoops as he walks. He waves toward the escort vehicle and introduces its driver as Kenn.

When the crane operator arrives, Alon positions the boat over the slings, checks to make sure the straps hang without kinks or folds. He whirligigs his finger in the air and the boat rises out of the water and lands quietly on the trailer, causing the suspension to buckle and its tires to bulge. Kenn stows the dinghy under the prow of the big boat, and the two men leave Dale and me to watch as *Betty Jane* ducks behind a mesquite tree like a puppy on a string.

We are excited. We are anxious. And we know nothing about rivers.

CHAPTER FIVE
Forty Days and Forty Nights

The next morning, *Betty Jane* sits on the trailer where Alon left her last night in the Applegate boatyard. Two men lean against her hull. Walt, Alon's father and the elder of the two, wears his Stetson like a Texas rancher with the brim turned up at the sides. Robert is the part-time help.

"Alon will be along shortly," Walt says around a chaw as big as a fist.

"That's him," Robert says as we hear a diesel truck start up across the water. Robert is not much for talking.

We follow the noise of the truck around the edge of the cove to the boatyard. Alon parks short of the gravel in the yard, climbs out and says, "'Mornin'."

He coaxes the Travelift to life, raises *Betty Jane* off the trailer and lowers her into the liftwell until her bottom gets wet, but she still hangs in the slings. The five of us gather around, two on one side and three on the other, crouch with our hands on our knees, and listen.

After a few minutes of nothing happening, Robert asks, "What're we lookin' fer?"

"Anathin'," Walt answers.

Still nothing. Nothing cracks. Nothing snaps. A bilge pump does not fire.

Robert, in an effort to be vigilant, reports a bubble.

Alon asks, "Are the pumps on?"

"Can't be off," Dale answers. "Hard wired directly to the battery."

"Someone oughtta g—" Alon begins, but a call hails from across the water.

"Whatcha doin'?" Rhoda asks, teasingly.

"Launching a boat," Alon answers.

"Don't look like it. Looks like five Okies staring at the water with their butts hanging out."

Alon smiles for the first time I've seen since last winter and says, "These are very tricky things, the likes of which a girl the likes of you t'wouldn't understand."

We boys giggle.

Undaunted, Rhoda fires back. "You remember that when your lunch ain't made."

"Aw," Alon waves and returns to the problem at hand. "Now, someone oughtta climb down 'ere and check 'em pumps."

Ain't Highport, I think to myself where there are legions of olive complected men to do this sort of work while an executive keeps the boat owner at bay.

I climb down the rusty pylons, land in the aft cockpit, and go below to inspect the cabins. I lift floorboards from stateroom to deckhouse and report, "Dry as a bone" to those waiting above. "Dry as a bone." In finding no damage, my excitement grows until I step into the deckhouse where the floor is wet, the ceiling is soaked, and the bulkheads are streaked with water.

"Uh-oh," I cry out.

"What?" Dale shouts.

"The deckhouse is sopping wet," I answer.

"The hull? The engine room?"

"No. The ceiling. The walls. The floor is a mess. The hull is fine except for a little standing water, but nothing's rushing in."

I stop to consider.

"It's rainwater. The deckhouse roof leaks like a sieve," I exclaim. "It's topside only."

"Well, you're gonna have to fix *that* before you go," Alon says. "You won't be so lucky as to find covered slips on transient docks. Not on the river."

Something we had not considered and another item to add to the list of repairs, but for the moment, we are glad she is seaworthy.

Alon points to two available slips in the boathouse directly across from the well.

"Which'un you wont?" he asks.

"The one I can hit," Dale snaps back and pulls *Betty Jane* into the cove.

"Welcome. Welcome. Welcome to Applegate," Rhoda says as we land. The man standing next to her, dressed exactly as I am in a white tee and bib overalls, is Bob Quackenbush. He's old enough to be my father and twice my size. He manages the gas dock.

"I'm Bob," he says with a wink and a smile. "You need anything, you see me."

"You got a Diet Coke?" I ask.

"You betcha. Follow me."

Doris Faye and I leave Rhoda and Dale to tie up.

———•———

When we get back, we find Dale alone taking in the neighbors. Boathouses with fifty-foot slips have generally the same tenants. There is a Silverton cruiser on one side, a Carver on the other, the ubiquitous '80s vintage Chris-Craft 410 down the catwalk.

"And there's the big ugly Trojan," Dales says, being uncharacteristically blunt about the boat moored across from *Betty Jane*. There had been one at Highport, a monster of a boat—rotten hull, cracked superstructure—ghastly.

I lower my voice to say, "You mean that beautifully restored vintage woody whose captain is on the bridge and has probably heard every word?"

"Yeah," Dale whispers. "That one."

We unpack the car, returning everything to its place on the boat, when the man presents himself. He says his name is Earl and his wife's name is Ruthella, whom he invariably calls Ruthie. He admires our work and asks the questions of one who has done it himself. No answer is too long. No minutiae is too specific. We are comrades-in-arms exchanging war stories.

"Got mine from right up 'aire," he says, pointing to the boatyard from which we have come. "Sat right next to t'other. Only difference was one faced north and t'other faced south. Mine's the north'n un. C'n still see where the keel rott'n' into the gravel up'air."

He doesn't want to board. He knows we're a mess. Instead, he invites us onto his boat. "After you get settled in an' all. Come by. We'll have a b'er." Acquaintances are easily made on the river. We all have boats and places we've either been to or want to go.

He and Ruthella have a son, Raymond, who is in the Army like his dad was. They've got two dachshunds. They've got this boat, *Eye Candy*, which Earl bought without really telling Ruthella who tries to make it as homey as possible.

They sold all they had in order to chase the dream of "driving it," as Ruthella says, to North Carolina and live with Raymond when he gets back from Iraq. I mention Dale's comment about their boat, but Earl just laughs a smoky laugh.

"Don't matter," he says, "I seen you coming back after following Quackenbush over to the gas dock and I says to Ruthie, 'Ruthie, that man has a perty boat and a perty dog, but the ugliest wife I've ever seen.'" He jabs me with his elbow, adding, "Talking about you, Alexander."

Eye Candy, the Hoelschers and their two dogs will be gone before sun-up. Quick departures are commonplace among river folks. They never say "Good-bye." They always say, "See you down the river," because they never know who is going to turn up, neither where nor when.

Dale and I have errands to run in town. We stop by the Carpenter house where Alon is reclining in his chair at one end of the porch; Rhoda is in her office at the other.

"Goin' to town," I call out the passenger window. "Need anything?"

"Naw, but how's yer boat?"

"Good."

Actually, she is better than we could have hoped; she did not suffer from transport at all.

"Good," Alon says, stretching out his full length. "Would it be all right if Robert and I got her into the barn tomorrow?"

"In the barn?" I ask. "I'd figure we'd be out in the yard."

"Hell no, man," Alon raises his head for emphasis, "You're my only customer."

"Sure," I answer. "We'll have to go to Dallas, though. Get my truck, some tools, and some supplies. Tomorrow afternoon is the soonest we'd be back."

"I got keys?"

"No," Dale answers, "We'll drop off a set on our way back out."

"Fine," Alon says, laying his head back down and closing his eyes.

By the next afternoon, *Betty Jane*, on tall jacks, is in the barn. Around her is a hodgepodge of lockers and shelves meant for inventory no longer kept in stock. Tools lie on benches. Scrap and remnants remain still clamped in vises.

———— ◆ ————

The next few weeks are going to be a trial. *Betty Jane* has always been something we have always done together, but Dale has a staph infection on his leg that keeps him out of the boatyard on doctor's orders. So, while Doris Faye and I go it alone, he will make a homestead out of a hotel room and order parts to be shipped here where a ball-point pen is special order and overnight means one week. I crawl under her bow and begin sanding.

Abraded red bottom paint, toxic and fine, goes everywhere and turns everything pink, including my dog. It clogs my respirator and clouds my goggles. It gets in my ears and around my eyes. It is in my nose. By the end of the day, it will have mixed with sweat and trickled down the creases in my skin to streak my underwear red. It is miserable work that I oddly enjoy. The scratch of sander against her bottom. The rumble that resonates through her hull. She's my boat.

"Whatcha been doin'?" Dale asks as he jumps out of the truck.

"Sanding your damned boat."

"Are you about to die?" he asks.

"Yes. Where's my lunch?"

The next morning I start removing planks.

Easy, easy, I remember Clay saying as he watched me pull the first screw out of the first plank back at Highport. Even though Clay no longer chewed tobacco, the habit of curling his lower lip when he spoke remained. It slurred his m's and obliterated his b's and p's. *Those old bhronze screws are old and soft. Just one light tap and lean into it. Lean, don't twist.*

Removal of planks is often the first sign the boat will never see water again.

Do not use a crow bhar, Clay said. *You'll sphlinter the edge and ruin the phlank. You'll have to phress it out from the* inside.

I press. I pry gently. If Dale were here he could catch from the outside whatever may come loose.

Careful...careful.

I inch a bit more and a bit more until I have pushed out enough to get a handhold on the outside. I unfold myself from inside the cabinet, climb down the ladder and stand to get the best leverage.

Don't tug. Lean. Lean out, feel the flex. Unfold it like a letter from your true love. Now take your bhar, that's it, phress, phress, don't phry...easy it does it...and...

Pop!

The first plank comes out intact. The second reveals the full extent of the damage. The third and fourth are out just to make sure. A section of the chine—rhymes with "shine"—is rotten, which prevents a watertight seal.

"CHINE," I say out loud like a curse, as Clay did.

Dale arrives with lunch. He sees the gap that smiles eerily down the starboard side of his boat. He sees a pile of rotted mahogany lying on the concrete and smells the acrid stench of rot. His usually sunny disposition evaporates. Shock and fear takes its place.

"Bad?" he asks hesitantly.

"Chine," I repeat as if it were an answer in itself.

"Oh."

Chine's fault is its function. It joins the side of the boat to its bottom. It follows the hull's contour from stern to prow, is difficult to manufacture, hard to get to, and prone to rot. It is a challenge especially when the nearest woodworker is a cabinet man in Tulsa, a hundred miles away.

"Let's eat," I say. "I'm hungry."

———— ♦ ————

We sit out under the cottonwood tree to listen to opening day unfold in the boathouse. Though not as effusive as Memorial Day at Texoma, it is the reunion of people who have not seen each other since last October.

Our empty slip is more noticeable as the distraction of new arrivals evaporates. Our slipmates are disappointed. They were expecting fresh ears to listen to their stories and a vintage Chris-Craft *non pareil* as a neighbor. They see our red F-150 and hear me working in the barn, but there is no boat. The women of the boathouse decide to send a snooping party.

I am back to work in *Betty Jane*'s belly when I hear a truck pull into the boatyard, three car doors slam, and Doris Faye's collar rattle as she gets up to greet a trio of men, owners of the biggest, grandest boats in the marina, sent to bid welcome.

"Hello, puppy," one of them says in a high falsetto. "Are you a nice puppy?"

"Well, look at all the pink dust."

"*You* look at the dust. *I* came to look at this boat."

"You did not. You came over here because Linda sent you."

"Sh-shush."

Their inspection begins on the port side and goes aft to the stern where they read aloud, "*Betty Jane*. Dallas, Texas."

"What do you s'pose they're doing up here?"

"What does anyone do here? They're going to Florida."

They shuffle back along the starboard side and stop abruptly when they see the gash in her side, the missing planks laid out on the floor.

"Uh-oh," one says,

"That's not good," says a second.

But the third, who will introduce himself as Morgan, says, "That's fine. It's just a few planks."

I throw out a large scrap to announce my presence.

They step up and peer in.

"Hey."

"Hey," I answer.

"Your boat?"

"You buyin'?" I ask, sticking out a dirty, bloody hand, "My name is Alexander."

Each are polite about saying what a pleasure it is to meet me.

"And your names are?" I ask.

"Oh, sorry. I'm Morgan. This is Barney."

"And I'm Owen."

"We're your neighbors," Morgan says. "I'm in the Silverton next to you in the boathouse."

"Great."

"And I'm three slips down from Morgan and Barney's next to me," Owen says, nodding. "We have boats."

I say, "Good. Boats are good to have on the river."

I am sweaty, frustrated, my hands are bleeding, and I am in no mood for polite conversation.

Owen, a little miffed, says, "Long as they float. *Yours* gonna float?"

"Gosh, I hope so. Otherwise I'm spending a lot of time and energy for no reason."

Morgan asks, "Up from Texas are you?"

"Why do you ask?" I say, not wanting to be interviewed.

Owen interjects, "Because you're a smartass and you're not from around here. And *that's* why."

Morgan tries to cover. "Because the hailing port on your stern says 'Dallas, Texas'," he says.

"We're up from Texoma last Monday."

"You and your wife?" Owen asks.

"No. My partner."

"Oh."

A few minutes of small talk pass as the idea formulates in Morgan's head.

"Is your partner with you?" Morgan inquires with care.

"He is in the office, I guess."

"You buy this boat together?" Barney asks.

"We buy everything together."

"What? You live together?" asks Owen, scoffing as if he has made a joke.

"Yes," I answer flatly.

We talk about our plans.

"No one goes north on the Mississippi," Barney says. "You'd be better going to Florida. Everyone goes to Florida."

"But we don't want to go to Florida. We want to get out of the heat."

"Well," Owen insists. "Everyone goes to Florida."

They ask about *Betty Jane's* age, length, and engines until suddenly Morgan blurts out, "Nice meeting you. Gotta go."

"No, we don't, Morgan."

"Morgan, we're just talkin'."

"We gotta go," Morgan says, giving the other two the bum's rush.

"Where are we going, Morgan?"

"What's the rush?"

"Where's the goddammed fire, Morgan?"

"Get in the car," Morgan says.

"*Lemme go, goddammit.*"

"I'll tell you when you get in the car...just get in the car."

"Well, all right, but I don't like being pushed."

Bam! Bam! Bam! Three doors slam over failed attempts at being nice.

"Glad to have met y—" Owen and Barney tried to say.

The Suburban spins off the gravel and onto the road, beating a retreat back to the boathouse.

Alon, propped up in his chair on the porch of his house, has watched all of this transaction that he can from between his bare feet resting on the ottoman. He lays his head back and pretends to be asleep as I get back to work.

———◆———

Reassembly is slow. *Betty Jane* is back in the water by the Fourth of July. My repairs hold, but we are two weeks behind schedule. We intended to be underway by now. We still have all the mechanical work to do and no projected departure date in sight. Our Texas registration has lapsed, and Oklahoma dates all of theirs July 1. It is decision time. Do we keep on or do we go home?

"What do you want to do?" Dale asks.

"I want to have dinner…in a restaurant with incandescent lighting and an atmosphere that does not waft of sweaty Okie and baby shit…I want table service with a menu I can hold in my hand. No Styro-plates, no breakaway prison utensils, and no disposable bar wear. I want a reason to put on a fresh shirt, pressed pants, a tie and a jacket. I want to polish my shoes, shave my face, and run pomade through my hair."

I feel defeated and try in vain to hide my tears.

Dale draws my convulsing overalls, filthy with dust and damp with sweat, close to his chest and says, "Poor baby, you can take the queen out of Dallas, but you cannot take Dallas out of the queen."

"F-f-f-fuck y-you," I mumble into his embrace.

"That's better. Now, how much do you have left to do tonight?"

"Nothing. I'm done except to sweep up and rinse the pink dust off my dog."

"Good. I'll be back."

He drives around to the gas dock, gets out, comes back, drives back around and asks me, who hasn't moved since he left, "Well? Are you ready?"

"No. For what?"

"Why not?"

"Because I've been wondering what you're doing."

"I've been planning a surprise. Get in. Where's Doris Faye? Let's go, the sun's going down."

"Where are we going? What are we going to do?"

"Just get in. We're going to get you cleaned up. Do you have a jacket and tie at the hotel?"

"I have a jacket and both ties."

"Good. We're going to Fort Smith."

"To Fort Smith?" I ask.

"Yeah."

"Why?"

"You know, Alexander, if you tell someone what the surprise is going to be, then it is no longer a surprise. But it is late, you are hungry, and I'm dropping you off at the shower house so you can get cleaned up, so you can probably work out the rest for yourself. Do you want the red tie or the blue one?"

"Blue...no, red...no...red."

He pulls the truck up to the cinderblock structure in the middle of the parking lot and says, poorly imitating the local accent, "Now, git outta my tru-uck,"

I protest. "Shampoo? Razor?"

"I'll git 'em, now, git."

I get out of the truck saying, "And feed my dog."

"I'll feed your dawg."

"Bye."

"And be sure to scrub 'em neck 'n' ears, they're nasty with red shit."

———◆———

Fort Smith, Arkansas, is midtown Manhattan compared to where we've been. People loiter around the honky-tonks, hang out of the tattoo parlors, and drink beer at the biker bars that line Garrison Avenue. Rolando's Cuban Kitchen is on the corner of Third and Garrison. Immaculate Conception Catholic Church, bathed in blue light, stands at one end of the main drag. The Old Fort defends against Indian attack at the other.

Cool, dry air conditioning is the first thing I notice when I step into the dining room full of smartly dressed couples gathered around tables set with china and crystal. Iron chandeliers cast a rosy glow off heavily stuccoed walls. Skillets flare up in the kitchen and middle-aged grandma waitresses in sleeveless dresses troll the dining room.

Maree brings my Diet Coke and Dale's Tecate with lime.

"May I have the *Plato Cubano*?" I say, then ask, "Is it really Castro's favorite as the menu claims?"

"Never known him to order anything else when he's in here," she snaps back, turning heavily madeup eyes to Dale, who orders the barbecued ribs.

Over our hot and aromatic entrees, Dale poses the question again, "What do you want to do? You wanna call it quits?"

It is a hard question. *You'll only regret the chances you let slip by in life. Not the failures.*

"No," I state without further self-discussion. "I do not want to throw in the towel."

"Good," Dale says, genuinely relieved at my answer. "I won't have to waste any time convincing you otherwise. You know we are already grossly over budget, don't you? And our nest egg diminishes exponentially with each passing day?"

"I don't care," I answer defiantly.

"Good," he says, gnawing the bone and asking, *"Flan* or *Tres Leches*?"

"Fresh peach pie à la mode," Maree interjects, scooping up the plates. "Coffee?"

"Yes, please."

Dale continues, "Then, we will have to register in Oklahoma. If we were passing through I wouldn't mind, but since this will be home for at least another month—"

Another month?

"—and then we're on the move, I'd like to be legal some-where in the interim and while underway."

He's bought in, I think to myself, relieving my concern that he was only along for the ride.

"Better hurry if you're gonna get a place to see the show," Maree says.

CHAPTER SIX
Amongst the County Set

U ntil last night in Fort Smith, our world consisted of Applegate and Sallisaw, Oklahoma. Sallisaw is a lone white outpost surrounded by Indian reservations. There are two truck stops, a Wal-Mart, several churches, and a Braum's Dairy Store across the highway from our hotel where we get ice cream every night. The paucity of goods and services in this southeastern corner of Oklahoma is one thing we urban dwellers have to get used to. The people are the other.

Our errand is to register *Betty Jane* in the Sooner state. We stop by the Carpenters' house on our way out.

"You have to go to a tag office," Rhoda volunteers, explaining that the state of Oklahoma licenses its routine business to independent franchisees called tag offices, "and do *not* go to that man in Sallisaw. Go see my friend Susan in Vian."

Dale and I are not interested in an expedition across Indian Territory on an infernally hot day. The tag office in Sallisaw should be fine for business conducted with a check and first-class stamp back home. But it is not.

A walrus of a man sits behind an ancient poster of Dinah Shore, in gown and heels, announcing the coming-soon arrival of the Eisenhower Interstate System already whizzing across the south side of town. He greets us with a slack

jaw and an index finger left hanging in the dial of the rotary
phone to make it obvious that we are interrupting.

"He'p ya?" he asks in almost one syllable.

Our answer bothers him to move across an office that
was new in 1950. He extends a pudgy white hand and, keeping his eyes fixed on the two of us, rifles through our papers,
finally muttering something inaudible in a disagreeable tone.

"I said, 'Got. To. See. It,'" he repeats, as if we were dull
or deaf or both.

Our explanations go unheeded. Hauling a wooden yacht
ten miles into town strictly for his convenience is impossible.

"Gotta see it," he repeats.

Letting *Betty Jane*'s documents fall like snowy leaves
onto the counter, he intimates that there probably is no such
vessel and as he turns to walk away, "Or at least there isn't
one *y'all* could claim."

Irritated and provoked, I storm out. I am not the first.
The screen door slamming behind me is already torn.

"Now what?" I demand when Dale gets into the truck.

"Rhoda said not to go to that man."

"I know."

"She suggested we go to see Susan in Vian."

"I know," I say, fuming. "But where the hell is Vian?"

"Turn right."

Vian—rhymes with Diane—is far enough away for the
unpleasantness of the last few minutes to get lost in row upon
row of emerald-green cornstalks glistening in the late morning sun. Hot wind blows through the cab like a scirocco.
Doris Faye, sitting between us, pants.

The National Bank of Vian, MeMe's Emporium, the Bee-
hive Salon de Botay, and a convenience store—which advertises
both having a drive-through and being the mayor's office—clus-

ter the central business district around a four-way stop. Folks line up on Main Street for the meatloaf lunchtime special at the Market Café. On the next corner, the man at the True Value hardware hawks John Deere riding mowers. But we see no tag office. We pull into the convenience store drive-through to ask directions. Glass doors open automatically on a woman wearing a green eyeshade and hunched over a computer printout.

"He'p ya?" she says without looking up.

"We're looking for the tag office," I answer.

"Where'd'ya come from?" she asks, training a ruler on her printouts.

"Sallisaw."

"Back-the-way-you-came-little-yellow-house-with-green-trim-on-the-right-side-across-from-the-Exxon-and-Bubba's-Burgers-can't-miss-it."

"Obviously, you can," I whisper to Dale.

She looks up. The ruby and turquoise chain attached to her glasses rests on her cheeks.

"You boys want a cold drink? Sure is hot out there. Mercy!"

We order a Diet Coke for me and a root beer for Dale.

"Coming right up. RubyLee, RubyLee. These gentlemen out here want a Diet Coke and root beer. Hop to."

Shortly, the last remaining slave freed by the Emancipation Proclamation and the only black woman, ancient and still in captivity in these parts, delivers the sodas. A loose-fitting garment hangs from her withered frame. Pink ribbons tie her plaited hair.

"One dollah," she says timidly through a mouth without teeth.

We pay her two dollars and explain she can't make any money selling cans of soda for fifty cents. She laughs and disappears. The woman in the eyeshade waves good-bye as I ask, "Where's the mayor's office?"

"You're looking at it," she says proudly. "I'm the clerk."

"Thank you," Dale says, seeing me draw breath, and ever watchful for sarcasm.

"B-but—"

"Just drive the truck," he urges, "Just drive the truck... just..." He waves towards the highway that is Cherokee Street in Sallisaw.

"What?" I protest. "I wasn't going to say nothing."

"Good," he answers. "Drive the truck."

———— ◆ ————

We find the two landmarks. The gas station blew down years ago, and a sign at Bubba's insists, "Yes! We're Open!" despite the judge's liquidation notice pasted to the door. The frame house across the street looks more like a private residence than a place of business. Hanging baskets line the porch, a wind chime announces our arrival into a room that contrasts sharply with the Sallisaw office. A woman in her mid-forties, dressed in a simple white blouse over a tailored beige skirt, is returning a vacuum cleaner to its closet.

"Hi," she says, "I wanted to get this done before the after-lunch rush."

She invites us to wait at the counter arranged with community service pamphlets, license plate frames, and bumper stickers praising Jesus. On the desk behind the U-shaped counter sit a color portrait of two boys and a black-and-white snapshot of a soldier in the jungle.

"My name is Susan," she says. "How can I help you?"

"We need to register a boat," I answer.

"Fine," she says in a laid-back drawl that elongates vowels. She reaches tentatively for the manila folder Dale has in his hands and unloads its contents onto the counter. She sorts through the title, the bill of sale, the Coast Guard registration, the proof of insurance and asks, "Where's your proof of moorage?"

We are dumbstruck.

She rephrases the question.

"Where's she tied up?"

"Oh," we exclaim together. "She's at Applegate. Rhoda sent us."

A change occurs. Susan's face softens. We are no longer strangers. We are Rhoda's friends. The difference is subtle, almost imperceptible, but we see it in her eyes.

She asks, "How's Alon?"

Alon is not good. He has stage four cancer of the colon metastasized to the brain, is stretched out in his recliner on the porch, and strung out on pain-killers; but it is not our place to say. Instead, I offer a vague, "As well as can be expected."

She shakes her head and reaches for the phone, punching the number from memory and pushing the Farrah Fawcett hairstyle out of her face.

"Rhoda? Susan. How are you?...How's Alon?" It is the beginning of a lesson that teaches us how things are done outside the big city. Discussion runs from the antics of Susan's younger son to the older one's being eager to drive, and the Fourth of July being fine except the cat peed on the firecrackers. Never does she mention the business at hand until finally, "Yeah, they're here. Just a minute, I'll see."

She cups the receiver.

"Did y'all go over to that man in Sallisaw first?"

Our faces tell the tale.

Susan relays our tacit confession.

"Yeah, I know. I *know*." She fingers the wedding band hanging on a chain around her neck. "Men are like that. You can't tell 'em nothing...Okay...Yes...Okay...'Bye...All right...'Bye."

Meanwhile, the noon seating at the Market Café has let out. Customers wanting to "do bidness" before going back to work trickle in. They find places in the rows of chairs salvaged from some church fellowship hall.

"Take a seat. I'll be right with you," Susan greets each new arrival while putting together our application.

They take off their hats, mop their brows, and state their business. Some need fishing licenses while others want to file liens. These are the people she's grown up with. Her kids play with their kids. Her parents are friends with their parents.

"You know the judge will never grant that, don't you?" she says. "Hasn't yet, has he? Have a seat."

"How are you's?" and "How ya been's?" circulate around the room as Susan, holding one hand to her ear to blot out any distraction, reads from State of Oklahoma Manual of Procedures.

"'All registrations must be pre-approved prior to issuance,'" she says out loud. "That cannot be right."

She reaches again for the phone. This time she dials Oklahoma City, the capital.

"Melinda? Susan...Uh-huh...Fine...You?...Good...Really?... Again?...Too bad...Listen, I've got these two guys from Texas here trying to register...What? Oh, I've got a host of customers in here. You know how it is the first day after a holiday especially at the first of the month...Uh-huh. Anyway, like I was saying, I've got these two guys in here trying to register a boat...Uh-huh...Well, the manual says...Well...Uh-huh...Well, I cannot very well go out and look at every single boat that comes in for registration, now can I?...I'm sorry, it's just...well, it's not...I know, but it's not...Yes, well, it's not... Okay, fine, but it's not on a trailer, it's at Alon's... Not good. Bad, really...I know...She's fine considering. I mean, if your husband was dyin' a slow painful death, how would you be?... Yeah, I just talked to her...Well, you know Rhoda. The house could be on fire and she'd run into the kitchen to save the weenies and marshmallows so the kids would have something to do...No, their children are grown and out. Chad's deployed God-knows-where and Casi's in school someplace..."

Dale and I find seats among the locals. Everyone is talking about corn. It is going to be bumper crop "if the weather stays good."

"Been awfully wet, though," says one.

"August is coming," says another while Susan continues to plead our case.

"Now, you know Alon is too sick to haul that boat up here...All right...I'll just have to drive out there after work and look at the hull plate...Okay...You, too...All right..."

Hull plate rings in my head. I pull Dale away from eavesdropping about pork bellies and well casings to ask, "Dale?"

"Huh?"

"Didn't you make a rubbing of the hull plate?"

"Yeah."

"Does she have it?"

"Think so."

"Check."

"No," he says and jumps up, waving the thin sheet over his head to get Susan's attention.

"Wait, wait," Susan calls into the receiver. "Melinda? Are you there? I have a rubbing of the hull plate. Will that work?...Yeah, I can read the hull number. Yeah, it matches. Okay. I'll send it. Thanks...'Bye."

Completely unflappable, Susan says to the room, "Sorry, y'all. You know how OKC has gotten about this stuff. These guys are trying to register a boat down at Alon's."

She feeds our application, the rubbing of the hull plate, and a copy of our lease that Rhoda faxed over into the machine and asks, "Now, who's next?"

Somehow the twenty or so men, ranging from white men in Stetsons to migrants in sombreros, sort themselves into an order according to their arrival with minimal disturbance in the conversation. Anything new in Sequoyah County is noteworthy. Our boat is new.

"What kinda boat is it?" asks a man wearing a silver and turquoise clasp on the bolo around his neck.

"A 1955 Chris-Craft cruiser," I answer.

"Is that that woodie Alon brought in last month?" asks another.

"Yes," Dale says, turning around.

"Man, that's a beautiful boat. Is that yourn? She's a beaut."

"Y'all got a boat?"

"Y'all the ones with the dog?"

"Yeah, she's in the truck, her name is Doris Faye," I say, pointing out the windows.

"Yeah, you oughtta go down to Alon's and look at their boat. Man."

"What kinda boat?"

"Mighty fine looking dog. Bet she's a good huntin' dog."

"They say it's a woodie, fine looking, too. I might just take my wife down and come see your boat."

"No, she's gun-shy," I say to one and to the other, "Wish you would come down and look at our boat."

"How's Alon?"

"Too bad."

The fax machine whirs. Susan gently moves the customer at the counter aside, explaining that all we need to do is pay, and then we'll be gone.

"Fine. Fine," says the man in overalls and clutching a car title.

The phone rings.

"It's Melinda," she says to us, then into the receiver, "Yeah. Yeah. I've got it right here…We figured…Well, that's all right as long as we got it…Yes…Thank you…Hi to Buster and the kids…Uh-huh…'Bye…Uh-huh, you too…'Bye. 'Bye." Then to us, "That'll be $106.83, gentlemen. Congratulations, *Betty Jane* is registered in Oklahoma."

———•———

The foray into the countryside has put us in solid with the county set. The cloud of mystery and suspicion that greeted us in this place where everyone knows everyone has dissipated. We are one of them—almost. The greetings are heartier; interest in our progress is sincere; offers to help come readily and from all quarters. So, too, comes a familiarity which I handle with varying degrees of grace.

———•———

Back in the water and registered, *Betty Jane* is viable boat. Chris and Robert are eager to investigate the oil leak in the starboard engine and Kenn wants to order the vinyl for the deckhouse roof. I walk up to the porch to ask about color samples.

"You're gonna want white," Kenn says.

Kenn is not usually antagonistic. He is a perfectionist looking out for the best interests of his client and to secure satisfaction in a job he is about to do. He and I are alike in this way.

"Right," I counter. "But the original specs call for palmetto green."

"What color *is* that?" Kenn says, peering over his bottle-end glasses, tinted brown against the relentless prairie sun.

"Well, we don't really know," I admit. "Whatever palmetto green was doesn't matter because we must to choose from what is currently available."

"You're gonna want white," Kenn says.

Alon nods.

"Certainly, we would consider white," I say. "I mean, white is what we just ripped off, but we'd also like it if you'd ask what greens are available."

Kenn reaches over and snubs out Alon's cigarette left smoldering in the ashtray, hands him another, and says to me, "But you're gonna want white."

I am accustomed to resistance in the face of innovation. Interior decorators, hired for their creativity, often had to either educate their clients or wait out their stubbornness.

"Fine. We're gonna want white," I say, pretending to relent. "But could you ask the shop to please send cuttings of the green they have in stock?"

While he was at National Coach in Fort Smith, Kenn upholstered the vinyl tops on all the Clinton administration's presidential limousines. He has expertise, but Alon has authority.

"No harm'n asking, is there, Kenn? I mean. Y' know?"

"Well, they're gonna want white."

"White" in these parts is invariably a two-syllable word with the vowel drawn out and doubled, but, the "i" begins to bite as discussion continues.

"Right," Alon agrees. "But these boys aren't from around here." Alon shoots me a wink. "An' they don't know 'bout the river or nuthin'. Don't you remember when we went to pick this boat up? These boys stumbled out onto the dock half-dressed, groggy eyed, 'thout no breakfast? Shoot, Kenn, the coffee wasn't even on. 'Member?"

Kenn nods.

"We're just gonna hafta go slow," Alon counsels.

Kenn nods.

Slow is the last thing we need to go.

Alon pulls his best friend by the shirt tail and whispers, "B'sides, they're the customer."

"Okay," Kenn allows. "But..."

"BUT THEY'RE GONNA WANT WHITE," Alon says, running interference. "Fine. Let the damn dog have his day and ask for samples of the damn green. C'mon, Kenn."

"What kinda green?"

"Kenn."

———— ◆ ————

A couple of days later, Rhoda walks down the boathouse triumphantly holding the envelope in her hand. Robert and Chris squat in the engine room wondering why Alon sent them for the wrong gasket and then argue about which one's going to tell him.

"Tell who what?" Rhoda interjects herself into the conversation.

The two guys lie quickly, "Nuthin'."

"If it's about my dope-headed husband lying up there in that recliner, I already know. I know better than you ever will know." Rhoda, defiant but not defensive, says, "So he's made a mistake and the gasket doesn't fit. Go down to Cheryl at NAPA. Tell 'er what happened and get the right thing."

The two men look stunned.

"If you get a move on you can get to town and back and get this done before five."

Chris and Robert scurry as much as anyone does out here.

She turns to us and says, "Well, other than that, how's it going? Anyway, I come to bring down this envelope from the upholstery shop."

Dale, more interested in the engine than the upholstery, lays the packet on the inside dashboard.

"Well? Aren't you gonna open it?" she asks.

I grab the envelope.

"Of course we are," I say, tearing the paper and letting its contents fall amongst spiderwebs mixed with sawdust.

Ten whites and off-whites embossed with various textures and finishes and four greens—a lighter and a darker shade in two different patterns.

"You need to go ahead and decide if Kenn's gonna get that order in." Then she smiles mischievously and adds, "But yer gonna want whi-ite."

Dale and I put our minds together. We discuss cleanability, heat gain, and the contrast of the green against the mahogany stained red. We exchange inanities, hoping the other will tip his hand.

"What we had was white."

"The hull's white."

"But the green looks nice, too."

"It'll be different."

"What we had was white."

"Which do you like?"

"Green's nice."

Finally, I cannot resist. "Kenn says, 'You're gonna want white.'"

We both tend toward the green but neither wants to suffer the "I told you so" when, after installation, we discover Kenn is right. Mature, logical debate devolves into several games of rock-paper-scissors, each round being disqualified for cheating, as yet another polling yields inconclusive results. The sunlight fades, and we have to decide.

Early the next morning, Kenn is at the marina on some errand concerning his sailboat. Judging from the looks of his truck, he is off to string a fence somewhere. Post hole diggers, cement-mixing hoes, shovels, and a wheelbarrow fill the bed. I catch up with him before he leaves.

"This one," I say, pressing the sample Dale and I agreed upon into his hand.

A syphilitic canker would be more favorably received.

"GREEN?" Kenn says with such scorn that the grackles on the lawn take flight.

"This green."

I press the sample deep into his flesh, like a knife.

"Green, REALLY?"

Blood rushes to his head. Veins pop out of his neck.

"Yes," I answer quietly. "Please."

His eyes set on the gravel drive. His jaw sets.

"You...are...going...to...want...WHITE," he snaps.

At this point, I am angry. I am not nice, kind, nor professional. I stacked finish samples like blocks and cut fabric samples like construction paper in my mother's showroom when these boys were chasing dung beetles down dirt holes.

I've watched creative genius solve impossible design problems in a trice. I respect the artistic temperament and Kenn is the consummate craftsman, but I have lost patience defending a decision that is ours to make. I am sarcastic and condescending.

"I know we are," I say, coolly. "But we'd like to see what green will look like. Surely you are correct and we'll instantly see the error of our decision, in which case you will enjoy the satisfaction of charging us twice, using the green as practice for a more perfect installation of the white."

Gasoline on the fire.

I don't care.

Kenn grips the wheel. I see the bones in his knuckles. He stares out the windshield and tromps on the gas. Spinning tires spray gravel across the water. The blue Dodge Ram careens up the hill. It narrowly misses Walt mowing the lawn. It roars past the house, screeches onto the pavement, and tears up the highway. Tools, bounced out of the back of the truck, lie in its wake.

"How'd that go?" Dale asks, setting out breakfast.

"Good."

———————◆———————

I repair the roof substrate during the next week. As I smooth the last of the blemishes, the weekenders arrive and collect behind my back. Finally, the one whose brother owns the vinyl shop in Oklahoma City says, "My brother says you're putting a green top on this boat."

"Yes," I answer, turning to see the mob that has assembled off *Betty Jane*'s bow, and call down to the clatter of Dale's washing up breakfast dishes to say, "Dale bring up the sample of the vinyl top and come out here, please. We have company."

Eight or ten boaters muse over the cutting. They rub it between their fingers and angle it toward the light. They pucker their lips, cluck their tongues, and raise their objections.

"Gonna be hot."

"Your gonna want white."

Nothing we say quells the unrest.

"What color is pal-met-to green, anyway?" A third says, stumbling over the unfamiliar word.

Meanwhile Morgan, almost invisible in yachting whites on his white boat, has been watching. He commands respect in the boathouse politics that Rhoda and Alon stay clear of as a matter of good business. Over a dashing physique, he wears the paunch of a life well-lived. White hair runs a fringe around his scalp.

"The massacre is over and you want to carp over ammo?" Morgan asks. "Look how good Alexander repaired the roof. None y'all thought it could be done," he says, casting an accusing eye.

Morgan's interest in us is personal. Later on in the summer, his wife, Linda, will explain: "He had a *Betty Jane* once, or almost did. It was a 1960 Owens, twenty-nine feet, Morgan's dream. But she was too much. Too much rot, too much time, too much money. Every weekend, every holiday, and weeks during the summer, we worked on her. The children hated her, bless their hearts; they were so bored. He became Captain Bligh. I was The Sea Hag.

"She always wanted something, *needed* something. Morgan never neglected me or the children, he'd never do that, y' understand. But, sometimes, he'd go out in the middle of the night just to check on her, be with 'er. Like some secret mistress or something. It got kinda creepy."

A shadow crosses her face.

"I was scared," she confesses haltingly. "I honestly didn't know what he would do. I knew he loved me. I knew he loved the kids. But I also knew we could not go on…Not like that. I said, 'Morgan, you have to decide between your family and that boat.' He said, 'I know. I know.' Bawling like a baby, he was. Poor thing's heartbroke…but…we just couldn't keep 'er. She was twenty-nine feet of nothing but work. We simply could not get ahead of the work."

She smiles as if relieved the crisis has passed once again.

"He chose us, but he wants to be doing what you're doing. He wants to be on a wooden boat sailing away somewhere."

After Kenn installs the new upholstery, we take *Betty Jane* for a sea trial to inspect the oil gasket installation and other upgrades. The sound of her engines draws a crowd. Dale drops her into reverse. She backs into the sun and, as she does, a green reflection flashes across the boathouse ceiling, causing those standing by to gasp.

"She really is the most beautiful boat I've ever seen," they say.

Kenn could not be prouder.

We make our way around the far side of Kerr Lake. All systems are go until I notice a white plume of steam coming out of the starboard tailpipe. A steamy exhaust, insufficient cooling somewhere, can come from a myriad of minor malfunctions. We will address the problem when we get back from Dallas. Dale wants to see his father before casting off, which we believe is imminent.

We find Roy in good spirits, regretting only that he cannot go with us. Betty, on the other hand, is not so enthusiastic. She wants to know when her son is coming home.

"Home is where Alexander is," Dale explains, kissing his mother.

CHAPTER SEVEN
The Widow Carpenter

We return to an Applegate in mourning. Alon has died. Those who used to come down every afternoon to have a beer by the water, stay away. The fishing boats that used to splash at the boatyard ramp at dawn and pull out at dusk don't launch. Cars that once parked at water's edge now circle the house as if to stare at the porch where Alon lay. The weekenders do not come. Robert is scarce. Rhoda is nowhere in sight. Only Walt comes down to the water. He sits on the gas dock and allows Bob Quackenbush to wipe his tears. Walt's brother, Oliver, stacks fresh plates of food next to the grief-stricken father and murmurs something about how he has to eat.

The memorial service is that forced celebration of life with upbeat music and images of Alon's gappy smile projected on screens. Afterwards, friends reacquaint each other with the minutia of their day-to-day lives. The excitement dissipates and an unshakable pall draws itself over the cove.

For the most part, we live-aboards keep to our own affairs. By day, we step to do whatever is necessary to keep the marina running; by night, we gather around a bonfire on the beach—rituals broken only by a frog croak or fin slap. Suddenly, after two or three weeks, the porch door slams. It is Rhoda. Her signature white tee glows in the moonlight as she approaches.

"Hi, Rhoda."

"Hi, Rhoda."

"Hi, Rhoda," we say like a warped recording.

"Hi, y'all. Good. I'm glad to see you all here. I'm gonna have a meeting tomorrow morning at the gas dock. Y'all are expected to attend, all y'all. See you, then."

We nod dumbly.

Having made the announcement she came to make, she turns to walk back but catches herself and says, "My husband is dead. I'm not," before marching back to the house.

At dawn, Bob Quackenbush, store manager and one of the first to introduce himself on our arrival, presides over a barbecue grill—turning out eggs, bacon, sausage, hash browns and toast to all comers.

"Coffee's on the counter," he says, waving a spatula. "Beer's in the cooler if you gotta have it. But you're paying for *that*, cash on the barrel head, you all, I'm not putting anything else on account, not for now. That goes for soft drinks, too. Rest of this's on Alon. Eat up."

The center of the store, which Rhoda purposely keeps clear of merchandise for gathering, is full of men—some in lawn chairs, others sitting on the floor, all with breakfast in their laps. Between extra helpings, conversation is light until Rhoda stands up, digs a cigarette out of her jeans, and before lighting it, says, "Y'all." She cups the flame, exhales fully and adds, "Y'ALL! We've got a marina to run here, if not for our own sake's, then for Alon's."

A round of applause, hoots, and hollers dispels the apprehension and anxiety that has pressed so mightily on us all. Applegate's got a leader, the woman who has been running it since Alon's first diagnosis. She glances at her clipboard and asks for volunteers. Dale will keep the laundry tidy. I'll haul the garbage out of the boathouse.

"I've assigned other jobs to people who aren't here so y'all don't start pokin' 'round what ain't your business," she says, sweeping an eye across the room. "Okay?"

"Yes, *ma'am*."

"Good. Now, from now on, 'til I say otherwise, we're gonna be meetin' down 'ere ev'ry mornin' at least 'til we can get this thing on an even keel. Breakfast to anyone who wants to pitch in. Right, Bob?"

"Right."

"Okay. Now, the first problem is," she says, pointing to us, "that these guys got steam in their exhaust. Who knows why?"

The item goes to open discussion.

"You're getting steam in your exhaust? Probably a cracked exhaust manifold."

"That's the steam, but what about the elevated water temperature?"

"Well, may be the steam but what about the consistent compression ranges?"

"And he's got a gunky spark plug on the number one cylinder."

"Well, that's a carburetion problem. He may be burning too rich."

"Okay, that could explain the overtemp, but what about the steam?"

———— ◆ ————

This isn't Texoma, we don't have mechanics and technicians at our disposal; we have this group of guys, each with a contribution to make. The process is slow and inexact and trying. But our safe passage will depend on the charity of strangers, so before we leave this place, I will have to learn patience. Patience precedes charity.

"The oil pan gasket we just replaced has nothing to do with it, right?" Rhoda asks.

"Right," we all say together.

Walt speaks up.

"What you need to do—," he turns to spit tobacco juice into a cup, "is start in the front with the cheapest thing, which'll be the water pump, and go from there. Look at it. Test it. And go on to the next thing."

"But I've already checked for leaks," I say.

"That's just where *I'd* start," he says, throwing up his hands.

"Anything else?" Rhoda asks her rally of men. "All right, then, let's get to work. And I'm expectin' to see every last one of you here tomorrow a.m., too, hear?"

"Yes'm."

Dale and I go back to the boat and trace the water's course from through-hull in the front of the engine to the exhaust manifold in the back, inspecting every component on the way except the water pump, which I've already done. We blame the thermostat that we can get from Cheryl at the NAPA in town. We install and test.

"Steam!" I call from the back of the boat.

Next is the thermostat housing, which could easily malfunction after twenty years. We order, wait, install, and test.

"STEAM!"

The cast iron exhaust manifolds are heavy and cumbersome. They are difficult to remove, but eventually they come out and lie on the dock where I can examine them. The water channels are clogged.

"That's the problem," Walt says. "Even if it ain't, you'll be needin' to replace 'em, if you can't vat 'em."

Vatting is to dip into corrosive agents. Once as ubiquitous to any shade-tree mechanic as Gojo, vatting is now banned by the EPA, except for the most sophisticated operators. The local network that we met at Susan's in Vian sends us along an uneven route of "damned government" to "I can't but I know a guy who might" until, at last, we arrive on the far side of Fort Smith.

"Can't vat. Don't know anybody who can. Guv'ment, y' know."

This man uses ultrasound.

"Will it do any good?" I ask.

"Don't know. Can't say it will. Don't know it won't."

"It's cheaper than new," Dale says.

"Worth a try," the man says. "Ready for you tomorrow."

Re-installation takes the two of us, new gaskets, and a toolbox full of wrenches; but we do it.

"STEAM!"

The last option is to buy new manifolds, which are expensive to manufacture and costly to ship. The closest pair is in Houston, Texas. One week delivery. I assemble the new manifolds, install, and test.

"STEAM!" I cry out.

It is the height of frustration. I drop the pram into the water and begin ramming the boathook up *Betty Jane's* exhaust pipe hoping to find a dead anything that could be blocking proper flow. Morgan, in his inimitably placid way, presents himself at our stern.

"It's in the front," he says quietly.

"WHAT?" I jab, deaf and blind with rage.

"It's in the front," he repeats.

His composure is maddening.

"Can't be," I insist while Dale wonders if I should be committed. "I checked it."

"Nevertheless," he says, taking a swig of his coffee cup. "It is."

Morgan returns to his cabin.

The next morning, we eschew the morning roundtable and refer the problem to Oliver and Walt privately.

"Did you switch the water pumps?" Oliver asks.

"No," I answered. "They're a pain in the ass. I checked them for leaks and didn't find anything."

"Still," Oliver says, "if the steam moves when the pump moves from starboard to port, then you've found the problem."

A demonically simple diagnostic, which yields the same result.

"STEAM!" I cry out from the back of the boat, but this time it is on the port side.

I take the offending pump to Oliver.

"Why, sure, there it is," he says, pointing with a pen-knife. "There's a crimp in the O-ring right there."

"Does it make a difference?" I ask.

"Without a groove in the casting to receive it, you're just crimping the O-ring when you tighten the cap. A flat gasket's what you need."

"I checked for leaks."

"Might not have leaked," Oliver explains. "Not water, that is. But it leaked air. It's called cavitation and happens when air mixes with water. It reduces efficiency."

Less water means less cooling. Something gets hot and steams.

Meanwhile, Robert cannot get the transmissions put back together without Alon.

"Okay," Rhoda says, pulling a cigarette out of her jeans. "ALL RIGHT," she shouts across the morning meeting. "Robert needs help in the machine shop. Who knows anything about transmissions?"

The round robin that bounced around the room over steam is more tentative and reserved about transmissions.

"My mother-in-law had a Buick once," begins a well-meaning but unqualified prospect.

"Did you work on the transmission?" Rhoda asks.

"No. Didn't need too. Ran like a top."

Giggles.

"Okay, now," she says over her glasses, like a schoolmarm restoring order.

She pulls from behind her back the Borg-Werner service manual she found in her office, opens it to the page marked with a bobby pin, and reveals an exploded diagram of the transmission in question and the instructions for its reassembly.

"I thought this looked a lot like my momma's Singer 401A Slant-O-Matic sewing machine."

Grown men slide onto the floor like children to a game. They trace with their fingers the movement of torque through the diagram and explain to each other that which they recognize.

"And I thought that if she could get that thing took apart cleaned, oiled, and put back together, running stitches between cleaning up breakfast and getting lunch for a bunch of farm hands; then we could figure this thing out, too."

Her ploy works. If a momma could do that, then these guys can whip this. Rhoda picks the manual off the floor and leads everyone to the shop where pieces and parts of two transmissions cover the floor—everyone except for Mr. Quackenbush, his wife, and me. There is a boat coming in.

CHAPTER EIGHT
John Bartlett, As I Live and Breathe

Five miles downstream from the gas dock, the lock doors open, releasing from its chamber the most hellacious noise of a single unmuffled gasoline engine pushing hard against the current.

"Must be John," Mrs. Quackenbush says, proceeding without pause to wipe the next jelly smear.

The noise gets louder as it approaches until finally it turns into the marina, revealing itself as a houseboat and filling the cove with all the imagined cacophony of the Second Coming. Only in the nick of time does its captain kill the one engine so that her nose gently presses into the dock and the stern swings around to a perfect landing.

A bald, shirtless, shoeless, sunburned-like-a-native man somewhere in his mid-to-late fifties alights. With one hand, he pulls a pair of khaki shorts into the groove of a waistline that runs under his beer belly. With the other, he loops a line nonchalantly around a cleat.

"Out on two; back on one," he quips to no one in particular, as if losing one engine while underway were *de rigueur*.

He is so abrupt, rough, crude—the kind of man which one does not meet in Grandmother's living room. I am instantly attracted to him. *If that ain't a river rat, I've never seen one.* Two blue eyes inked to the back of his skull stare back at me as he struts into the store and demands that someone get him a beer.

His wife is closer to my age than to his and made up to match the hot pink and acid green ensemble she is wearing. It is neither tasteful nor subdued, but she carries it off as indomitably chic.

"Hi, my name is Kara," she says, stepping daintily onto the dock.

She owns The Magic Marker, a tattoo parlor in Fort Smith; he is rich in a way no one talks about; and judging from their boat, they both spend a lot of time on the river.

Enjoy Enjoy is a fifty-foot fiberglass Gibson, the workhorse of houseboats, around twenty-five years old and not the show-stopping beauty that is *Betty Jane*. Severe exposure has oxidized the gel coat, rust stains trail off the fittings, ragged towels beat against the railings, and bungee cords lash an open flame barbecue onto the stern, directly over the fuel tanks. The mufflers are cut out in order to increase fuel efficiency, and a Jolly Roger with a red kerchief tied over one eye snaps in the wind over the bridge. They have been gone for over three years, but news of their arrival brings folks down to the gas dock. Kara holds boaters' wide-eyed attention with her telling of how they survived Hurricane Katrina.

"…John kept saying, 'We're gonna make it, Kara. We're gonna make it.' But we *didn't* make it."

"But—," John tries to interrupt.

"BUT we didn't make it," Kara insists.

John says, "BUT if we hadda made it, we coulda had shot up the Tennessee-Tombigbee as far as we wanted an' been safe."

Kara rolls her eyes.

"But...we *didn't make it*, did we? We tied up to some trees in the Mississippi Bayou. It's a wonder we didn't get blown out to sea and drowned."

"Not with a deckhand like you on board, honey bunny," John says, pressing his gut into the small of her back and wrapping his arms around her waist.

"Yeah," Kara says, brushing off his advances. "The storm surge is coming in, and he says, 'Someone's got to go out there and re-tie 'em lines,' and pushes a rope at me."

"Now, now," John corrects, wagging his finger. "I offert you a rope."

"Pushed."

"Whichever of us went out there hadda have line tied 'round her pretty little waist in case she got blow'd overboard...or sumthin'."

"Anyway," Kara continues, "there was water everywhere. Water blowing around the boat, in the boat, under the boat. Nothing was dry...nothing. We were rockin' so bad I thought we would capsize."

John jitterbugs and gyrates as if on wind-tossed decks.

"When all of a sudden, the ropes started binding horribly against the trees," she says.

John contorts his face like tortured lines.

"It's a wonder they didn't rip the cleats right out of the deck."

John abruptly stops his pantomime.

"Outta *Enjoy Enjoy's* deck?" he asks, feigning shock over her assertion. "She's as solid as that Rock of Gibraltar."

"Ha!" Kara says, repeating a guttural, "Ha!" before continuing. "Anyway, he says, 'Honey bunny, if I go out there and get washed overboard and the boat comes down on my head, which it surely will do and knock me out at least, if not kill me.'"

John draws breath to interject, but her frown preempts his interruption.

"Anyway, he says, 'Then you'll be a lonely widow woman in a storm with no one to help you wrestlin' with the guilt, grief, and worry, and all over my corpse floatin' out to sea with no one to blame but your own silly selfish self. Why, you'd never be able to live with yourself,' is what he said."

"You know all that'd be true," John insists with hands outstretched.

"I'd chance it," she says.

"Whereas if *she* hadda got washed overboard, I'dda been big an' strong enough to haul her limp, delicate frame over the rail an' I'dda give her mouth-to-mouth resuscitation," John smiles, adding, "I do mouth-to-mouth real good, don't I, hon?"

"Ha! As drunk as you were? I'd probably suffocate like Mama Cass. Did I tell y'all that we were pie-eyed?"

"'Twas a *storm*," John insists.

"It was *bourbon*. And despite just having my hair done," she primps. "I went out. He was right. There was no way I could've rescued him if anything happened."

"She was my brave little trooper. I helped her on with her PFD and opened the sliding glass door an' all like a gentleman."

John snuggles up to his bride just as a beer burp falls involuntarily out of his mouth.

"Gross," Kara says, pushing him away again. "He shoved me out with a rope and a life jacket. Water poured into the deckhouse and rushed down the middle of the boat into the bilge like a river. I've never seen so much water."

"She shimmied 'em lines up 'em trees just like a rat."

"And almost drowned standing straight up."

"Yeah, but we did it...what a night."

John shakes his head and grins.

Kara throws her arms around his bull neck, pulls him close and says, "Yeah, what a night."

They berth *Enjoy Enjoy* two slips down from *Betty Jane*.

———————◆———————

As much as I love John Bartlett—a Cajun as it turns out, the kind that passes out in a deckchair with a fishing pole in his hands—John Bartlett loves *Betty Jane*. He smiles at her varnished decks, so large we can see the spaces between his teeth. He caresses her woodwork and pats her nose whenever he walks by. When we take her out to test the re-geared transmissions, John is on the bridge with Dale while I stuff myself in the engine room, laying hands on anything that looks hot.

"Cool as a cucumber," I call over the engine noise, "Cool as a cucumber...John, can you check the exhaust for steam."

"Cain't."

"Why not?"

"Cause I'm busy screaming *Yee-Ha* on the bridge."

He demonstrates.

"*Yeeee-HAAAAA. Yeeeee-HAAAAA.* See?"

"Don't bother," Dale interjects. "The gauges are fine."

"Gauges were fine last time," I say.

"Little ste'm ain't nothin'. *Enjoy Enjoy* steams...a little."

Dale and I answer together, "We know."

"WHAD'YEW MEAN?"

Giddy with the results of our tests, we return to the slip and are eager to finally get underway but Dale, the more cautious of the two, suggests, "Before we shove off for good, we better have a shake-down cruise."

"*Bonne idée,*" John says in anglicized French. "Where'y goin'?"

A shake-down cruise is a trial run, longer than a test cruise. *Betty Jane* needs a shade over the bridge to protect us from the sun and rain, a cover over the helm and its instruments, and a raincoat for the pram. The sailmaker at Applegate is too shaken up by Alon's death to do the work, so we take referrals and find that the hands-down favorite among the locals is Tucker Duck and Rubber in Fort Smith, forty miles downstream and an easy day trip. We'll spend the night there, meet Tucker's sales representative, and return the next day. *Betty Jane* will show us how she handles against a current.

We start out as folks are getting up, hugging their cups of coffee and enjoying the first smoke of the day. Among them are John and Kara, standing by to see us off. Though they don't want to go, John, always shirtless and shoeless, has plenty to say about how to get there and what to expect. He plants his feet on the dock and pretends to be at our helm.

"Now, th' garrison is goin' to be over this-a-way." John raises his right arm to indicate the old fort. "And then th' river's gonna swing around that-a-way." He indicates left. "Y' gonna see some islands and stuff pert' soon after that the Mitland bridge goes over."

The Midland Bridge is where U.S. 64 crosses over the river from Fort Smith to Van Buren and on to I-40 and points east.

"Now," John says, changing hands on a make-believe wheel between his legs. "If you look over yonder"—he waves at shoulder height—"you're gonna see Em'rald Cove on t'other side of a tow." Which is what river men call an island. "And jus' as 'at tow give out, you gonna wanna pull hard t' port and sail into the gas dock neat and perty. But don't'y do it. It's shallah." John frowns severely at the word, shallah. "That's bad."

He changes his grip, leaning his belly into the pretend wheel so to free both hands.

"Y' look downstream." He points straight ahead with arms outstretched. "There's a gravel depot on river left. Y' head for that gravel depot, past the marina, past the bridge, y' follah?"

Dale nods.

"Look 'aire on yer chart." John points to a non-existent map. "See it?"

Dale glances at the real map on his real bridge and nods.

"Go all th' way down to that gravel depot and come 'bout."

John flips an about-face to indicate the reversed heading.

"Now, y' hug that shoreline an' come up to th' gas dock with her nose 'nto th' current. Git me?"

Dale nods.

"Good. Have fun. Tell Art I sent y'."

"Cast all lines," Dale says.

"Let 'em go, John," Kara says, reaching out to grab her husband's arm.

"One more thing 'fore y' go."

He clasps my head between his hands. I can feel his breath on my lips, taste the tobacco and coffee in his breath.

"If you need anything, *anything*, you call me. Kara and I'll come git y'. I mean it."

"Let 'em go, John."

"'Sides, I need a reason t' git 'way from these Okies, anyway."

"Let 'em go, John."

"'Bye. Have fun," he says. "Now where's my coffee. Hon, do you have a cigarette?"

We pull out.

Rhoda, sitting in the office with her coffee, watches us leave. Her voice comes over the radio, "*Betty Jane. Betty Jane.* This is Applegate. Over. Applegate to *Betty Jane.* Over."

Knowing only the Texoma radio protocol used for dinner reservations and gossip, we are unsure how to respond.

Rhoda persists.

"If you can hear me, *Betty Jane,* you call me when you get there. Copy?"

"*Copy?*" she repeats.

Dale presses the button on the microphone and says, "Yeah. Okay. Thanks."

"You say, 'Copy,' *Betty Jane,*" Rhoda instructs. "It means, understood, or in your Texanese, 'Yeah. Okay.'"

"Copy," Dale mimics dutifully.

"Good. Now, hail the lock before you get too far down. 'Lock Fifteen, Lock Fifteen this is *Betty Jane.*' Copy?"

"Copy," Dale says confidently.

"Good. Applegate out. That means, 'Bye."

We slip by the breakwater and push through the harbor mouth into open river and are a couple of miles downstream before the lock comes into view. There, Dale reaches for the mike to hail, "Lock Fifteen, Lock Fifteen, this is *Betty Jane.*"

"*Betty Jane. Betty Jane.* This is Fifteen. Got you in visual. Doors're open. Green light's on. C'mon down."

———•———

Finally, we are on our way, into the greater river community, the grapevine of barge captains, lockmasters, and marina operators that keeps its finger on the river's pulse. They've kept up with our successes and setbacks since we arrived. The master is glad to see us.

"Been a long summer," he says, hanging over the chamber wall. "I seen ya. I'm up to the marina time t' time. Awfully pretty in the daylight. That dog hunt? Anyway, I'll let ya down slow and gentle, bein' as it's your first time an' all. Ya won't feel nothin' at first, but I'll blow the horn so ya'll know I'm goin'. She's might' fine."

He spits brown tobacco juice between sentences, watches to make sure we tie up properly, and when we shut down the engines, he asks, "Y'all know not to restart 'til I blow the horn 'gain, right?"

"Right," we say together.

"Fine. Le's go."

He pops into the little yellow buggy that lockmasters use to run the circuit from one end of the chamber to the other and disappears. The klaxon sounds. The casters on the floating bollards moan like whale song as we make our descent, revealing the thick green carpet of moss that clings to the usually submerged part of the walls. At the bottom, the downstream doors open up on to a river running away from the dam. We have left Kerr Lake and Applegate Cove and entered the free-flowing Arkansas river.

Lock Fourteen is expecting us.

"Fifteen cawled and sed you was a beaut. How far ya' goin'? I'll let 'em know ya coming. Directly or stopping for lunch? Okay, should be there about two, judgin' from y' progress. River's runnin' clean, three knots. Y' know not to cross over at E'mld Cove, right? Fine. Le's go."

The "i" in fine is always open and elongated like a diphthong. "Le's go" has no "t" and swoops up at the end.

I fend the boat away from the wall while Dale checks the engine room. He finds that the starboard transmission is running hotter than port.

"We need to keep an eye on that," he says.

The klaxon sounds the all-clear. We are on our way to Van Buren, Fort Smith's sister city, on the opposite side of the river.

As the day and the starboard transmission grow hotter, a shadow falls across Dale's face. He doesn't say anything, but he is worried and getting more so as the afternoon drags on. Fortunately, Fort Smith appears on river right, exactly as John described. We pass the islands and see the bridge, below which is the marina, a single boathouse butted up against the old wharfs that were there in the steamboating days. I see Ruthella Hoelscher sitting on *Eye Candy*'s bow working a crossword puzzle. Her two dachshunds are asleep at her feet.

"Blow the horns," I tell Dale.

The horns I mean are not the two electric ones installed at the factory for signaling courtesies like hellos and good-byes. The horns I mean are the ones John King had installed at the front of the deckhouse. They are chrome-plated trumpets that, backed by 125 pounds of air pressure, bloat like a semi on steroids. Dale pulls the handle. An obnoxious roar resonates down the valley. Ruthella looks up.

She gets to her feet, waves, and cups her hand around her mouth, but we cannot hear her over our own engines. Her call only panics the dogs. While she runs to the stern to find Earl, we follow John's instructions to the letter and arrive at the gas dock where the Hoelschers are waiting.

"You're here! You're here!" Ruthella gushes, the two dogs yapping at her feet. "Welcome to Emerald Cove. Art's not here. He's off to birth a grandchild in Vegas. We're minding the store. How are you? How was your trip? You look fine. Gosh, we are so glad you are here."

Earl recognizes concern on a captain's face.

"Ruthie, hush," he says to his wife, and then to Dale, "What's wrong?"

"The starboard transmission runs hot. I have to call Rhoda."

While he and Earl discuss various causes and solutions, Ruthella and I find us a berth right next to hers. Emerald Cove is not so well protected from the mainstream as Applegate, and floating debris fills the slips. I push fallen trees back into the current while she talks.

"Yeah, we left y'all just after you got there. Pulled out on our way to North Carolina and got this far before we had to pull in for repairs...that old boat of ours...It had bugs when Earl found it, y' know...Yeah, I figured you did...Anyway, we were pulled in here. Then the rains ke'p' comin,' probably shouldn't been out in it in the first place. I was happily sitting on the bridge when Earl said, 'Ruthie, we gotta pull in here.' Like I was gonna argue. Well, here we are. We're s'posed to be fixin' our boat, but y' know Earl, always into someone else's business. He'll do anything. I won't be surprised if he comes in one day and says, 'Ruthie, I'm gonna dig a basement under so-and-so's boat. What do you think of that?' He would, too...gosh, it's good to see you two."

Rhoda arrives later in the evening with a laser thermometer, instructions to take regular readings of both the port and starboard engines, and to call if we run into any problems.

"No bother," she said. "Casi and I were gonna come over here anyway to do some shopping and have dinner."

The next morning, Tucker Duck and Rubber cannot guarantee us a completion date. A freak hailstorm last April blew out all the awnings in town and has kept them busy. But Earl finds a nearby automotive shop that specializes in ragtops. The owner says he has a new man, Juan, perfect for this kind of work, but he speaks no English. Hand gestures and rudimentary drawings show how we want the sunshade, the helm cover, and a raincoat for the dinghy. We order the goods, expecting to be back in a week, and shove off back to Applegate for *Betty Jane*'s first time to push upstream.

The mood is tense. Her engines spin faster, therefore louder, against what has now grown to a five-knot current, murky and debris-filled, which makes semi-submerged hazards harder to see. Against the current, water now piles up at her bow against planks that have heretofore been high and dry. They have not yet swollen with the new wet; their seams have not closed.

"...and your bow leaks like a sieve," I add to a report that includes clogged bilge pumps rising and operating temperatures, doing nothing to allay Dale's fears.

We eat our lunch silently, hoping we get home safely, and almost do, until—late in the afternoon, within a couple of miles of Lock Fifteen—a transmission alarm goes off. It is certainly starboard.

"Dammit," is all Dale can say, yet somehow relieved that the other shoe has finally dropped.

I climb into the engine room and settle between the two eight-cylinder engines, a comfortable place. The warm moist smell of combustion fills the air; the propellers dig into the current and the river splashes against her hull.

Dale telephones Applegate where Rhoda is at the gas dock stocking coolers with beer and soda pop. Tomorrow is Saturday. Everyone will be eager to squeeze out the last bit of summer before schools starts and the days get short.

"Just below Fifteen and negative," he answers her questions about our location and if the engine is shut down. His speech is taut and carefully stripped of inflection. "No," he repeats.

Rhoda gives clear and calm instruction: we have to cool the transmission. Either we leave the engine running, which circulates fluid with the unnerving alarm squealing in our ears, or we shut down the starboard engine, enjoy the quiet, and risk that it not restart. In either case, we have to immobilize the shaft. A propeller freewheeling in the current builds up as much friction in the crankcase as it does underway.

I say, "Right. I know how to do that," when I overhear Dale question Rhoda about blocking the prop.

He looks askance at me through the hatch.

I repeat, "I do."

"You do?"

"Yes."

"How?"

"Does it matter, dammit? Hand me something that I can wedge between the shaft and the hull. Something with teeth like a pipe wrench."

"Call you back," Dale says into the phone.

He runs down the ladder into the deckhouse and passes me the first thing that comes to hand, a pair of vise grips.

"All right. Go on the bridge and put the shaft in neutral. You'll have to compensate for the loss of power with the port—"

"Yeah, yeah."

We decide to leave the engine running and suffer the incessant alarm in hopes that circulating fluid will speed the cooling.

"Is starboard disengaged?"

"Yes."

"Okay, look, you have to slow down because starboard is still spinning too fast in the draft for me to grab a hold."

"What are you doing?"

"I've got to get these pliers locked around the shaft so that the handle pushes against the hull and the jaws stop the propeller. I cannot set the lock at twelve-hundred rpm. If I can't make it stick, we'll have to go to plan B."

"What's Plan B?"

"Let's see if Plan A works first."

Dale disengages both propellers. The hum of momentum—the engines, the turbulence against the hull—gets quieter as *Betty Jane* begins to drift. In the moment when the propellers stop, I snap the grips onto the starboard shaft.

"Blocked!" I call up to the bridge.

"Good," Dale says, reengaging the port engine. He hails the lock that has come into view. "Lock Fifteen, Lock Fifteen, this is *Betty Jane*. Over."

"Go to channel fourteen, Cap'n,"

Dale retunes.

"How's yer trip? Heard ya got to Emerald Cove awright." he says, "Been lookin' for y'all since you left out of Van Buren this morn'n. Taking yer time, ain't ya?"

His patter ends suddenly when he recognizes the distinctive and disconcerting alarm in the background. His tone becomes official.

"Is that an alarm, Captain?"

"We've got an overheated transmission. Starboard side."

"Have you got her bound?"

"Affirmative. The starboard engine is running. Hoping that will cool her down. We don't want to cut the engine for fear we cannot restart. Over."

Dale's worry turns to rage as he recounts in his mind the decisions we should have made to prevent getting to this point. We should have done all this at Texoma where there are expert mechanics. We should have checked out the facilities at Little Rock before deciding to come to Applegate. We should have bought new transmissions. But it is too late now.

"What's the temp?" The master asks.

"What's the temp?" Dale calls down.

I point the laser thermometer at the starboard casing.

"…230…no change," I answer.

Dale relays my reading.

"Stand by, *Betty Jane*."

Standing-by is different than Giving-a-sec or Waiting-a-mo, which we have also heard from lock towers. Stand-by is an official term that implies something—a clearance, a decision, an authority—is in the balance. At the moment, *Betty Jane* is not the luxury yacht they have adopted as a mascot. She is a potential bomb.

Fire hazards on board are real. Three combustion engines and all the electrical and fuel connections are crammed together in the confines of the engine room. Engine overheating, an errant electrical spark, or accumulated gasoline vapors can cause a sudden and devastating explosion. A lock is federal land, a potential terrorist target; the master has risks to assess and protocols to follow while we wait.

Minutes drag; our minds race.

The radio cracks: "You're cleared to come in, Captain."

We have lockage.

"Doors are open. Light is green. And, *Betty Jane*, I want you to tie up at the upper end to your starboard side, near an e-vac-u-a-tion ladder on the shore side, so I can keep an eye on you. Do you copy?"

"Copy," Dale answers smartly.

Meanwhile back at Applegate, the crowd at the gas dock grows. Bob has put on a fresh pot of coffee, free in times of trial, but everyone'd rather have a beer.

"Cold ones're in back," Rhoda says with phone in hand. "I'm standing by."

Speculations of worry and trepidation circulate quietly around the room until John busts in.

"They're *fine*," he says in his usual bravado, "Now, someone hand me a cigarette. They're not on fire, aground, or sinking yet, are they? And I want a beer, too."

His bluster in the face of danger and calamity is legendary, a direct contrast to Alon's reserve.

"'Fore long Alexander'll hang on that damn air horn he loves so much an' scare all 'em damn fish outta the water from 'ere to Tulsa."

He pops the tab off his beer and breathes in the first drag off his cigarette.

"'Ems boys best not tarry 'fore Kara and I take a notion t' just go fetch they white asses up 'ere. Ain't that right, Kara?"

Volunteers raise their hands, saying, "I'm going," "I'm going," while we, on the river, enter the lock chamber.

The transmission has cooled, the alarm has quit, and the emergency has passed, but the master appears at the top of the lock wall, anyway. He dispenses a huge chaw of tobacco into a paper cup.

"Your fuel shut down, Cap-tain?"

"Yessir," Dale answers.

"Shut down your electric, too, just for safety's sake. Are your PFD's cinched down nice and tight?"

"Yessir," we answer together.

"Can you breathe?"

"Yessir."

"Then they're not tight enough, Captain. Cinch them up. Cinch them up tight." He waits and watches as we pull our

PFD's as tight as corsets. "Now, if anything happens, I want you two to scamper up one of those e-vac-u-a-tion ladders." He stumbles over the official word and points to one off our stern and another at our bow.

"And what about Doris Faye?" I ask about my dog who is also wearing a PFD.

"Throw her overboard."

My jaw drops.

"She'll know what to do. She'll be all right," he assures. "Trust me. I have a dog."

With that, his head disappears. The valves open; the water rushes in. *Betty Jane* jerks and twists from side to side. The lines slap, and the fenders pinch. We fight hard to keep her from scraping the wall. It is fast. It is scary. We find out later that emergency lock-ups come with bragging rights.

The upper doors open on calm waters and a setting sun. I pull the air horns and we cruise the five miles back to Applegate and into the cove. Well-wishers wave and call from the end of the boathouse, "Welcome. Welcome home," and a swarm of men clamor to get on board before we've even landed, saying, "Don't shut down, Cap'n. Don't shut down." The sun sets on us safely in port.

Rhoda grabs Dale, "Buy ya a beer, sailor?"

Someone takes Doris Faye, and John guides me to the far end of the boathouse where the water is deepest. He picks me up by the butt of my overalls and throws me headlong into the cove.

I come up sputtering and cussing. Eyes closed, John is waving his cigarette over the water and murmuring some Cajun gris-gris mumbo-jumbo that ends with, "You are now a river rat. You belong to the river. Muddy water runs in your veins from now on."

He lets the smoke trail into the air before clamping the cigarette between his teeth.

"Gimme yer hand, boy. Water's n' place for som'uns what can't swim."

"I can too swim," I protest.

"Cain't prove it by me. An' pull off 'em wet bibs."

I hesitate.

"Got somethin' you don't want me to see, do y'? Scared I'm gonna have it out with y'?"

I shake my head.

"Okay, then, hand 'em 'ere. Like as not, you've already caught yer death."

I hand over my overalls. The water's chill, the heat of the summer night soothe the strain of tension and concern of the last two days. The heft and warmth of John's arm across my shoulders causes an erection to rise between my legs. I have to smile. It's Mother.

Lowest common denominator, her complaint about Dale.

She raised me to be her daughter, her acolyte, her companion, but I had lived that life. She would have preferred that my lovers be female. Failing in that she would have wanted him to be some decorator twink, someone she could conscript, someone she could intimidate, someone who looked good at parties. Someone who could sew would be even better.

Hand sewn window dressings hang so much prettier when someone really understands drape.

Dale was none of those things.

He was pudgy, balding, severely myopic, wore double-knit polyester, worked in a windowless basement, lived in a decidedly un-chic postal code, came from dirt farmers, and did not know or care who Vivian Watson was. He was heaven.

But Mother insisted that I study Isabel O'Neil's treatise on furniture finishing, be fluent in antique restoration, and watch carefully as craftsmen built the finest furniture in the country. Without her tutelage, *Betty Jane* would not have been possible and I would not be here.

Walking down the middle of some boathouse in the middle of nowhere Oklahoma in the arms of a man with eyes in the back of his head. Naked.

Yes, ma'am, I answer. *Because this is the part you denied me. The love and affection of my own father.*

Whether Mitchell was too drunk to honor his visitations or was kept away is immaterial. So, too, is my sexual orientation, the product of suspected stereotype: "strong mother, distant father." I've known I was different since I was a boy, known what to call it since puberty. But the void, the absence has always been there. Now, here is a man whom I respect, who respects me, and has no interest in my penis one way or the other.

John stops. He explains that he *was* afraid during Katrina; it was *his* fault that they did not find a hurricane hole; and what if something *had* happened to Kara?

His eyes trace the joists in the boathouse ceiling. We continue on. He stops.

"God, what it must be like to be y'all. I mean, being like y'all an' goin' deep into country full of men like me—*them,*" he says, pointing to the crowd, which has moved to the gas dock. "An' what for? 'Cuz you don't know no better? 'Cuz yer stupid?"

He tilts his head down to light a cigarette. The tobacco sizzles. The flame turns his face orange like a lantern.

"No, y'all've answered the river's call. Takes guts. Most men just buy boats, sit on 'em, say, 'Ain't this nice,' but wonder, 'Where is the thrill?' 'Where is the adventure?' You'll find it if y' haven't already."

We arrive at *Betty Jane,* dark and abandoned.

"Now, go git dressed."

I watch John walk down the boathouse, across the cat-walk and the little spit of dry land between it and the next the ramp to the gas dock. I see it. I see the John Bartlett whom everyone recognizes.

He stands at the doorway, the light from the gas dock cuts a sharp line across his toes. He takes a moment, a deep breath. He leaves everything that just transpired between us behind in the dark, and, in a trice, reassumes that role of John Bartlett whom everyone knows.

"Will *someone* hand me a *goddam* beer?" he bellows as he wades into the crowd.

When she thinks I am not looking, I catch Mother's eye. She is gazing at the woman opposite her, across a table covered in fabric swatches, paint chips, catalog photos, and blueprints of a house. The woman is Mother's client, a type, here and most often, dressed in a fine luncheon ensemble and real jewels. The jacket of her designer suit hangs daintily on the back of her chair. Her purse perches next to matching shoes. She does not notice Mother's gaze.

The two were Junior Leaguers together. They shared the same upbringing, education, and expectations for the future. In similar gowns, they married similar men in similar churches; began similar families; and sent similar children into the world to continue similar lives. Except one day, Mother set Father's belongings on the porch.

She parlayed decoupaged screens of her own creation into a job selling fine French reproduction furniture. She opened her own business, recruited her own manufacturers, and bought her own inventory. Divorce made her feel ashamed, therefore she enlisted her new acquaintances: talents so extraordinary that while debating next season's color they absently folded cocktail napkins into miniature Baroque corbels and twisted swizzle sticks into tiny Régence table legs. A constant cloud of cigarette smoke clung to the ceiling. The pungent aroma of bathtub gin permeated the air.

The only limits to her success would be that she competed in a predominately gay man's world where, ironically, her second husband was a fag. Twenty years prior to their wedding, he was a buyer at Neiman-Marcus where she worked in sales. He moved to New York and followed a career similar to hers. But when Nixon-era stagflation hit the city hard, he sold his showroom and returned to Dallas where it was revealed why he left—the threat of criminal proceedings for homosexual activities. Mother, to be blunt, was a fag-hag. And she was lonely, wanted someone to share her life with, and he filled the bill. How she juggled the sexual equation I do not know.

Disgraced and subject to giggles and snickers behind her back, Mother resorted to deriding the men who helped set her up in business, referring to their partners as "whatevers." She called networking "kissing the queers," and, perversely, she outed gay men who, otherwise, were happily married-with-children. Then she married exactly what she had for so long railed against. And so they boycotted, forcing Mother to cater to the decorator whose client was of the type previously described. How far she had deviated from her parents' expectations!

In an effort to compensate, she sent me to her high school, then to an east coast liberal arts college, just as she had been. But in my junior year, I went to Florence, Italy. I fell in with the group of artists and craftsmen who maintained the city's art and architectural treasures. They needed a model.

I was their ignudo—the name given to naked male figures who drape the Sistine Ceiling and pose on the sides of Egyptian vases. I was their prize—housed, educated, fed and cared for like a beloved apprentice. I was their toy—sex in exchange for immersion into ars gratia artis, the opportunity to write glowing letters home about how well I was settling in and the understanding that nudity is a state of unfettered liberty, comfort with oneself, and emotional well-being. My Italian was fluent but my studies suffered.

Rather than face the shame of academic failure, I ran home. There I worked diligently and tirelessly at the show-room. I could do nothing else; I knew nothing else; I had planned for nothing else. There, I was her solace. I was the loyal devotee who—even from an early age—repeated every word, imitated every movement, and memorized her lessons faithfully. Until I met Dale Harris, that is. Then I became a traitor, another of Mother's public humiliations, one more disappointment in a life full of disappointments.

And so: across from her, at the table covered in fabric swatches, paint chips, catalog photos, and blueprints of a house, sits the client, the Junior Leaguer. She is approving the decoration of guest rooms for grandchildren who will come to visit, unaware that she is being examined and that she is the mirror in which Mother and I must examine our own relationship.

Mother will never have suites of guest rooms; I will never present her with grandchildren. Instead, we are ransomed to each other in a perilous dynamic. I am the baby boy whom she brought into the world and must shelter from its cruel-ties. I am the whipping boy she punishes for all that has gone wrong in her life.

Only in her dying do I break free.

CHAPTER NINE
The Truth About Alon

The transmission is Applegate's problem. For our part, Dale and I are ready to go. We strip the dock. The clotheslines are down. The string lights are packed away. The lumber, locker, tools, paint cans, boxes of rags, and sawhorses are loaded in the truck and on their way to Dallas. Dale will attend to his parents for a few days; I will return in the Cadillac. Rhoda has requested that one of us be on board while they run test cruises.

John Bartlett, our captain in Dale's absence, slaloms *Betty Jane* in and out of navigation buoys at unsafe speeds. New batches of diagnosticians bounce around the engine room while John screams, "Ya-HOO" or "Yee-Haa" at the top of his lungs. Sometimes it's Robert and Kenn and me; sometimes it's Robert and Chris and me, Robert and me, or Robert and Kenn and Chris and me. Finally, Robert gets so befuddled that he takes to whirling his index fingers in opposite directions whenever he has to discuss counter-rotating engines.

"I don't know," he says, "I don't know what I did."

September turns to October before Rhoda says, "We gotta get these boys on the river. Winter's coming."

She tells us to go away for a couple of weeks, promising to get the problem solved by the time we get back. We return to find a brandee-new transmission gleaming where the defective one once was. It is mid-October and the last social event of the season, the one that closes Applegate for the winter, the birthday party of Alon and Rhoda's daughter, Casi.

People come from across the county to help get ready. The men sweep out the pavilion, knock down the wasps' nests, and gather all the available Coleman lanterns to put in the overhanging pecan tree. The women stay in the house. They bread catfish caught from the river; prepare fixin's of beans, cole slaw, and potato salad; bake cookies, cakes, and pies. All under Rhoda's watchful eye.

"Y'll keep those fat fryers out from under the roofline, hear?" she calls from the porch to the men on the lawn. "I don't want nuthin', *nuthin'*, catchin' on fire, hear? 'Member what happened last year?"

Lanterns glitter in the tree like giant fireflies and the air gets chilly. The bonfire burns next to the water where it always has. Friends and neighbors help each other out of cars and trucks parked on the lawn before parties slowly separate by gender. Children chase dogs and each other across the freshly mown grass. The mood is light and the conversation bubbling, but, occasionally, a roving eye allows itself to settle on the spot where Alon once was. A table and two chairs take the place of the recliner, the meds, the fan.

Catfish filets bubble in the bucket fryers set in the yard. Cooler lids snap closed and beer cans spew as news of our departure, scheduled for tomorrow morning, spreads. We are wished warm good-byes and good luck.

"These are the guys I told you about with the wooden boat," they say, introducing us to family members for the first and last time.

Some ask if we have to leave. Others wish we would stay for the winter. But it is a river trip. Even if we get no farther than Little Rock before cold weather is upon us, we want to get some miles under our keel, for pride's sake if for no other; we said we were going down the river and we are.

Mounds of fish, crackling hot, tumble onto the tables set in the middle of the shelter. Rhoda cuts someone's much-too-long prayer short by saying, "Let's eat!" before the amen.

They worry that we will not settle in well at the new marina, forgetting that we settled in here. They understand our ambition and wonder what it would be like to pick up and go, but they'll miss us anyway.

"Well...'Bye," they say.

The children, full of dinner, fall asleep in the warmth of their daddies' laps. The dogs, full of whatever people fed them, pile up on the far side of the fire. Folks hug and wish each other "Happy holidays" because most will not see each other until next spring. They climb back into their vehicles and drive away. Taillights creep up the drive; gravel crunches under tires.

We're glad that they came and glad they went because it is time for the live-aboards, we who have lived and worked together for the last five months, to clean up. The last of the beer comes out of slushy ice, and so, too, does the truth about Alon.

"Yeah, me and Kenn's gotta go pick up this antique Chris built back in the '50s sometime," Alon told those around the marina before coming to haul our boat. "Man, is she a beauty, too. Mahogany and chrome and all. You can shave in them decks. Better'n forty feet long. These guys've done some work on 'er and're gonna take 'er down the river. Cincinnati or som'aire's like that."

In fact, Alon had not yet seen *Betty Jane*; he only knew what we had told him during our January visit. But Alon took risks. He suspected that we were the only business Applegate would see in 2008 and promised anything to get it. He knew he was going to have to figure something out about those transmissions, and he knew that overnight delivery did not exist. He knew we were gay for which he knew he'd take some heat. He figured that if he got us out of the boathouse, hidden in the shed before Memorial Day weekend, we'd be out of sight or gone or, at least, about to be gone before anyone noticed. As the bonfire dies down, the details of what transpired last Memorial Day weekend unfold. It is a story we have heard before in these last few day before our departure.

The details, like who said what, change to avoid laying blame at any one person's feet. It goes generally like this: Morgan's Suburban left the boathouse, drove around the cove, and pulled up to the work barn. It came back, flew down the drive, and stopped just short of the water. Three men got out; three men walked into the boathouse; three men led a mob up to the porch where Alon pretended to be asleep.

"Alon," he heard someone say. "Alon."

Some suggested that it wasn't that important and that they should come back later. Others were angry and wanted to air their grievances.

"*Alon.*"

Alon opened his eyes as if suddenly conscious that someone was calling his name, stretched his full length, and blinked from the sun's reflection off the water.

"Hey," he said groggily, rubbing his hands over his face. "Wow, everyone's here. 'Sup?"

Their spokesman, nervous and wound up, stammered, "Alon...w-w-we are just not going have no q-q-q-queers around here and th-th-that's just the end of it."

The crowd's support rustled like leaves across the grass.

"You hear me, Alon? We are not having no sissies around this marina."

"Okay," Alon said.

He lit a cigarette, blew out the deep inhalation, and waited as the fan oscillated in the corner and the awkward silence weighed heavily on the mob. Then, he shrugged, saying, "Thanks for letting me know. Is that all you wanted?"

"We mean it, Alon."

"I said, 'Okay.' What do you want me to do, put up a sign?"

"Well, what're you going to do about it?"

"'Bout what?"

Pain wrenched Alon's guts as he straightened up in his chair.

"Oh, come off it, Alon. You know good and well them two guys working on that boat in the shed there is...is...," he whispered, "*gay.*"

"Well, what I know is that a bunch of y'all went snoopin' over to my yard. You went into my shed, saw what you saw, heard what you heard, and now's comin' ov' here to tell me m' business. I 'spect all you *know*'s that there's a man, probably curled up inside his boat above a pile of rotten shit on the floor. He's a nice fellah, too, and probably introduced hisself 'fore y'all bothered, if I'm guessin' right. Am I?"

Alon paused to let the facts sink in.

"An' I know that t'other man's alone with my wife in her office spendin' money orderin' parts so I'd appreciate if you'd keep yer caterwaulin' down and your accusations to yourself...unless someone got *mo-lest-ed*...Did anyone get *mo-lest-ed* an' wanna talk 'bout it?"

Alon flashed a smile around the crowd. One or two started to drift back to their boats; others doodled in the grass with their boots. But some were adamant.

"Alon," one insisted in low tones, "this is a family place. We bring our wives and children down here and we don't want any of that... that ho-mo-sex-u-al stuff going on around here."

"So, what's the problem? I got two guys and one boat all leaving by the end of next month...Oh, and a dog."

"Christ, Alon, did we tell ya? Even their goddamn dog is *pink*."

Alon could not help but laugh, no matter how much it hurt, but it inflamed the righteous.

"The point is, Alon—" they tried to say, but Alon raised his hand to interrupt.

The rabble persisted. "Now, look here, Alon—"

"NO! YOU look here. THEM BOYS IS MONEY IN THE BANK," Alon roared.

Nothing moved.

"An' if I find out that our guests get even the tiniest little whiff of foul around here so help me God—"

Alon did not finish. He did not have to. The ones whose slip rents were overdue, had outstanding fuel receipts, or unpaid service invoices retreated quietly down the hill. The others stood struck by the sudden understanding that Alon may not have been as out of touch as they had suspected.

He had made a judgement about Dale and me on that cold January day when we sat in his and Rhoda's living room, icicles hanging from the eaves, and discussed his hauling *Betty Jane* to Applegate Cove. Whether it was us, our boat, our business, or a combination of the three we cannot know, but we had a quality he admired and wanted in his marina. Within days of arrival, Dale was at Rhoda's desk, poring over parts catalogs, and I was in the barn, tearing a hole in *Betty Jane's* side, proving correct Alon's assessment of us. We were capable and accomplished men, regardless of our proclivities. It was an assessment he was willing to defend, a legacy he wanted to leave behind. It is why Alon was so loved and the loss of him so grievous.

From the looks on the faces of those gathered around the fading embers, it was obvious they offered this story by way of apology. They had misjudged us; Alon had not. And they were grateful to have learned differently. Though most were not the kind of men to say so outright, they could not let us leave the next morning without saying, in this, their own circuitous way, that they were glad to have known us. It was their own special, "See you down the river."

The tale is one which Dale and I hold rather than readily share—as a dockside anecdote, it does not do justice to the majesty of the situation or the people involved. But Applegate does creep, slowly and over time, into our daily consciousness; always, in the center of it, is Alon. We will watch ourselves look off into the distance and will start snapping our fingers in the air when we cannot remember some detail and say, "Aw, hell, hon, what's the name..." We will imitate his gappy smile whenever we want to look pleased. "Brandee new" will slip into our patter.

Likewise I can imagine someone around a campfire somewhere saying, "'Wonder whatever happ'n'd to 'em pee-cu-yer boys Alon brought down to Applegate that time. 'Wonder what they's dewin'. Don't yew? Don't yew ever wonder 'bout 'em boys?"

Then they will shake their heads and laugh, not in derision but in that way folks do about family.

———•———

The hour is late. The party is over. We douse the lights, tamp down the fire, and go to our boats and our beds. Dale and Doris Faye get in *Betty Jane* when I turn and see John Bartlett staggering across the catwalk on his way to Kara, already on board *Enjoy Enjoy*. A cigarette clings to his lower lip.

He ambles unsteadily up to me, takes my head in between his hands and looks me in the eye like he does, except this time he is a little out of focus from his drinking too much beer.

"If you need anythin', 'thin' 'tall," he says, "no matter where y' are, no matter what people say, y' call me. I'll be there. I'll come git y.'"

I nod away the sentiment, figuring that it is booze talking, but he insists, "I *mean* it."

His right eye wells up, a tear runs down the length of a cheek and stains the Hawaiian shirt he wore especially for the party. And, then, another and another.

"John, are you crying?"

"No, goddammit, y' idiot. 'T's t'is goddammed cigar'tte smoke got in my goddamn eye. God*dam*mit."

He throws his arms around me, pulls me into his chest where for the last time I breath in the rank aroma of sweaty Cajun, reeking of beer and cigarettes. I memorize it.

The next morning, fog covers the river like a duvet. Bob and Rhoda are on hand to see us off. A white flag—triangular with a red dot at its center, the nautical pennant for the number "1," heralding our first day out—flies off her stern.

Bob Quackenbush shouts, "Better get that goddammed Jap flag off your stern before you get beyond where people don't already know you're peculiar," and Dale hails the lock.

"Lock Fifteen. Lock Fifteen. This is *Betty Jane*. Over."

We never see our friends at Applegate again. The place will be deserted when we return, the week before Thanksgiving. The leaves will be off the trees, the gas dock closed for the season, and the parking lot empty except for the car we have come to collect. We will take a moment, in that lonely quiet, to see Applegate as we did that very first time two summers ago when Rhoda gloated over her new gas dock.

It was an insignificant nothing of a place, a shallow inlet flooded by a dam in the middle of nowhere—a couple of boathouses, a Travelift, and a work barn—still is. But it is the single largest contributor to our successful completion of the trip. Everything we learned over the last five months will come to bear somewhere along the way, starting at Ozark, Arkansas.

CHAPTER TEN
The Daily Grind

Ozark, an alpine village nestled in the mountains of the same name, is about sixty-four river miles below Applegate. Along the way, we stop over at Emerald Cove, Ruthella and Earl again our hosts, eat at Rolando's Cuban Kitchen, and ride the steam-driven Ferris wheel on Fort Smith's levee. But at Ozark, we learn what to expect from a life lived on the water.

MECHANICAL FAILURE:

While we slept—anchored alone in the middle of the river, out of port, and away from friends—our batteries completely discharged. The all-around mast light, which marks our position to passing traffic, went out. A dense fog settled in the valley. The pumps stopped. The bilge filled with water. And I wake up to a strange rhythm—stroke-*splash,* stroke-*splash.*

"'Sup?" I ask, turning over in my bunk to find Dale at the manual pump.

"We're sinking," he answers, somewhat amused that we cheated Imminent Demise once again, somewhat put out that his electrical design has failed, somewhat smug that the apparent redundancy of restoring the manual pump has paid off, after all.

"That's nice," I say and, overlooking the absence of java aroma that usually comes from the galley, ask, "Where's Madam's coffee?"

"Madam's *barca* is cold, dark, and dead in the water until Madam's captain can get a charge on Madam's batteries, Madam," he answers between strokes. "We have no electricity."

FOUL WEATHER:
The view outside is a uniformly gray.
"Not even for coffee?"
"Not even for coffee."
"Bother," I huff.
Stroke-*splash*. Stroke-*splash*.

OBLIGATION, ADVERSITY, AND INCONVENIENCE:
"I suppose I should get up."
"Dog needs to pee," Dale says.
The Dalmatian under my blankets chases a bunny in her sleep.
"She doesn't think so."
"Still."
Stroke-*splash*. Stroke-*splash*.

I cite fog as a reason not to get out of bed, "We are not going anywhere, not in this soup. Not without radar, which we don't have."

"We still have a bilge full of water, no coffee, no heat, and no breakfast."

Stroke-*splash*. Stroke-*splash*.

"Fine," I relent and stagger onto the aft deck to pull on shorts hung out to dry the night before but still wet, now, with dew. The PFD snugged around my chest is a cold shock. We launch the pram.

Getting clear of the big boat, Doris Faye and I hear the genset turn over once only; crossing the water we hear the starboard engine not crank, and tying up at one of the flimsy docks set out from shore for the purpose; we hear the low signature rumble of the port engine unsettling the morning's peace.

Good, I think to myself. *She's up and running,* thanks to another redundancy, a sort of jumper cable system, permanently installed for emergencies just like this.

Doris Faye and I tour the Army Corps of Engineers campground, developed as part of the lock and dam infrastructure, and return to *Betty Jane* where the galley is warm and filled with the sound of frying eggs and bacon. Newly spun electricity pulses into the batteries.

CHANGE IN PLAN:

The fog lifts around noon, too late to make our next port of call before sunset, so I suggest we see the sights.

"We don't really need anything," Dale says after a morning of dozing and reading. "And we can pretty well see it all from here."

Ozark is a simple street grid of church steeples, two-story houses, and single-level businesses.

I say, "If nothing else we will have a town lunch and pick up a few groceries."

We leave Doris Faye behind and row the mile-plus distance across the lake, up a tributary marked by a railroad trestle, and on to the municipal dock. We stow our PFD's under *Pramela's* overturned hull, lock her to a railing, and take the oars with us.

LOCAL ADVICE:

We approach the first person we see, a man in a beat-up truck, like mine, eating a meager lunch. He's a paint contrac-

tor, judging by his clothes. We ask for a lunch recommenda-
tion. Guidebooks are only accurate at time of printing. The
better information comes from asking.

I say, "Where do a couple of sailors get a plate lunch
around here?"

"That yer bowt?" he answers. "Nice bowt."

Betty Jane's reflection ripples on the water. She is long
and lean, like the *Queen Mary*, set against the tree-lined park
on the far bank. The breeze pushes her playfully at the end
of her anchor rode.

"Mus' b' nice t' have a bowt like 'at," he adds, swatting
at his salt-and-pepper beard and chasing the crumbs off his
tee-shirt and into the footwell.

He points with his index and second fingers as if to say
something but stops, interrupted by a honking goose that
brings Doris Faye onto the aft cockpit to investigate.

"That yer dawg?" the man asks.

"Yes."

"Nice dawg."

PATIENCE:

He fumbles in his shirt pocket for a crumpled package,
lovingly straightens out the last cigarette, finds a match,
opens the truck door to strike it, closes the door, lights his
smoke, tosses the spent match out the window, and lays
his head back to enjoy the cigarette, his only luxury. We've
learned to wait.

"He hunt?"

"No. She's gun-shy."

"Tew bad."

My question isn't hard. Lunch is somewhere, but from
his point of view, we are strangers—strangers dressed in over-

alls, shorts, and wearing floppy hats, granted, but strangers nonetheless who walk around town carrying oars and shopping bags in their arms. He wants to be sure before aiding and abetting.

"Y' fish?"

"No."

"Don't hunt, an' don't fish, an' th' just ride around in they li'l wood boat," he mumbles to himself before turning for the first time to look at us directly.

"Y' go down Commerce Street. Th's here's Commerce Street." His hand waves at the viaduct we've just floated under. "Go thataway 'til you get t' Mama's. She'll feed you good."

EXPLORATION:

We strike out in the direction indicated until we find a storefront indistinguishable from all the others except for a hand-made plywood sign leaned against a car bumper promoting Mexican Chicken as today's special. Mama's is an expanse of beige linoleum, a waitstation and soda fountain between an equally make-shift kitchen and a few mismatched tables and chairs. Bare fluorescent tubes run the length of the room.

REMINDERS OF SALLISAW:

Our waitress is a young woman, almost twenty, looking like the test dummy from the local beauty school. What appears to be stray Oreo cookie crumbs around her mouth is actually purple lip liner, the application of which still needs practice. Her style sense comes from her favorite rockers whose stage costumes expose as much as legally possible. She is desperate to be acceptably different.

She looks us up and down.

"Yer feet muddy?" she asks.

"No."

"C'mon then. Lean 'em oars in the corner there. Sit any-where's."

At one o'clock, late by rural standards, we are the only customers.

"Whatcha drinkin'?"

She drops glasses of water and menus on the table. Grainy photocopies slipped into transparent sleeves list the fare as the usual mutations of burgers and fries with meatloaf and fried chicken as the plate lunch standouts.

"An' we got Meskin Chickin," she says, smacking green gum around a tongue stud. "Whattayas gonna git?"

I ask about the special.

She tucks the gum in the corner of her mouth in order to yell at the ceiling, "MOM, this man here wants t'know what's Meskin Chickin."

A large woman, who has been disciplining a deep fryer since we arrived, puts the fry basket aside with deliberation, wipes her hands on a greasy apron, and begins a labored trek towards the front. She looks cross and unpleasant, and, for the five-dollar cost of lunch, I can take a chance.

"Never mind," I say, "I'll just have that."

"NEVER MIND," the teenager screams.

The woman, visibly relieved, returns to hectoring her machine.

Dale orders the meat loaf.

Cuisine:

Mexican Chicken is canned chicken, Rotel, tortilla strips, and Campbell's Nacho Cheese soup, sprinkled with grated Monterey Jack and baked. It is Arkansas's Hot Brown.

"Where's the grocery store?" Dale asks.

"Where're y' parked?"

"We've come off the river—," Dale begins but is interrupted.

"Oh, I figur'd 'twas sumthin' like 'at. You look kinda ster-range," she says, approaching a Valley Girl inflection.

"—and the refrigerator in our boat is tiny—"

"Gosh, you sh'd see ours. Little ol' bitty thing. Don't keep nuthin' cold, neither. That's why we don't serve anythin' *à la mode.*" She leans down to whisper the secret. "That means with ice cream."

"—and we need some produce and some milk," Dale finishes.

As a point of reference, I reiterate that our boat is at the city dock.

"Right, I seen y' oars."

She puts one hand on her hip to consider and begins an oral registry of who lives where in Ozark, smacking her gum for punctuation.

"The white wood Methodist church's on the left, it's the one that's got 'em green shutters, y' know—*smack-smack-smack*—'cause the woman down the street sells 'maters, cukes, and onions right outta her very own garden. Got the best oakrah in the county. Wins prizes for it an' all, she does—*smack-smack*—an' 'er suster brings her fresh milk off'n her fa-a-arm—*smack.* Her suster's got a farm 'round'ere sum'eres. You'll hafta sweettalk her for some of that, though. But she might let yew have sum o' 'er fresh eggs—*smack-smack-smack*—An' ask if she's got any homemade corned beef. Makes the best sandwiches. Mmmm."

She rubs her belly.

Smack.

NEW FRIENDS:

We find the house. The woman opens up her kitchen, full for our picking.

"Brought it all in this morning," she says, "on account of it's gonna freeze, you know it?" And had no idea what she was going to do with it all.

"The Good Lord sent ya. He did."

Dale carries bags full of fresh greens, tomatoes for *sugo,* and baby okra—small and tender enough for sautéing whole—back to the pram. I have milk, eggs, and the coveted corned beef. We have to lie flat in the bottom of the boat in order to clear the low-hanging utility mains over the creek, and just before reaching the river, I turn abruptly into waterworks lagoon.

SIGHTSEEING:

"Where are we going?" asks Dale, irritated with the sudden change of plan.

"I want to check something out."

"Well, what is it?"

It is an olive drab cinder block building with all the architectural interest of a bunker. It used to be a filling station; the awning still reaches for the highway, but where pumps used to be, a portable sign would flash "GUNS! GUNS! GUNS!" to passing motorists except that all the bulbs have fallen victim to target practice and lie in shards, glittering on the blacktop like a starry night.

"Well?" Dale asks.

"It is what guide books call local color and is why we are here."

CHILDHOOD MEMORIES:

Guns are from summers on my great-uncle Eddie's ranch in the Texas hill country. Guns were like prostitutes, a delicate subject—never brandished, never advertised, never discussed in mixed company, and never the province of children. Guns are for killing things, like varmints. Raccoons getting into the corn crib, bobcats taking baby goats and fawns, turtles gutting fish left on a line—they were all varmints. Rattlesnakes, as a rule, were shot left-handed while shifting gears.

My two older brothers piled in the back of an army surplus Willys jeep. I rode shotgun in my grandfather's lap. We sat in a natural blind of junipers and grapevines and waited under an August full moon until animals cooped up in some shady den came out to forage. Eddie blew across a piece of cellophane. He said it sounded like an animal in distress.

One night, he put down the cellophane, waved his hand across the grass for us to keep quiet though we barely even breathed, silently picked up his rifle and aimed across the pasture. Bounding with the grace and beauty that only wild things have was a fox as red as those illustrated in children's books, complete with a black tip on his tail. He smiled, or panted, in anticipation of a kill, not expecting a gun to discharge.

He hit the earth and skidded across sun-withered grass with a bullet shot precisely through his heart.

"Stay back. Stay back," my uncle said to us boys, eager to see. "What if I only stunned 'im?"

His body went across the hood of the jeep while I wrestled with a child's outrage at witnessing an act seemingly so malicious and unfair. Eddie took my narrow shoulders in his hands and explained that ranching is a rite—a rancher, like trappers and hunters and fisherman, does his job out of love for God's creatures—"…the other way is a long lingering death of sickness and not enough to eat. And we can't have that, can we?"

It was a rite performed by God-fearing men who all traded at Harriman's on the courthouse square in Georgetown. For all the world to see, Harriman's was a newsstand where my grandfather, Pap, an avid reader, took us to buy anything from *Dennis the Menace* and *The New York Times* to Simon & Schuster's latest release. Dark oak cabinets lined the walls and displayed rifles behind beveled glass and locked doors. The ammunition was locked in drawers below. There was a black man who kept the cases polished and the white tile floor mopped and always dismissed my grandfather's apologies for our smudging the glass, saying, "'Thout no chillens, Mis'er Vinther, I gots no job."

Today, Georgetown is a suburb of Austin, part of the I-35 semi-conductor corridor. Harrigan's is gone, so is the ranch. Big box stores advertise hunting equipment and sporting rifles on prime-time television.

"I'll stay here," Dale says.

JUDGEMENT:

The light is poor, the aisles are dark. Everything is painted brown or green. Crossbows are stacked within convenient reach. Live and snap traps, snares and pit covers list their features across plastic wrappings. Rifles rack up the walls and collapsible blinds hang from the ceiling like giant cave crickets. Camouflage does not mask the fact that this is bloodlust.

"He'p ya?" a male voice asks.

DISCOMFORT:

It is a deep voice, low and quiet, disciplined to not startle prey. I turn. I see no one. I feel self-conscious. I have no real business here. Other than curiosity, quickly turning self-righteous: I am trespassing. I ask for my default need, a diet Coke.

"Below the nightcrawlers and next to the deer musk."

I know nothing about either. I amble aimlessly around clips and magazines, remembering that hollow points explode on impact and make a bigger mess than necessary if one knows how to aim.

"In the cool cases. In the back. To your right. Look down. See the night crawlers? Now, look about chest high."

The icy bottle in my hand is reassuring. I have business. I have a reason to be here. I head towards the voice coming from behind a case full of opened knives, blades exposed. The serrated ones are particularly gruesome looking.

"That it?" asks a man standing as big as a tree and dressed in twigs and leaves.

Two black eyes sparkle behind a bush of beard and mustache of the same unfathomable darkness. I stare. He stares back. I stare more. He is Native American and French. Osage and Cherokee Indians settled here; Ozark was popular with European hunters and trappers, supplying the eighteenth century fashion trade with feathers and furs.

WONDER:

He is a man of the forest. This is his shop. Unlike the waitress who dreams of getting out of this one-horse town as soon as possible, the paint contractor struggling to feed his family, or me, running away from home, this man exudes the calm of someone contented to be exactly where he is, like my uncle Eddie, like the black man at Harriman's.

It is in Ozark that we come of age as boaters. We learn the protocols, fashion the templates that will serve us throughout the rest of the trip. Ozark is where boating becomes a life-style rather than an amusement.

CHAPTER ELEVEN
Spadra, A Fantasy

That night we observed austere conservation measures—no lights, no heat, no hot supper. We huddled up in our jackets and read. But none of it made any difference. The next morning, Dale is at the manual pump, stroking and splashing.

"We're sinking," I say, rolling out of bed to row the dog ashore.

"And we're going to keep on sinking until we can get a decent charge on these batteries," Dale says over breakfast.

"But we're socked in, Cap'n."

Dale takes a long look at the gray soup outside his porthole.

"I can just barely make out the shoreline," he says. "By the time we clean up breakfast and get ready to go, the fog should be lifted enough to get to the lock."

"Dead slow."

"Dead slow," he repeats. "And it won't be a bad idea to take a look at the charts before we go."

The Arkansas river below Lock Twelve runs straight as a string. These are the headwaters of Lake Dardanelle, the most challenging water we will run. Extreme turbulence pushes warning buoys away from the hazards they mark or washes them away completely. The Army Corps of Engineers cannot map shoals as quickly as they come and go. Barges routinely scrape bottom as they push through. Consequently, an advisory—rubber-stamped in red ink on every page of every chart—warns, "Captains will stay within marked navigation buoys," or in local parlance, "You can go to Hell on the Dardanelle."

We leave the foul weather pinched behind the mountains above the dam and, below, enter a fjord steep with rugged walls soaring into a clear blue sky. *Betty Jane* bounces and weaves in the narrow flume. A river has never seemed this beautiful since my childhood summers on the South San Gabriel.

The South San Gabriel River marked the northern boundary of the ranch. It was a Texas river which, almost everywhere else, would be called a creek or a slough. It flooded in the spring, dried up in autumn, and, in the heat of summer, was high enough for my brothers and me to float down to the fern bank on inner tubes. We packed a picnic lunch, watched dragonflies mate, and chased schools of fish across shallow ponds. Canyon wrens sang diatonic scales down ravines, snowy in July with cotttonwood seed. The fern bank was a cliff, white as Dover but north-facing and much smaller. Natural springs permeated the limestone to irrigate a variety of fern, algae and lichen. I wanted to be nowhere else; the South San Gabriel was the first river I ever loved.

The jagged peaks below Lock Twelve flatten out over the course of the day. By late afternoon, Dardanelle becomes a flooded meadow, a watery plain. Spadra—rhymes with Audra—Creek, marked by a train trestle on the opposite bank, will be our overnight moorage. We heed John Bartlett's warning: *Don't g' thataway. Don't you cut crosslots*, he said. *You'll be tired, hungry, an' wanna beer. Spadra's a long day. But don't you do it. You follow that chart*. He jabbed his finger at a pretend map on his imaginary helm. *Dardanelle's no place t' get clever. G' all t' way down.* He pointed to where the sailing line would cross the river if he had a map. *And you come 'bout.* He jumped an about-face as he does to indicate the reversed course. *An' y' push back up nice 'n' easy. It'll add a half-hour or more t' y' arrival 'pendin' on current, but 't's better 'an groundin' 'er.*

We follow his advice explicitly. Hugging the opposite bank and pushing upstream, *Betty Jane's* exhausts echo off the limestone bank, pitted and stained by erosion. A landing, tied between two trees, looks inviting as the sun begins to set, except it lacks electricity.

"I need shore power," Dale says as we pass by. "Just a little bit farther. The trestle's just ahead."

Dale is not as enamored with tying up on the river as I am. He prefers off-river moorage. Spadra is definitely off the river.

We duck under the railroad bridge, black with creosote, and leave behind a river that reflects fiery reds, oranges, and yellows. Spadra Creek is purple, indigo, and green. The channel narrows; the banks close in. Squirrels and blue jays scamper through the trees. Deer forage. We believe that we have taken a wrong turn. Suddenly, a fishing boat whips out from behind where a three-legged goat is grazing in front of a stand of trees. The boat slows down to meet us. It, too, seems fantastic.

A Rubenesque woman, perched on the bow, drags a vee in the water with her toe. She wears a gauzy white diaphanous sun dress and a broad Audrey Hepburn hat over scads of auburn hair. She interrupts her nibbling of a pimiento cheese sandwich to ask, "How're y'all?" through a heart-shaped mouth waxed red. "Y'all off the rivah?"

Her pilot is a phantom, seen only as bright cigarette ember burning through a cloud of over-rich exhaust.

"Hi d'ye," he says as he passes by.

They turn under the bridge, dragging a plume of blue smoke behind them, and head out onto the river which, from here, looks like the firebox blazing inside a dark locomotive.

"Did you see that?" I ask.

"Yeah."

"Good. Just checking."

———◆———

We continue on. Spadra Marina, which has even less room to maneuver than Emerald Cove, is around the bend. A single gas pump marks the fuel dock. Houseboats tie into open slips on one side. Skiffs and runabouts crowd in a boathouse on the other. The office sits precariously atop a twenty-foot escarpment. The docks are very low. I am going to have to jump. They are also very waterlogged because when I land, the pier gives way under my weight.

"You are kidding me!" I scream, sputtering and spitting as the dock recoils, pushing me back out of the water.

"What?" Dale yells.

"NO CLEATS!"

Eye bolts, instead of the butterfly cleats I assumed to be standard, are irregularly placed and too small to thread any of our lines through. Without a place to secure a rope, thirteen tons of Betty Jane threaten to pin me against the sheer rock face.

"REVERSE PROP!" I call as a voice from above hails, "You're here. Been expectin' yah."

Guidebooks suggest calling ahead for overnight dockage, but marinas never answer the phone. Recorded greetings insist that "Your call is important to us" and that "We will call back," but they never do. It is the river community, barge captains and lock masters, that keeps track of our progress. *Betty Jane* is distinctive that way.

Bursting out of the office and tripping down a single flight of stairs three treads at a time, is a short, stocky fireplug of a man, dressed in camouflage from head to toe. He sticks out a meaty hand and says, "I'm Larry." Violet eyes, set into a fiery beard and mustache, sparkle over a devilish smile.

"Is this where we tie up?" I ask.

"No place finer on the rivah," he answers. "But you might want to throw a line off 'er stern, though."

"And tie it to what?" I demand. "What if we get a blow?"

The dock, such as it is, barely reaches to *Betty Jane's* middle. She is huge by comparison. One strong gust of wind and she will wipe out most of the other boats.

Larry takes off his granny glasses, presses them to his pursed lips, and surveys the situation as if for the first time.

"We'll run a line 'cross the water over to that there tree over there to...to that there island over there...See? Tripod won't mind. He's my goat. He's only got three legs. Get it?"

"But what about other traffic coming through?"

"Son," he says with the familiarity of one smart-ass recognizing another. "If there's gonna be any foul weather, there ain't gonna be no traffic. Now, ain't that right?"

I change the subject.

"Why is everyone since Ozark dressed up like a tree?"

Larry jumps in shock and disbelief. His eyes narrow.

"Bowhuntin' opened last Monday, son. Where the hell have you been?"

More to the point, where the hell are we?

"Now," Larry says, "You need power and water. Okay, I'll fetch it."

He vaults up the stairs, three at a time, and returns with a hose and an extension cord, one leaky and the other frayed, running side-by-side down the incline from Lord-knows-where.

I knot a moorage that looks more like occupational therapy than anything nautical and call, "We're here. Shut 'er down."

———•———

Betty Jane is only a momentary disturbance to Spadra's enchantment. When her engines go quiet, birds swoop down to skim bugs off the water; turtles poke up their heads; fish jump under a sky going from pink to violet. We climb up to the harbormaster's office where a tall Bradford pear tree heralds fall with awe-inspiring brilliance.

"You eat dinner at The Pasta House in Clarksville," Larry says. "Groceries are at the Walmart. My Dodge Neon is in the parking lot. Help yourself." He does not look up from stirring the chaos he keeps under the counter. "Showers are in the campground."

"Is that the campground where we passed a dock tied out in the river?" Dale asks.

"Yep. That's the one. Out the drive and turn right. Just past the train tracks. If you run my car into the river, you've gone too far. And get the new fishing rod out of the back seat if you do, and just let her sink. I'm late on my payments, anyway."

"Do we need to sign anything?" I ask.

"I've got yer boat, son."

Larry calls me son.

We snatch our towels and shampoo out of the boat and walk down the two ruts covered in blacktop to the campground where we find no cars, no tents, no RVs, no campers. The shower house is locked, but a sign propped against an open door of a fifth-wheel trailer nearby says, "Park Hostess." Our knock interrupts an in-home spa day and *Wheel of Fortune*.

She appears at the door with curlers in her hair, a mudpack on her face, two cucumber slices between fingers, and says, "Showers are for campers," before asking, "Whattayawant?" She rattles the screen door to make sure it is locked.

"We need a bath," I say, stating the obvious.

"Hush!" She screams at her yappy dog before asking us, "Are you campers?"

"No."

"Showers are for campers."

She pokes the last of a Ding Dong into her mouth and wads the cellophane into the pocket of her housecoat. The filling squishes out from between her lips.

"May we pay for a shower?" I ask.

"No. Like I said, showers are for campers."

Applause draws her attention to the TV.

"Can we rent a campsite and then take a shower?"

Forcing herself to forego the game, she turns back around, squints at us suspiciously as if we are hiding a thirty-foot Airstream under our towels and asks, "Where's your gear?"

"On the boat. At the marina. Larry said we could come over here and get a shower."

"Well, you can't!" she screeches.

A long pent-up grudge against her neighbor breaks forth, citing section and sub-section of the Arkansas Parks and Recreation Department Use and Maintenance Code, stopping only to catch her breath before launching a second more lengthy invective against "that man who is always sending people over here," so vivid and well phrased that I wish for pen and paper. I am tempted to applaud.

Dale grabs my arm to drag me away and says, "Thank you, ma'am."

"But it was just getting good," I complain.

"We'll shower on the boat."

"Well, that beauty treatment is pretty much shot. I can tell you that."

Larry is surprised to see us back so soon. We explain what happened.

"Well, I got a shower behind the shop," he says.

A new shower in a freshly remodeled bathroom with lots of hot water, a vanity to shave in, and a hook to hang our clothes on.

"What the f—?" I begin.

"Don't ask," Dale says. "Be grateful."

———— ◆ ————

The next morning we have breakfast in the marina restaurant—a few modular dining tables salvaged from a defunct Arby's, a microwave, and a refrigerator posted with a sign that says, "Hot Pockets—$1.50." Larry is drinking coffee.

"Coffee's free to slipholders and transients. Help yourself and take a seat," he says.

We ask about a place to take *Pramela*.

"You can go all the way up this draw here. Just beyond 'em trees is a wide shallow pool full of fish. You fish?"

"No."

He tugs at his beard trying to imagine a couple of men who don't know it is hunting season and don't fish. Fishing is why Spadra is here. The camp store is an angler's paradise. Rods—from bamboo to state-of-the-art graphite—lie neatly across ceiling trusses. Nets, lines, and lures—from hand-tied flies to wriggly rubber worms—are organized in bins. Nightcrawlers are live in the cooler next to the stink bait, and crickets sing all night under a light bulb in a cage outside.

Larry recovers from his consternation and says, "Well, anyway, you can canoe up that draw there. While you're gone, can I show your boat to a couple of friends?"

I supply my usual answer. "Sure. Keys are in the helm. Take her for a spin if you like, but mind the water moccasins in the bilge," which will turn out not to be so funny after all. "They usually don't bite but they're mating and the male's likely to be a little nervous."

"Awww," Larry waves us off, not really sure if we are kidding or not.

He pulls his camouflaged telephone out of his camouflaged overalls, flips it open, dials a number, and says greedily, "Guess what I got in my dock," as Doris Faye, Dale, and I head up to higher water.

Finally...Finally, I think to myself.

Finally, Dale and I can spend some time together. *Betty Jane* is safely tied up under Larry's watchful eye. He's probably giving tours to all his country cousins while we are alone in our dinghy floating in a pond. There is a duck, a goose, a turtle. A great blue heron squawks as it takes flight. The trees are shedding their leaves. One drops here; another drops there. Something rustles on the shore. Doris Faye sniffs the water as Dale and I look at each other.

We talk about the last six months. We laugh at our mistakes, grieve our disappointments, and wonder at our victories. But there is a question we must answer: what happens next? I have my heart set on cruising up the Mississippi, if only for bragging rights, but Dale still favors another over-the-road transport.

"Look, Huck," he argues. "Everyone we know thought you were nuts for hatching this plan. They are certain of it after all the trouble we've gone through. And now they're beginning to wonder about me. Bragging rights to whom? Most of our friends don't know port from starboard, stem from stern, and the two who did are dead. We didn't know, either, until suddenly, one spring, we got a wild hair to buy this leaky tub."

His voice becomes shrill.

"And ain't she grand?" I ask.

He won't be distracted.

"If you just have to cruise the Big River, I'll go with you as long as we end up in a northern state." Dale, a born Wisconsinite, is tired of living in the South. It is his only condition for making the trip. "But I do not see the point in going all the way down to Pine Bluff so we can turn around and go all the way up to Memphis so we can sweat it out all the way to Cape Girardeau. Even at that, we'll need to install topside fuel tanks."

Between the Arkansas and Ohio rivers, the Mississippi is not controlled. Broad floodplains make development along its banks impossible, except at Memphis. We will have to make special arrangements for food, fuel, and fresh water to be trucked down to the shore. We will cruise all day, every day, for weeks at a time in fair weather or foul, spending nights alone at anchor—without exception. All the while pushing against the current. The best time to be on the Mississippi would be right now during the fall drought, except we are too late and too far away. By the time we make the Ohio, all facilities will be closed for the season, if they are not already. We'll have to wait another year.

"And gas is five dollars at the pump," he says. "No telling what it will be brought-down. It's more economical to haul."

Dale lets me weigh the option against the advice of those at Applegate.

Morgan and Owen have been down the Arkansas and the Mississippi as far as the Gulf. Barney goes every year to Fort Lauderdale. Morgan tells harrowing tales about near collisions with tankers on the Intercoastal Waterway. Both say there's nothing to see below Little Rock. And I've seen cornfields on both sides of a river before.

"Okay," I decide. "Let's haul."

"Good. Now, I have another matter," Dale says gravely.

"What's that?"

"It's starting to rain."

———◆———

In my deliberations, I failed to notice the drops of rain sending concentric circles across the pond.

"The real rain is just about to hit," I say, pulling oars at a steady pace.

Rain, heavier than a drizzle but not so much as a shower, descends upon us as we approach the gas dock where a shiny black coil has lodged itself between the pier's flotation and decking.

"I'll let you and the dog out over on the other side of the gas pump."

"Why?" Dale asks, grabbing a hold as I come about sharply. "I don't see anything."

"Exactly. It is a snake."

A water moccasin, engorged on minnow and perch and unable to swim, squeezes itself between the dock's layers of floatation and decking so it can sleep off the feast in proximity to the water without being in it. We'd see them often at the ranch.

Despite our whisperings, we've been overheard. Fishermen, not yet mentioned because they blend in with the forest, live in a sort of stasis by the water. Their movements are slow, their skin is tinged green, and their clothes exude a damp and musty odor. Only the occasional puff of cigarette smoke gives away their positions around the cove. They are everywhere. Our mention of a snake sends up the alarm and brings them out of hiding.

"Larry," says one angler. "LARRY!"

"What're yew hollerin' about?" asks a second.

"Can you keep it down?" asks a third.

A fourth *shh-shhes*.

A fifth complains, "You're scarin' the goddamned fish."

The first whispers across the water, "But there's a *s-s-snake*," hissing the final word for emphasis.

"What kind of snake?"

"A water moccasin snake," I announce in full voice.

"Shh-shh-shh-shh-shh," echoes around the cove.

But the silence is broken and a chorus of men take action against the intruder.

"LARRY. LARREEEE. You gotta sna-a-a-ake!" they call up to the office.

Larry pokes the point of his red beard out the screen door.

"What? Whatthehell is up? Can't you see I'm on the goddammed phone? Shut up all this hollerin'. You'll scare the goddamned fish."

The anglers whisper almost inaudibly, "*Snake.*"

Larry's eyes open wide as he mouths silently, "What kinda snake?"

"The kind that eats *fish*."

Like the venomous-viper-whose-bite-is-lethal part does not matter?

"Call you back," Larry says as he slides his phone into a slit in his tree costume. He grabs a pistol and bounds down the stairs.

"Where?" he asks.

I point out the slithery shadow wedged under the dock. Larry squints to get a look. He pats down his coveralls. From one of its many pockets and pouches, he extracts his granny glasses and bangs them onto his face. He spreads his feet wide and leans over the water.

"Here?" he asks, without uttering a sound.

I wave him farther down.

He steps gingerly.

"Here?"

I wave him farther.

"Here?"

"There," I nod.

He bends his knees, rests his belly against his thighs, and cantilevers his butt over the water. Slowly he sights his target. His finger begins to squeeze when suddenly both his eyes spring open, and he stands bolt upright. Apoplectic with shock and horror, Larry gasps.

"B-B-B-But, that's J-J-Jasper," he wails.

"Is it?" Four asks, being quick to explain. "Well, *I* really didn't get a good look at 'im. *HE,*" accusing me, "*HE* just said there was a snake."

"Yes, well," Larry spits until his upset settles into indignation. "Well, I've got better things to do than to hold you ladies' hands every time something goes squiggle in the water. I got a marina to run. I'm putting in for grants, y' know. I'm gonna fix up this place, y' know."

He marches off the dock. The vibration of which barely causes Jasper to shift his head, yawn, showing me his cottony mouth, and send his forked tongue out once to probe the air before lying still again. The screen door slams.

A soft, benevolent rain draws a curtain around the marina. Diesel trains rumble low and heavy along the waterfront. Their horns echo down the valley, and the trestle creaks under their weight. Forgotten cups of peppermint tea cool on the dresser as dreams from far, far away arrive one after the other. This is where we are. This is Spadra.

CHAPTER TWELVE
The Long Stretch

Charlie's Hidden Harbor promises "Life's real fine above Lock Nine," but unlike highways and interstates, the river is pristine, devoid of signage, advisories, or advertisements. Charlie's is so well concealed that Dale and I do not see it and decide to anchor out below the dam. However, as Dale makes his final approach to the lock, I spy a break in the shoreline off our stern, the marina entrance. We come about and almost immediately wish we hadn't. If Spadra was small; Charlie's is miniscule.

Precious little water separates the gas dock from the harbor mouth. Riprap, an erosion control of jagged rock piled against the shoreline and a hazard to propellers, further narrows the margin for error. The shallow-water alarms scream. A fierce wind roars up our stern. Nerves are frayed. Tempers flare as Dale tries to walk *Betty Jane* into port like a crab. But every gain in the bow comes at a loss at the stern. I stand on the foredeck, alone and out of earshot, and think to myself, *Desperate times call for desperate measures.* I cinch the PFD tightly around my chest, gather the line in my hand, and curl my toes around the bow rail. I blow an I-love-you kiss to Dale whose face is red and contorted with protest.

He yells, "No. NO. NO!"

But it is too late; I've jumped.

I vault the chasm between boat and dock. The rope unfurls loop by loop. The wind pushes me off course. My hat blows away. I land hard but still have the rope in hand, and *it* is still tied to the boat.

"Line on, Cap'n. Bring your stern in," I scream over the wind as I wrap the rope around a standard cleat.

Dale is furious.

"...of all the foolhardy...irresponsible...dumbest...GOD-DAMMIT, Alexander!"

He is really mad.

"What? Sorry, love, cannot hear you over this ceaseless wind."

A man walks up. He is handsome in that spit-and-polished-retired-military sort of way—starched shirt, creased pants. His hair is jet black—slicked down, combed straight back, immovable. His smile is warm and toothy.

"Hi, my name is Charlie," he says.

"My name is Alexander. That's Dale. There's my dog, Doris Faye, and the boat is *Betty Jane*. Now you've met the entire family. Oh, and that's *Pramela*, the baby, hanging off the davits at the back."

"This all right, right here?" asks Dale, now calmer and concerned about where we've tied the boat. *Betty Jane* obliterates any view of gas dock from the river.

"No place else to put y'," Charley says, speaking the truth.

"What if someone wants to buy gas?" I ask.

"Did you see anyone behind you?" Charley answers.

"No."

"Ain't no one gonna want to buy gas."

Business is bad. Fuel prices are high, and people don't cruise like they used to.

"Used to," Charley remembers, "entire families would pile on a big cruiser like this, well, not exactly like this." He pulls out a comb and combs his hair in a window. "Used to they'd go down to Florida. Everybody goes to Florida, y' know. And back in time for school. No more. You're the first big boat I've seen all season."

"Can't be, Charlie," I say. "*Candy's Nightmare* left out of Applegate right after Memorial Day. And that other man going to the West Coast via Panama left out of Emerald Cove first of the month."

"Didn't stop here."

Probably couldn't find it.

The entrance to Charlie's is hidden behind an Arrival Point, a pair of mammoth pylons sticking out of the water to mark the lock zone. The lock zone is federal land where private enterprise is prohibited by law. Charlie's is the exception.

A small office stands at the end of the catwalk. Two or three sailers rot on stands in a small boatyard next to a vegetable garden overlooking the river. A single boathouse shelters ski boats and party barges. Mobile homes park under shade trees on higher ground. Charlie was a pilot for commercial air lines. He was Air Force before that. The marina is something for him to do while his wife is at work. He pulls a rack of chairs salvaged from an airport concourse to provide the three of us a place to eat lunch on the dock. When Doris Faye and I return from our walk, he says, "Dale tells me that y'all fix houses."

"We did. Most recently we've been working on this boat."

"And, man, ain't she pretty?"

"Thank you," Dale says, pushing the standard boat lunch of chips, fruit, and a sandwich through the hatch. "I got Diet Coke, Diet Ginger Ale, Jumex, and branch water. Who wants what?"

Charlie has never heard of Jumex, our staple of fruit nectars from Mexico.

"I'll try one of them," he says, then asks, "Where're you gonna winter?"

"Little Rock," we answer simultaneously with Dale adding, "We expect to haul out in the spring,"

I interject, "But we haven't made any plans yet."

Charlie's eyes light up. His hand fumbles for his cellphone, and then for the glasses off his head before jabbing at the keypad with manicured fingers. The call goes through.

"Is Ray there? Where the Sam Hill is he? Gimme his cell."

Charlie hangs up and re-dials.

"Ray? Ray? You asshole. What'er yer doing? Well, get fucked." Charlie explains that he and Ray are good friends, then turns back to the call. "Well, look, Ray, I've got these guys here, they got a beautiful boat. They need a slip for the winter, you got one?...I dunno..."

Charley shifts his glasses back to the top of his head and measures the length of our boat against the length of his dock.

"Fifty feet oughtta do it...You don't?...Hmmmm. Well, throw out one of those dead-beat relatives sponging off ya and put these guys in...I know she's your wife, but this is a boat...Hell yeah, it's a nice boat...Well, see what you can do. Call me back? Don't shoot your dick off, you asshole. 'Bye."

The phone goes back in his pocket.

"Ray's only got a forty-two-foot slip empty right now. He runs a nice family business, Ray does. You'll like Ray's. Except right now he's hunting. Ray cares about nothing more than hunting, not even boats. You go to Ray's when you get down there. He'll take care of you."

John Bartlett had told us about Ray's.

"Fer shelter off t' river, ain't no bett'r than Ray's. Five or so miles up t' Great Maumelle mashed up 'gainst a bluff. Come rain 'r snow 'r flood 'r storm, ain't nuthin' gonna git y' at Ray's. T'onliest t'other place is Little Rock Yacht. But, man, come spring an' th' Little Maumelle turns a-loose. Best hold on, 'r yer in N'awlins 'fore y' know it. B'sides, you won't get in 't Little Rock Yacht. No one I know gets in 't Little Rock Yacht."

Charlie takes a bite of his sandwich and says, "Now, about my father's house."

Dale and I look confused, so Charlie starts again.

"I mean to say, my Daddy died, and I got the house. It needs a little work. I figure with your boat at Ray's you might want to live in town over the winter. Maybe fix the place up a little while you're there since y'all know about fixing things up and everything."

Dale and I consider the possibility.

"I mean, having somebody in there will save me the trouble of winterizing, but, of course, you'll have to pay utilities."

"Of course," we say together.

Neither of us has given any thought to winter. We agree to call when we get to Little Rock. Maybe we can swing a deal.

————◆————

We trade car service for lunch at Charlie's favorite Mexican restaurant in Morrilton while we're tied up at his marina. But the fair weather is over. A depression in the Gulf has become a tropical storm.

"Rain's coming," Charlie says on the third morning. "You gotta git. I'm not running you off, y' know, but—"

But we'll have to make a run for it. Locks Eight and Nine are above Little Rock Yacht, which may have cover but doesn't return our calls. Ray's is farther down the Arkansas plus five miles back up the Great Maumelle. Ray has cover. Charlie has made the decision for us.

"I've already called the lock; they're waiting for you."

"Well, we are not in the habit of keeping lockmasters waiting," Dale says, "Let's go."

We suck down our coffee and toss the dishes in the sink. Doris Faye and I go ashore while Dale starts the engine. The first bands of storm that will hector us all day rise up from the southern horizon.

"No. No. No," Charlie says when we try to pay for dockage. "Won't have it. Don't try to make me. Call me, now. Call me and tell you got there all right, hear?"

I cast the last line as Dale powers through the breakwater. The wind is back.

"Call me about my Daddy's house, promise?...'Bye," he says, waving. "SEE YOU DOWN THE RIVAH!"

We are through Lock Nine with no delay. But the cruise is not fun. The clouds are low. The wind is cold. At Lock Eight, we have to wait.

"Lock Eight. Lock Eight. This is *Betty Jane* requesting lockdown. Over."

The lockmaster says, "Thirty minutes, Cap'n."

Thirty minutes is the time it takes to cycle a lock chamber once. It is the standard, universal answer given whenever a lock is unavailable. It has no bearing on anything.

The barges locking up are too long or wide to lock through in one piece. They have to be broken down, locked through in pieces, and reassembled on this upper side. Rain begins to spit. *Betty Jane* treads water while I slide windows closed, batten down hatches, and snap her new rain bonnet over the helm. I grab the binoculars and look downstream at the lock.

"The radar is spinning on top of the pushboat below the chamber. I don't see anything locked through yet. No change from fifteen minutes ago. Whattayou wanna do?"

"What do you mean?" Dale asks.

"I mean we can either stay out here with the wind blowing us all over creation. By the way, there is a dredge and some empty gondolas over there we need to not hit."

"I saw 'em."

"Or we can tie up at that Arrival Point over there."

"APs are for barges."

"Okay. So you want to stay out here in the middle of the river not running into shit for who knows how long?"

"Not really," Dale says.

"So let's tie up. It's not like the AP will explode the moment we throw a rope on it."

Dale turns the wheel and we tie up with her nose downstream and her stern into the wind just like at Charlie's. We don't know what we are doing. If we did, we'd know to turn around.

"Not right," I complain.

She's restless and cannot get comfortable. The wind blows her bow into the bank, the ropes complain, the cleat moans.

"She's going to beat herself against that AP until she bleeds," I say. "We have to come about."

"Really?" Dale asks, protesting the need to get back into the mainstream, broadsiding her to the wind in order for us to still be breaking the law.

"Yes, really. I've seen what Clay had to do to fix a banged up nose. No, thank you. Besides, I can probably do it myself. I'll just untie her and walk the line to the nose."

"Not this close to shore, you're not," Dale says. "Just a minute and I'll restart the engines."

We put nose to the wind, tying the rope to her bow. She falls naturally in line with both the current and the wind, like a kite on a string.

"Much better," I say.

"And the windshield catches the rain that was running down my back."

———————•———————

At last, the pushboat is through the lock. Deckhands are retying the last few gondolas when her captain sounds her airhorns—*B-L-O-O-O-A-T!*

We take no notice.

She insists, *B-L-O-O-O-O-O-O-O-A-T!*

Dale suddenly springs to action. He falls rather than climbs down the aft ladder to the cockpit, raises the hatches to turn on the fuel, and begins to order me about.

"Untie that line. Get your PFD on. And do something with the dog," he says, starting the engines. "And tell me if I've got pretty water coming out the tailpipes."

"What is going on?"

Dale gives the T-handle mounted on the helm a long and forceful tug.

B-L-O-O-O-O-O-O-O-A-T, Betty Jane's airhorns echo across the valley.

"What's the deal?" I ask, shinnying down the gunwales, slick with rain, to untie our moorings. Then, back to the stern to inspect the discharge. "Pretty water, port. Pretty water, starboard. What's going on?"

"That man wants his parking space and we're in it. Now fend off that side while I push up and come about."

"How do you kn—?"

"Just do it," Dale says.

"Here we go."

We wait in the middle of the river as the pushboat shoves away from the lock wall.

"Okay," I say impatiently. "We're out here untied and adrift in the wind and the rain. Let's go."

"Wait for it..." Dale says, holding up a finger.

The barge ties up where we just vacated. He lets out another *B-L-O-O-O-O-O-O-O-A-T!*

"Wait for it..."

"*Betty Jane. Betty Jane.* This is Toad Suck, over."

"There it is," he says, picking up the mike. "This is *Betty Jane*, over."

"Doors're open. Light's green. C'mon in, the water is *fine*."

"What just happened?" I ask.

"You heard the man. We're locking down. And you better get a move on because that storm isn't letting up and the light's fading and we've already fiddlefarted around here for three hours. Let's not just stand around and hold court. Let's *go*."

Dale drops *Betty Jane* into gear, and as she picks up speed, I deploy fenders and decide where we will tie up.

"Starboard side, far end."

"Roger that."

"We say, 'Copy.'"

Dale smirks.

The lock doors close behind us. The master's head pops up over the parapet. He is a fat man as fat men often are in the country. He was probably a fat baby, a fat child, a fat adolescent, and now in his late twenties he moves with the grace and aplomb of one who has never known any difference.

"Whar in tarnation have y'all been?" he asks like a mother who has been kept waiting. "I've been a-here a-waitin' an' a-waitin' fer ya since I don't r'member when."

"We've been at Charlie's," I offer apologetically.

"I know where you've been, shoot. Ev'ry mornin' I come to work an' say, 'They come? They come?' I say. They say, 'Naw, ain't come yet.' Now, yer here. Ev'rybody upriver says yer sumptin' to see. They was right, too...Hi, dawg."

He waves at Doris Faye.

"That dawg hunt?...Tew bad."

I ask why we had to wait for barges after they had cleared the lock.

"'Cuz, I cain't 'ave tew vessels in the lock zone t' same time. Small craft, like y'all, they ride for free, but comm'cial, 'em boys pay. I let tew boats in. 'Un says it's on t'other's bill. T'other says, ''T'ain't.' An' pert soon, no one's paid. Shoot. 'At boy, 'aire," the master throws his head back to indicate the captain now shuttling barges between the dredge and the AP. "'At boy, he sez ain't no scope in deadheading empty barges. He sez I oughta let 'im ride up fer free since 'ee ain't got no load. I sez, 'You bring me a bowt like yern, I let you ride fer free.'"

A smile folds his face many times over. "'At boy ain't got no bowt like yern. 'Sides, Uncle Sam sez, 'No free rides for no barges...When 'at ol' boy blowed at t' AP, 'cuz heesa releas'n the lock to y'alls. That's when I called yew."

He looks at the weather.

"Nasty day fer a bowt ride."

"We know," Dale says. "We've got cover at Ray's if we can make it. Little Rock Yacht if we can't, but they don't call back."

"Yer ain't gonna make Ray's. The next band 'a rain is up yer stern already. Luttle Rock's best, an', no, I don't 'spect they call yew back."

Wonder what that means?

"Ken ya go down kinda fast?"

"Emergency lock up at Fifteen," I answer proudly.

"Yew ken go fast, then," master says, pouring himself in his cart to make swift preparations.

"Le's go," he calls over the radio, and we are down.

———— ◆ ————

NOAA, National Oceanic & Atmospheric Administration, forecasts "heavy rain, strafing winds, and lightning" with warnings to small craft to stay off the river. The canvas over the bridge flaps violently. *Betty Jane* vaults the choppy water, drenching us with wind-blown spray. The engines, spun up to maintain steerage over the rushing current, whine loudly. We pitch. We toss. Doris Faye is beside herself with worry.

"NOT GOING TO MAKE RAY'S," I scream at Dale.

"NO."

"WHAT ARE WE GOING TO DO IF THERE'S NO SPACE AT LITTLE ROCK?"

"WHAT?"

"WHAT ARE WE GOING TO DO IF THERE'S NO SPACE AT LITTLE ROCK?"

"THROW THE HOOK."

"ARE NOT. WE CAN'T LAUNCH *PRAMELA* IN THIS. EVEN IF WE COULD, I CAN'T GET BACK. DORIS FAYE IS NOT GOING TO SHIT ON BOARD AND I DON'T WANT TO TEACH HER TO."

Dale adjusts course to compensate for the cross-winds ricocheting off the bluffs.

"WE'LL SQUAT," he says.

"WHAT?"

"WE'LL SQUAT ON THE GAS DOCK. NO ONE IS GOING TO DENY US SAFE HARBOR."

Betty Jane rolls into a wave, toppling to the floor anything not held down. The pots and pans rattle in the galley. Something crashes in the stateroom. Dale goes below to investigate, and while in the dry, he consults the charts.

"Too little too late," he says, handing me my rain gear, "But it will help keep you warm." We hunker down like two fans in ballpark deluge. It is the bottom of the tenth inning with no score and two outs. Suddenly, there is a hit.

Dale points to a volcanic cinder cone coming through the mist and says, "See that?"

"Yeah."

"That's Mt. Maumelle. It's French for 'tit'."

"We say, 'breast,' but go ahead. So?"

"That means shelter is close by. The Little Maumelle runs alongside us here and breaks out in to the mainstream shortly. That's where the marina is."

"Really?" I ask in disbelief.

"Yeah."

"Thank God."

Like Emerald Cove in Van Buren, Little Rock Yacht Club is a line of boathouses sheltered from the mainstream by a tow. The accordion roofline of smaller boathouses zig-zag above the sandbar. Larger houses, farther down, open to the river through a break in the shoal.

Dale asks, "Did you see any vacancies on the way down?"

"No. But there's the gas dock with an attendant's shed on the end. Let's tie up there and find out what's what."

He wheels the boat around like a bullwhip and lands us closer to the dock than we were at Charlie's. I jump.

"Line on!"

The rain has abated, but the wind slams the stern into the dock.

———•———

"You're here!"

Doris Faye and I peek into the hut to see a layer of dust covering a shuffle of paper. A chair is overturned and the telephone pulled out of the wall.

"Door's locked. The operating hours are apparently obsolete, but here's a phone number we can try."

I call out the digits.

"Yeah, I know. That's the number I've been calling since Charlie's."

Dale scrapes the electronics off the bridge. Doris Faye and I go for our walk.

In addition to the boathouses on the river, boathouses line two sides of a man-made lagoon inside the gas dock, and a service bay floats farther downstream. But the truly unique feature of Little Rock Yacht is Travelifts—not one but two. The Arkansas only has three. Applegate has the third.

The outbuildings are in good repair, the boats are clean, the lawns are mowed, and the parking lots are freshly striped. But there are no people, no cars, until Doris Faye and I hear one approach. I wave to attract attention, but it veers away. We follow. We corner it. There is no way out but to run us over. It gives up. The passenger window lowers a fraction and the doors lock.

The driver is a woman in her seventies fresh from a standing appointment at the beauty parlor. Her complexion is flawless. Her red lips match her red nails. She is warm and dry in a dark tweed suit wrapped in a London Fog. The aroma of dinner—meatloaf smothered in ketchup, mashed potatoes full of butter, still warm from the oven, and carefully wrapped in foil—wafts from the seat beside her. I am a man with a dog in a storm. I skip the introductions and get to the point.

"We need help."

She doesn't doubt it.

"That's my boat."

She raises an eyebrow.

"We need safe dockage."

She glances at a sign.

"I know. They don't answer. They don't call back."

At last she moves, keeping her eyes on me the whole time. She feels around in her purse and produces a cellphone, unfolds it to make sure that it is on and lays it next to the dinner. She speaks.

"Well, I suppose you could find Shawn."

"Shawn?"

"Yes, he lives on a boat around here somewhere. I am sure I don't know which one. Perhaps you should look for his car."

"What does he drive?"

"Now how should I know that?"

As I am wearing a yellow-with-black-trim PFD and looking like a half-drowned bumblebee, she stares at me.

The window slides shut, the brake comes off, and the beige Skylark threatens to roll over me or my dog if we do not move. Doris Faye and I return to the boat.

"I say, wee bit of a blow, Cap'n.'"

"I'll say," Dale says. "What's up?"

"I couldn't get any contact information, but there's an empty slip across the lagoon. At least it looks empty.

I found a sign posted with the number we've been calling, and there is supposed to be a guy named Shawn who looks out for the place, owns the place, is buried on the place. Hell, I don't know."

"Nobody would be on the water on a night like this."

"If they are, they're going to want their slip."

"If they are, they're back by now," Dale says.

"I don't know if it's big enough, though."

"We're sure as hell gonna find out," Dale says, climbing back up to the bridge. "We've got to get warm and dry one way or the other."

———◆———

We pull in as far as we can, leaving the bow out in the rain. Dale cuts the engines, covers the helm, and steps into the deckhouse when the sky opens up—*KABOOM!*—and the phone rings.

"Hello? HELLO?"

Whoever it is cannot hear over the corrugated roof, beaten like kettle drums by the rain. Lightning strikes interrupt the signal and garble the message. Dale screams into the phone.

"Yes? Yes? We're here…I SAID, 'WE'RE HERE'…I DON'T KNOW."

Loud noises frustrate and confuse Dale, the musician.

"Where are we?" he asks me.

"WHAT?"

"WHERE ARE WE?"

"Little Rock."

My answer pisses him off.

"No. No. No. What slip? What house?"

"I don't know."

He glares beseechingly.

"Well, I don't."

Walls of water blow sideways through the boathouse, obscuring everything beyond our stanchions, but I manage to make out the boat in the next slip.

"Red stripe," I answer, pulling my head in from the storm.

"WHAT?"

"RED...STRIPE," I repeat. "The boat in the next slip has a big red stripe. It is an aluminum houseboat...thirty feet."

"Red stripe," Dale relays into the phone. "Hello? HELLO?"

We lose the connection.

I swab down the cabins from stem to stern.

"This must be like what John and Kara went through," I say to Dale, who is busy warming soup and brewing hot coffee.

"Yeah, but theirs was Katrina. This is the remnants of a tropical storm."

Torrents of rain are torrents of rain, but during a lull, we hear a knock. A tall man in his thirties and soaked to the skin stands opposite our deckhouse hatch.

"You Dale?" he asks.

"No. I'm Alexander."

"I'm Shawn."

"Come in out of the weather."

He is unkempt and ill-shaven as most live-aboard men are, including us.

"No wood boats," he tells us.

We laugh.

"No. I'm serious. No wood boats."

"No, you're not," I contest.

"Yeah, I am. The rule is 'No wood boats'."

"It may be the rule, but it's also blowing a bloody gale out there!"

Dale suggests that we stay overnight and see what tomorrow brings.

"We've got a slip at Ray's waiting for us, and we've called here for the last three days without response."

"Well?" I ask, knowing that no sheriff would throw us back onto the river on a night like this.

"I know," Shawn confesses. "But you gotta be outta here by first thing tomorrow morning. And if you're not, you gotta call this number."

Shawn lays a damp business card on the desk and leaves.

"Really?" I ask facetiously.

Dale says, "I'll call in the morning."

A gun-shy Doris Faye quivers on my bunk as thunder rumbles and shakes the boathouse into the wee hours. I cannot sleep. Instead, I pet her soft coat and remind her of the places we visited and people we met over the last six months until the rain dwindles to drops of water falling off the boathouse roof. Dawn takes us completely by surprise. The sky is blue, the breeze is slight, and the day looks like a fresh laundry, hung out to dry in the sun.

Dale dials the number. A cheerful voice answers.

"Good morning, Hastings Holdings. Just a moment, please."

"This is Steven. How can I help you, Mr. Harris?...No, we don't allow wooden boats."

Dale cites the transport from Texas to Sallisaw. He mentions the five months in retrofit. He offers Rhoda as a reference. "...and any of the lockmasters and marina operators along the way."

Steve asks, "Over the road, then, here?"

"Yes, sir. And we'll want to haul out in the spring."

"I've got business over there. Why don't I come and look at your boat. We'll have to do that before we agree to haul you out anyway. I'll talk to Shawn."

"Fine," Dale says. "We need to get our car back at Applegate and run some errands. We've been on the river for two weeks."

We agree to meet in the late afternoon, but while we are at the barber, Steve calls back.

Hastings Holdings is real estate. Steve is Mr. Hastings's son-in-law. He has employed one of our favorite tactics as property investors. He has gone alone to check our story prior to our appointment. He has snooped around *Betty Jane* and been charmed. His voice is brimming with enthusiasm.

"Yes, you can stay," he gushes. "We have two fifty-foot slips you can choose from. Hauling out will be no problem. I'm bringing my father-in-law down to see your boat this weekend. Is that all right? He'll be thrilled."

Dale advises against disturbing the snakes in the bilge. "None of us got a lot of sleep last night."

"I bet. You kidding? Good. I left a lease agreement on your gunwales, I hope that was okay. The rate is the same for either slip, and you'll contract directly with the utility company for electric service. If you have any questions, this is my direct line."

Dale grins from ear to ear.

"What?" I ask.

"We're in at Little Rock Yacht."

"John Bartlett won't believe it."

CHAPTER THIRTEEN
Living the Dream, Man, Living the Dream

Having gotten *Betty Jane* settled, we have to see about ourselves. Charlie, back at Lock Nine, offered us his father's house rent-free in lieu of the cost of utilities and repairs we would make over the winter. But Charlie remembers his father's house as it was when Dad was still living in it. The one we see is no longer habitable. Rather than take an apartment for the next few months, we decide to stay on the boat until we haul out and transport to the Tennessee in the spring. In the meantime, we enjoy the Arkansas capital. Little Rock offers Peter Max at the Clinton Library, Andy Warhol at the Arkansas Arts Center, and MetLive in HD at the local cinema. Eventually, dogwood blooms dot the hillsides, the Little Maumelle floods, and *Eye Candy* pulls into the gas dock.

"Hello! Hello!" Ruthella says, pulling off her hat and mopping her brow. "Well, we made it."

Earl has been working steadily on *Eye Candy* since we saw her last. The bridge is glassed-in and has air conditioning powered by a home-center generator strapped onto the swim deck and fed by five-gallon gas tanks lashed to the bow.

"Yes, here we are, though I really don't know why, to tell you the truth. Earl said something about repairs...No, no trouble." She redraws a mouth in heavy lipstick, using the chrome of *Eye Candy*'s rub rail as a mirror. "He just wants to pull in to do something or other before we got too far downriver."

They have a passenger.

"Yes, Earl got him from somewhere. Brought him home like a stray, saying, 'You know, Ruthie, I'm just gettin' too ol' to crawl 'round this ol' boat. He'll be worth it for all the chores he can do. And he don't eat nuthin' but beer.' You know how Earl is."

Eye Candy and *Betty Jane* are here for the same reason. Little Rock Yacht has the last Travelift above Vicksburg, Mississippi. Both boats need a haul-out—*Eye Candy* for repairs; *Betty Jane* for the three-hundred mile transport to Aqua Yacht Harbor in Iuka, Mississippi. We both want the same lift. *Eye Candy* needs the strength and size of the larger lift. I want the versatility of the adjustable straps.

On the morning we are scheduled to go, our trucker and his escort are in the parking lot. Dale is packing the last bits into the car. Steve has been by to check on where to put the slings and promised to call when it is time to come over to the liftwell. We should be loaded and on the way in time to splash the Tennessee river by this afternoon. But seven o'clock becomes eight, then nine, with no word. Not only is the sun getting high, but I resent having gotten up so early to do nothing. I resent that my contractors are having to wait. I resent standing around.

"Fuck, what is taking so long?" I demand.

Dale shrugs.

"Well, should we call?"

"They know we are here. They know we are waiting. They know how to reach us."

When the phone rings, it is Steve, calling to say it will be a few more minutes. A constant in boating is that time is not measured in seconds, minutes, or hours as it is on land, but in mornings, afternoons, and evenings. Dale suggests Doris Faye and I walk off the frustration. We return with a report.

"The problem is not with the lift," I say, defiantly. "The problem is with Earl's big-ass Trojan that is at the head of the liftwell and the three Arkies sitting under its busted hull."

"What?"

"*Eye Candy* is hanging in the slings of the Travelift I reserved two weeks ago. Her keel is in the dirt."

"Not good," Dale says.

"Not good. Worse is that we have a pair of contractors cooling their heels. And it is getting hot and...and...FUCK!"

"Now, let's just slow down a minute..."

"*What?*"

"Steve would not have called and said it would be a little while longer if he meant we could not lift at all. What about the second lift?"

"It's small, it'll pinch her hull. The pulleys are not adjustable, I want the larger lift I reserved two weeks ago."

"You mentioned that."

"And—"

"And you are not getting your way."

"And I am not getting my way. Yes."

"Well, histrionics will not change that. Solutions can. What do you want to do?"

"I *want* to get out of here."

"Bad enough to use the smaller lift and assume all the risk and inconvenience that implies."

"I reserved the larger lift precisely bec—"

"Bad enough to use the smaller lift?" Dale reiterates.

"It's probably broken, too."

"Fine," Dale says. "When your attitude achieves adolescence, we can resume this conversation. In the meantime, I've been up since before dawn. I think I'll go lie down."

I pull myself together.

"Yes. The smaller, narrower, less accommodating lift with the non-adjustable pulleys will be okay. Not great. Not what I had planned. But it will do."

"Shall I call Steve and suggest that we use the smaller lift?"

"Yes."

The phone rings before Dale can dial.

It is Steve who, after Dale has offered our magnanimous concession, says, "Good. 'Cause that's all I got. I had to set *Eye Candy* down at the head of the well. We don't have any jack stands so I have to leave her in the slings. We could not find the straps for the second lift—"

"I'm not going to tell Alexander that."

"What?" I ask.

"I had to send my son after another pair."

"I'm not going to tell Alexander that, either."

"WHAT?" I ask.

"Are two straps going to be all right?"

"You're going to ask Alexander that."

"*WHAT!*" I exclaim.

I take the phone and listen to Steve's explanation.

"*Two* straps?" I ask. "That concentrates the entire weight of the boat on only four points." I take a breath to begin a rant, but Dale holds up his preemptory finger. Reminding me of the choice, he says softly, "Yes or no?"

"What do *you* think?"

"I think—" Steve begins.

"Sorry, not you. I was asking Dale."

"Oh."

"I'm not the one who will have to repair the damage," Dale answers.

I'm too put out to be civil so I agree to two straps and hand the phone to Dale.

"Fine," Dale tells Steve on my behalf. "That'll be great. Thanks."

"I don't know about 'Great.'"

"We'll be right over," Dale says, before pushing "end" on the cellphone.

———◆———

The scene at the liftwell is tragic. *Eye Candy* barely made it to shore before having to be set down. She lists. Her starboard side pushes against the sling, the only thing that keeps her upright. Her keel is sunk in the mud. The generator runs to keep the boat cool for dogs barking inside. Their paws muddy the glass and ruin the paint. There is a gash in the bow. The missing planks, black with rot, bake in the sun. Earl and Ruthella and their rummy sit in the shadow of their wreck on whatever they can find.

"Stand by, Cap'n," Steve calls to us.

His teenaged son and the new man—the one whom, yesterday, we had to teach how to pump out holding tanks—thread the new straps onto the narrower Travelift.

"See? You get new straps," Dale says brightly.

"See? None of us have the slightest notion what we are doing," I answer.

"Fine."

"*Fine.*"

Steve gives a crash tutorial on crane operation to the new hire. The Travelift starts, a few tests, a few mistakes, the slings drop below the surface.

"Okay," Steve calls.

Dale pulls *Betty Jane* over the submerged slings perfectly.

"Nicely done," Steve says as he walks back to his man to give the next instruction.

The straps snug around *Betty Jane* and lift her just out of the water when I slash my hand across my throat. I need to check the slings for any kinks and binds below the surface as I had seen Alon and Kenn do. The crane stops, but an ominous *thump...thump...thump* resonates throughout the hull. The Travelift is too far forward in the well.

"STEVE! STEVE!" I scream, severely upset, "MY GODDAMMED BOAT IS BANGING INTO YOUR GOD-DAMMED WALL!"

Billy, the transport driver and himself a calming force who has not moved since these follies began, stirs. He gets up from his truck, squints against the sun in his eyes, walks slowly across the asphalt; a bit of belly peeks out from beneath his tank top.

He places two meaty hands on *Betty Jane's* nose and leans forward to fend her from the wall. The cleavage of his buttocks, soft, pale, and rising out of his pants, is distracting, but I have a boat to haul. The thumping stops.

Steve scrambles up and over the crane operator to correct the error, causing *Betty Jane* to lunge forward and pushing Billy onto his back. His escort driver, Debbie, a woman dressed in a magenta blouse and canary yellow pedal pushers, floats to his side like a bubble about to burst.

"Oh, my Lo-ord," she says, taking the Christ's name in vain across two syllables.

Debbie is a mother of four boys, not Billy's, and grand-mother to two more, not Billy's. An ample bust and generous hip make her middle-aged midriff appear wasp-like. She is as comely and inviting as an overstuffed sofa at the end of a hard day, and, to Billy, she is the perfect companion. Both of their first marriages ended in divorce, their houses are sold, their kids are grown and out. They are free to haul boats from coast-to-coast together.

"She lets me do anything…any-thing," he says with an appetite for Christmas morning in his eyes.

Meanwhile, Ruthella distracts herself with what I am doing.

"Why does Alexander keep sticking that pole in the wa-ter?" she asks her husband who, she believes, knows every-thing about boats.

"He's checkin' to see if 'em straps're twisted or bindin' below the waterline. He's got a soft spot in the chine behind the locker in the stateroom which is why he's bein' such a bitch about where they put 'em straps, and he don't want no damage to his paint. Don't blame 'im."

Earl studies me through tendrils of cigarette smoke.

"Do *you* know how to do that?" Ruthella asks him.

"No," Earl answers flatly, letting a sour mood take hold. "If I did, you think we'd be sittin' here with my bow broke in the mud?"

Ruthella, ever the optimist, says, "Oh, Earl, these things just happen. You know how wooden boats are."

She dismisses the entire mishap with a playful slap on his shoulder, but Earl is disappointed and upset. I know how he feels. A beached vessel with no sail date in sight gnaws at the gut. He has told me twice over the past week about what happened.

"I thought that leak'd close up once we'd gotten out of Emerald Cove," he'd explained when Doris Faye and I saw him earlier this morning. "I hoped 'twas just planks being dry in rough water. Twelve, y' know. But, by Charlie's, I know'd 'tweren't no leaky seam. Had to be sumthin' worse. By Toad Suck, I had to tell Ruthella that we wasn't goin' to make Vicksburg. Thank God I got a helper."

Ruthella tries to cheer Earl up.

"How's he know to do that?" she says.

"Do what?" Earl asks, lost in his own despair.

"I didn't 'spect no rotten chine, no sir-ee. Busted plank, maybe, but not no damned busted chine. An' y' know if there's a good place to have a busted chine, the bow ain't it. I got no jack stands. Don't know how we're gonna hold 'er up while we work on 'er. I got no workbench," he had said to me.

Does it get any worse? I wondered.

"*That,*" Ruthella says, pointing to my sounding the straps.

"What?"

Yes, it does get worse. Worse is being beached with no sail date in sight while your friends launch. Envy is a sickening shade of green.

"Earl."

"What, *Ruthie*?...'Cuz he's smart, Ruthie. 'Cuz he's smart."

———◆———

The truth is that Dale and I are aping what Highport did with twenty guys, what Alon and Kenn did with two. We've learned a lot since that dark morning at Texoma. Here is proof. I don't like the placement of the aft strap. I suggest moving it. Steve resists. Too far forward and the boat is out of balance. Too far back and it bends the propeller shafts. He doesn't want to take the risk. I don't want to tell him about the rotten chine. He, not wanting two old wooden boats with broken chines to close both lifts, may scrub my haul-out and send the transporter away. We argue.

Debbie intervenes.

"Y'all," she says, waiting to get our attention, "Y'all can fight all day and it makes no matter to me."

She rests her hands on her hips.

"But I am telling y'all, menopause makes a pretty girl hot so if you don't mind, I'm going to find me some shade somewhere with a nice tall margarita in it. And y'all can just let me know what you decide. All right?"

She strings "right" out into the swelter with the daintiest of pinkies flinging away the sweat that erodes her perfectly powdered forehead.

"Now, before I hafta go, I wanna know, are we going to lift or not?"

I look at Dale who shrugs. I look at Steve who looks back at me. The only thing that can change is that *Eye Candy* will miraculously get out of the larger crane, which is not likely. I whirligig my finger over my head.

"Good," Debbie says, bouncing back to the shade of her truck. "It would be an awful shame to have lunch without accomplishing anything this entire morning."

Betty Jane rises up and settles on Billy's trailer with a clunk. It isn't a perfect landing; but they aren't Alon and Kenn.

"There. That's better," Debbie says, sending Steve's son, with tape measure in hand, to the top of *Betty Jane's* bridge while she opens the Arkansas Department of Transportation manual in her lap. Her lips move as she reads.

"I gotta have less than fourteen foot-six, boys. Fourteen-six," she calls out, pushing a cigarette into a bright orange holder with a gold stripe around the end.

Billy crouches down to read the measurement.

"Fourteen foot, nine inches," he says.

"Not good enough, boys," she hollers back. "Not good enough."

Billy suggests we let a little air out of the tires and shows the teenager how to use the pressure gauge. Fourteen-six and one-half is the new measurement.

"Fine," Debbie smarts off. "Real fine if this boat don't need a top when it gets to where it's going. Them folks at Aqua Yacht are going to be some fair impressed with a bridge-less boat. Bet they've never seen one b'fore. I need more, boys, *more*. Liable to be one or two low-hanging trees in Iuka, Mississippi."

She waits for suggestions.

"Bet there are. Bet there are some low-hanging trees in Eye-YEW-kah, Mississippi...Now, let's think of something."

Steve suggests we take off the propellers.

Two brass propellers lie in the sun. The crane spins up. *Betty Jane* swings forward and back before easing down once again on the length of her keel.

"Fourteen-four," Billy calls out.

Applause and cheers comes from those gathered on the levee to watch.

"Thank *you*," Debbie says like the homecoming queen she most likely once was.

Spectators walk down for a closer look.

"Where're you going?" one asks.

"Cincinnati, via the Tennessee and Ohio rivers," I answer.

"Why don't you just truck her? Cincinnati is only eleven hours away."

Earl has walked up and answers for me.

"Because," he says thoughtfully. "Because a boat'll go places the land never heard about. You a boater, sir?"

"No."

Earl does not mask his pity. He leans forward, letting the shadow of his river hat fall on the toe of his boot as he composes his response. He shakes his head, and says, "Then you can't understand." His eyes trace a line to the distant upriver. "It's called 'Living the dream'," he says and walks away. Earl's got more to do than talk to landlubbers.

CHAPTER FOURTEEN
Adventure

Our launch is scheduled for three-thirty the following afternoon at Aqua Yacht Harbor. I am in the harbormaster's office when the flash of a familiar white hull zooms by the window at a speed I think is unsafe. But before I can get out the door to complain, Billy has turned a perfect doughnut and placed *Betty Jane* precisely under the Travelift. Yard hands set upon her like bees to honey.

Billy doesn't take time to get out. Instead, he calls down from the cab, "Rode like a high-dollar whore," just like Alon had said a year earlier. He drives away as soon as *Betty Jane* is lifted, waving good-bye out the window as he goes. Debbie is waiting at the top of the hill. I watch them drive away as *Betty Jane* splashes quietly into Pickwick Lake on the Tennessee River. It is three-thirty at Aqua Yacht Harbor outside Iuka, Mississippi.

Aqua Yacht Harbor's prominence in the boating community lies in its location. By land, it does not appear to be anything. It is on Route 57, an unimportant road that barely warrants the double yellow line down its middle. Twenty miles to the south, Iuka hosts a pizza joint and a place called, simply, Family Restaurant, which started my addiction to shrimp-'n'-grits. Twenty miles to the north, Savannah, Tennessee, is big enough to support some nationally franchised restaurants and retail, including a big box home improvement center. Everything else in this northeastern corner of the Magnolia State is deep deciduous forest, so intensely green as to be almost blue.

By water, however, Aqua is at the center of the Tennessee-Tombigbee Waterway. The Tennessee river flows north. The Tombigbee River flows south to connect the Ohio River to the Gulf of Mexico and provide an alternate route to the Mississippi, as it does for us. Everyone stops here, from the Loopers circumnavigating the eastern United States on the Great Circle Loop to the snowbirds migrating from their Midwestern porches to various tropical lanais and back, that is, everyone. Consequently, Aqua sets the standard by which the rest of the Tennessee does business, to a greater or lesser extent.

The place buzzes with the launching, retrieving, and washing of boats and the care of their crews. Workshops whir. Service bays bang. The ship's store caters to every need or want, and Café St. Clair serves lunch and dinner at waterside. Aqua is DeWitte Loe's Highport before the fall. We tie up at the service dock, center stage, where there is a yard hand standing by who introduces us to the Tennessee River mantra: "Welcome to Aqua Yacht. We're glad you're here."

Slipholders in flip-flops and diners in summer whites come by to admire the swoops and curves of an iconic age in yacht design. They forget table reservations and family appointments in order to relive some part of their childhoods. Dale and I lean on the decks sharing cans of cold beans and Vienna sausages as they tell of uncles and grandpas who "all had boats just like this." At last they say, "Well," by way of introducing themselves; then, "Welcome. We're glad you're here," and, "Good night," before taking up the business for which they had come.

The next morning the service manager arrives to explain that the only mechanic on his staff old enough to remember how—and young enough to be physically able—to set the timing and the dwell on our engines is currently serving jury duty. We decline his offer to install new electronic ignitions because we are not confident we can get service, no matter how guaranteed, where we are going. God knows where we are going. A ten-year-old with a butter knife can fix what we have. We will wait for Tim and his panel to reach a verdict.

In the meantime, Deep South weather keeps all but the saltiest sailors in port. Clear blue mornings turn tornadic green by afternoon. Wind blows, thunder claps, and, despite the new vinyl top, the deckhouse roof leaks. Not as badly, but it does. We scramble to move bunks and drawers out of the wet and to keep lockers empty of drainage.

The jury acquits the defendant, and Tim arrives. He and Dale go down Memory Lane as they relive working on the family car with Dad. The morning is spent cranking engines, listening and fussing until *Betty Jane* purrs. Dale, eager to get underway, is up before dawn the next day.

"Get up. Get up," he says, vaulting over the engine room with coffee in hand.

Jackrabbit starts have never been my strength, and ten days of indolence have done nothing to change that. I am comfortable here. The showers are hot, the pool is cool, and the food is excellent.

"Get up," he says, having returned to the galley to flip hot cakes and pour juice. "We've got quite a cruise ahead of us, a lock to get through, and it's going to be a scorcher."

———◆———

Our next stop is Clifton, Tennessee, sixty miles downstream, already a long day without allowing time to get through a lock, which, we learned at Toad Suck Ferry, is anyone's guess. Pickwick Lock and Dam are just around the bend. We have to settle our bill, top off fuel and fresh water tanks, and buy ice cream, which we enjoy religiously at every opportunity, even after a hearty breakfast, because *Betty Jane's* refrigerator cannot make ice. Vacation homes look down through darkened windows on Pickwick Lake sparkling with the first rays of sunlight as we push away from the gas dock. It is already eighty degrees and humid.

"Gonna be a scorcher," Dale repeats.

Pickwick Lake is the playground of power brokers, legislators, and celebrities from across the region. Their fishing camps—sporting terraced acres, gazebos, swimming pools, and tennis courts—get more impressive as we approach the big part of the lake. Their personal watercraft, tiny sailers, and ultra-fast ski boats, tied at private docks, bob in our wake. The grandest and most opulent estate is opposite the lock in full view of anyone coming or going.

"Pickwick Lock. Pickwick Lock. This is *Betty Jane*. Over."

I scan the horizon with the binoculars while we wait for an answer. The lake is empty except for what appears to be a tiny white dot against the dam, a gray expanse of concrete as impenetrable as any wall. The lock is to our left.

"Go to fourteen, Cap'n."

The dot is a boat. She's taller than we are, longer than we are, newer than we are, more up-to-date and better equipped than we are—typical of everything we've been around for the past week. A radar array spins on top of her fly bridge. All her hatches are closed, which means she is heavily air conditioned. She is treading water, which means she is waiting to lock. She is monitoring her radio because when the master says, "C'mon down, *Betty Jane*," she's off like a shot.

"Plowing a wake and digging a hole," I report, handing the glasses to Dale for a look.

"Guess she's going to ram the gates."

"Must is."

We take our time. Dale is not an aggressive captain. There is no need to be. Boating is time-consuming. Tying up takes time. Shutting down takes time. Restarting takes time. We cruise at around eight miles an hour. When we arrive, the other boat has moored discourteously at the near end of the chamber. *Adventure* is painted across her stern. She's from Minnesota.

"How do?" I ask amiably as we squeeze by, dead slow.

Captains are responsible for damage their wakes may do.

Two couples, dressed for luncheon at the club, stare down from on high. Lavender scented air conditioning falls from their only open door onto our nearly-naked sweaty bodies. They don't speak. They don't smile. They wait stock still. One of the women catches the sweater that falls from her shoulders.

"Oh, it's like that, is it?" I say when we are beyond earshot. "Snots."

"Now, now," Dale gently corrects. "Remember: one moment's snot is the next moment's rescue."

True, but these are not folks like the folks on the Arkansas were folks. These folks are snots.

We loop a bollard on the far end of the chamber, making room for late arrivals as courtesy has taught us to do. The klaxon sounds. We begin our descent as I tick off another offense—*Adventure* has not shut down.

Before the lower doors open fully and lock into place and before the klaxon signals the all-clear, *Adventure* is off. She passes us narrowly, causing *Betty Jane* to rock and our ropes to snap. We fight to keep her from scraping the aggregate wall. It is unlikely that we will see them again, which will be fine.

"Welcome to the Great Circle Loop and the Tennessee River," I call astern.

"LOOPERS!" Dale says, shaking his fist at their wake.

—————◆—————

The scene below the lock is Third World. The river flows through little more than a ditch. Everything bears a uniform coating of dingy beige dust. Abandoned vehicles park below trailer homes on stilts. Unwashed children come to the beach. They wave dirty hands and smile toothless smiles.

On river right is Cherry Mansion where Union generals Grant, Smith, Buell, and Wallace heard the Battle of Shiloh start while sitting down to breakfast at Mrs. Cherry's table. Above the mansion, on the top of the bluff and not visible from the river, is a Huddle House restaurant. Farther into town is the United Methodist Church where we attended church last Sunday. The church itself is suggestively Grecian with an imposing colonnade facing the street. Freshly painted white both inside and out, it houses a nave that is comfortable, if too generous for the size of the congregation.

Their pastor was on retreat the Sunday we visited and left key members to offer their vision of the church's future. Each of the three admitted that Reverend had limited their bit to no more than five minutes, but, begging the indulgence of the assembled, explained that their fervor and commitment required "a little more time." Each restated what had already been said, uniformly casting into the nearly empty nave the first speaker's idiomatic, "I wanna see butts in pews." Loved ones nodded adoringly from the front two rows as Dale and I sat in the middle, halfway back, alone. Finally, we were dismissed with lunch, not God, being foremost in our minds.

We stood, conspicuous in our deviation from the common gene pool, waiting for a welcome or at least an inquiry of who we might be but got none. I did what we had learned to do elsewhere. I asked. The encounter was awkward. The head usher was sent for and gotten.

"Hamburgers on the corner," he said.

But we don't eat a lot of hamburgers. So we got in the Cadillac and headed into town where we found Margie's restaurant and a dining room full of all the people with whom we had just spent the morning. We were not invited. We did not belong. Life on the Tennessee is not all, "Welcome. We're glad you're here."

————— ◆ —————

Clifton Marina comes up on river right, early in the afternoon, leaving plenty of time for the heat accumulated in the engine room to dissipate before bedtime. Chosen for its amenities—dock power, dock water, showers, and convenience to town—we hope to pick up a few grocery items or maybe get dinner in town.

A wiry woman draped in a breezy white dress with lots of gold jewelry like an Egyptian princess calls, "Here. Pull in here," and points to the transient dock. "Welcome. We're glad you're here. Are you the ones who phoned?" She pushes away the blonde hair spun around her head like sugar, and says, "Throw me a line."

I am not going to throw this woman one of our lines. Though she is still completely capable, she has no idea what she is asking. The lines she is used to catching are new, just-out-of-the-box, kept-pristine-in-canvas-bags-embroidered-with-the-vessel's-name lines. Our lines are nasty. Salvaged or stolen off other boats somewhere between here and Texas, they are frayed and caked with dried-on slime from spending too many nights in the mud. Besides, I don't throw my lines to a woman my mother's age wearing a white dress.

"Sure?" she asks.

"Sure. He's sure," Dale says. "He's jumped onto docks lower than yours. He does it to show off, you understand. One day he'll kill himself and that will be that."

"You fellahs are a mess. Come in for some cool iced tea when you get tied up." She turns to go back inside, commenting more to herself than us, "Man, it's hot out here."

It is hot and without a breath of wind.

Inside is cool, dry, and smelling of candy bars and pine cabinetry. Clifton Marina is new. Blue and white vinyl floor tiles gleam under multiple coats of wax. Crisp newspapers from both coasts hang on the wall. Cigarettes and chewing tobacco are within easy reach of the register. Our hostess has donned an apron and stands behind an impressive display of meats and cheeses, crisp iceberg lettuce, and home-grown 'maters as red as garnets.

"Here," she says, handing over two tall glasses of ice splashed with water. "Drink. And when you've finished those I'll hand you another."

Beets, cucumbers, carrots, and eggs—all pickled and in jars—line the counter. Bags of chips hang on the wall.

"May I fix you something?"

We cannot say no. A lot of time and money has been spent to make this marina as hospitable as the Aqua model but on a much smaller scale. There is no pool, service department, nor ship's store *per se*. But it has dock power, potable water, this woman with sandwich fixings and a bread knife. Dale and I split a smoked turkey on rye.

"You got any chutney?" I ask. "I like chutney on my turkey sandwiches."

She looks.

"No. But I've got some cranberry relish. How's that?"

"Fine."

I look at some photographs while we wait; photographs are part of marina life. Applegate collected pictures of the local kids mugging for the camera. Spadra kept pictures of fish. Even Charlie had pictures of his grandkids pinned up in that shack he called an office. But these are of a construction site, this construction site. They show the building of the marina from digging out the embayment to stocking the shelves. A horseshoe hangs next to an empty frame, anticipating the first dollar made.

I notice a man standing nearby. He introduces himself. He is a retired professional in town who has always had an interest in the river. He is the owner and the developer of the marina. He wants to narrate the photographs.

"They laid all the boathouse flotation and decking out on the bottom of the marina bed and then poked a hole in the levee," he says, gesturing from one image to the next. "Everything just came right up as the river rushed in."

The enthusiasm had not faded from his wrinkled eyes, but few of his guests take an interest. They had not rebuilt a wooden boat. The trials and victories are similar enough that we trade war stories, laugh at our own mistakes until his face darkens.

"But business is not good. Economy's bad, y' know."

The day-to-day routine is not as exciting as building a marina from dry land.

"You wanna buy it?" he asks.

"We already have a project floating at your dock."

"And she is a beaut."

Dale breaks an awkward silence.

"But we would like to buy some groceries. Is there a town? Is there a car?" he asks.

The man explains that there is a courtesy car but it is already out, taken by the people who came in before us. He points to *Adventure* floating ahead of *Betty Jane*. He imagines they cannot be too long, there aren't that many places to go; but if we wanted to walk, Clifton is only about a half-mile away.

"Grocery's on the corner. And there's only one corner."

"Like Vian," I whisper to Dale.

———— ♦ ————

C & G Grocery belongs more to the world below the lock. A sign—"NO STEELING"—greets the customer. To reiterate the point, a second sign ripped from the same corrugated box and scribed by the same hand in big black marker says—"STEELING IS A CRIME." A third enumerates the consequences: "STEELERS WILL BE PORSECUTED," crossed out and written "PERSECUTED," which is then crossed out and written, "PROSECUTED."

The produce is wilted. The cookie aisle offers two choices, opened Lorna Doons or unopened Oreo's. The meat is off-putting, but the milk in the cooler is probably all right. We pick up some cans of soup to be served over ice and root vegetables to go in salads. The clerk is unused to credit cards. The manager with the grease stain on his tie comes to help before we amble wearily back to the boat.

We are exhausted from heat, staying nourished and hydrated, and the numbing drone of engines still wears in our ears. Sixty-four miles is too long to cruise in a single day, especially when it is not necessary. The shipstrike clock in the deckhouse sounds two bells. It's nine o'clock. I am concerned about the possibility of rain.

"Go to sleep," Dale says into his pillow.

"But I see clouds on the horizon."

"Lie down. Close your eyes. You won't see clouds."

The next morning, the distinctive burble of *Betty Jane*'s exhaust calls *Adventure*'s first mate away from his breakfast.

"Isn't a more beautiful sound in the world," he says.

His name is Barney and is no way like the Barney we met at Applegate Cove. Barney is stocky, tan, has lots of sunbleached hair, and is golf course fit for his sixty-plus years of age.

The rest of his crew climbs gingerly down the ladder built into the side of their boat for the purpose. Their captain is named Dale, too. He is tall, dark-headed, missing his left arm and wears concern on his face at all times. His wife, Marjorie, is well-groomed in a china doll way, seems a little fey, and does not say much. Ellen, who appears to be a once-athletic woman of Norwegian stock, is still fit and spry. Both she and Barney are widowed.

"My dad used to drive over from Minneapolis to St. Clair to test drive these babies directly out of the factory," Barney says, eyeing the length of our boat.

The others stand around pleasantly for as long as they think is polite before Their Dale carefully guides his wife back on board, followed by Ellen.

Barney asks, "Can I help you cast off?"

"No, thanks," I answer.

Casting off is the conclusion of a rite, born of habit, that silently ticks off a mental list of don't-forgets. Since once leaving *The King and I* without bilge pump protection before she was bought, Dale and I disconnect the shore power a certain way. We disconnect dock water a certain way. I stow the hose; he tests the radio. We both check battery switches and seacocks. Is there water on the bridge and is the coffee pot unplugged? Our Dale looks around the boat for any hindrance to a safe launch, he toots the horns twice for departure and calls, "Cast all lines." Our hostess runs out onto the dock. Today's costume is a taupe knit dress, deceptively casual except that its cut and drape are decidedly couture.

"'Bye," she says, jangling her bracelets as she waves, "'Bye."

"See you down the river," Dale says, and we push into the mainstream.

The river widens and deepens and slows as it gets farther away from the dam. Cruising would be easier except for the wind, which, though completely absent yesterday, is howling out of the Gulf today. After forty-five river miles, Dale asks, "Here at Cuba Landing? Or Pebble Isle, another twenty miles."

"Here!" I answer. "I'm hot. The wind is unbearable. Another twenty miles puts us longer on the water than yesterday. Besides, I see shade."

A row of sycamore trees stand on the shoal that separates Blue Creek from the river and shelters the marina.

———— ◆ ————

Cuba Landing is a simple affair. A large gas dock and simple office furnished with a desk, a chair, and an unhappy woman to collect rents and fees. An ice locker, securely locked at night, soda machines and a weedy gravel parking lot. The power pedestals need paint and the electrical connections are corroded. It is more like Charlie's than Aqua.

The fuel attendant is genuinely Goth, from the heavily mascaraed eyes and blanched out lips to the leather, studs, and chains slung across a tall and gaunt body. He greets us with the hail that is standard on the Tennessee River.

"Welcome. We're glad you're here," he says, as he has been trained, and asks, "Need gas?" which rhymes with "mace."

He belongs in any urban jungle, but Cuba Landing is an old ferry landing in the middle of a wilderness triangulated by Waverly and New Johnsonville, Tennessee. One day he will be a captain of industry, the catalyst for great social justice, national chairman of the Rotary Club, or CEO of some digital on-line shopping conglomerate, but today he is just somebody's unemployed, no-good nephew trying to be hip in this sweltering backwater. And he's cool with it.

"No, thanks. Just overnight dockage."

"Okay. Throw me a line and pull behind this other boat."

The other boat is *Adventure,* which has overtaken us somewhere along the way. The hatches are closed, the boat is quiet, and the courtesy car is gone. We aren't going anywhere without transport, and it is useless to try to cool the cabins until the sun goes down and at least some of the engine heat has dissipated. We lie very still on our bunks, drink water, and hold books in front of our faces.

Around midnight, an alarm startles us awake. Our power is out and the air conditioning is off. We climb out onto the dock to investigate. *Adventure's* crew is already there.

The men are in gym shorts and tee-shirts, the women in silken robes with Chinese embroidery. Power appears to be out everywhere except for a few lights in boathouses upstream.

Their Dale goes to find an emergency number while Our Dale rummages around his cache of electrical tools and supplies.

"Here," he says, handing out a lash-up of meters and connectors he has assembled. "Go to the other pedestals and see if you can find some power. I'll look to see what I can do here."

Their Dale returns. He is quite agitated because Marjorie suffers from Alzheimer's disease. Moving her at this time of night will be difficult. He has tried the various numbers posted on the door but gets no answer, not even voice mail.

"Thank God you're here," he mumbles, touching the sleeve of Ellen's robe while trying to think of what to do.

Marjorie cannot stay here. The heat exacerbates her condition. He doesn't know where the closest hotel is, on-line locators have not been built yet, and connectivity is spotty here in the bush. He becomes frantic.

"Darn it, Barney," he says.

Standing at the nearest pedestal, Our Dale says, "The cord's hot and the breaker will not reset." He calls to me across the dock, "What you got?"

"Nothing yet," I answer.

The three men discuss the options. They are afraid of running the generators because there is no breeze to carry off the exhaust. No one wants to go poking around an unfamiliar marina in the middle of the night. A trip to Pebble Isle is equally inadvisable. Marjorie interrupts the discussion.

"Oh, look. A shooting star," she says. "What shall we wish for?"

"Cool air," Ellen answers.

"Power!" I call from across the dock.

"Great. How much and what kind?" Our Dale asks.

"Just a minute."

Their Dale says, "I have to have fifty amps of one-ten."

"I can't get a read. The breakers are worn. I can't see the rating," I say.

"Look on the pedestal," Our Dale says.

"Nothing. Perhaps a more skilled electrician could help."

Our Dale comes over and applies the meter.

"Fifty amps at one-twenty."

The crowd cheers, with Marjorie chiming in a bit late.

"See? That's how a captain-first mate relationship should be," Their Dale says.

Barney answers back, "But *you* won't let *me* do anything."

Marjorie cuts in, "He was like that as a baby. Never wanted *anyone* to help him with *anything*. It really bothered the cat, too."

Who gets the power?

Their Dale insists that we take it, which is absurd. They have the more pressing need. Rather than argue, Our Dale says flatly, "Can't."

"Why not?" Their Dale insists on knowing.

"I don't have the right connectors to step down one fifty-amp receptacle to two thirty-amp.

Bullshit, I think to myself. Our Dale has enough equipment in that locker to open his own power company if he wants to. *But if that is how he wants to play it...*

Their Dale says, "I don't think my lines will reach that far, and, even if they did, I wouldn't want to draw that much power across such a distance."

I suggest moving the boat. Barney agrees.

"You'd do that for me?" Their Dale asks in disbelief.

If Applegate taught us anything, it was to look out for each other.

"It's easy," Barney says, "We'll just ease *Betty Jane* back. Pull *Adventure* around and walk her over to the other side of the dock."

Their Dale is not sure.

Marjorie is tired of standing. She asks Ellen, "When is our table going to be ready? Where's the bar? I could use some iced tea. Wouldn't you like some iced tea?"

"Sure we can," Barney insists. "Me and Alex on the dock. The two captains on the bridges." Barney strips off his tee-shirt and starts giving orders. "Get your docking lamps on. Aim your searchlights so *we* can see what *we're* doing. Turn on your navigation lights so that *you* can see what *you're* doing. Now, ladies, you step right over here out of the way."

"Isn't this thrilling?" Marjorie asks.

The Dales climb to their helms while Barney and I untie the lines.

"Tow back," Our Dale calls with naval solemnity.

Barney and I pull *Betty Jane*.

"C'mon, lads. Put your backs to it. We haven't got all night," Our Dale says.

"I think that it is already all night," Barney quips.

"No talking in the ranks," Their Dale says.

Betty Jane picks up momentum.

"That's it. Steady. Steady," says Their Dale.

She has speed now. The end of the dock forces me to either drop line or swim.

"STOP!" says Our Dale.

Barney ties the bow, I tie the stern.

"Okay, boys, we're going to go nice and slow," Their Dale says, helping his wife aboard. "We'll tow her back and push her stern away from the dock on my mark. Dale, you get on the bow of your boat. Ellen, you fend off our starboard aft quarter. Marjorie, dear, you come up here and sit with me. Barney help me with her." He settles her in a club chair on the bridge and says, "Now, dear, when you see a waiter, order a round of iced tea for all of us."

"Make mine a beer," says Barney.

Their Dale: "We'll pass on my port side, swing her around your stern and tie her to the new moorage."

"Right," Barney and I say, playing the clowns.

"Ready?" asks Their Dale. "Okay, fellahs, pull."

The big white fiberglass luxury yacht that towers over ours and was wedged against the marina office is now on the opposite side of the dock. Their windows are snapped shut against the heat, the air conditioning on.

"Thank you," Their Dale says with the gratitude of a thirsty man who has been given a glass of water.

"Yes, thank you," Ellen repeats, before going to her cabin.

"See you in the morning," Barney says brightly, his shirt slung across his back.

But Marjorie, momentarily forgotten and left behind, remains with her head resting against the door frame. Behind her is an over-under dual oven, a microwave, and a dishwasher in a galley of white Corian countertops and stainless steel appliances.

She gazes up at the stars on this moonless night. Cool air begins to fall from their boat onto our sweat-drenched bodies. She offers us a beer, if she can remember where they are. She's had a lovely evening. She cannot remember when she ever enjoyed dancing so much.

CHAPTER FIFTEEN
The Mercy of Strangers

Twenty miles below Cuba Landing is New Johnsonville, Tennessee. Its marina, Pebble Isle Marina, is where we will leave *Betty Jane* while we take a break from the river. An attendant stands by to catch our lines.

"It's a Chris! It's a Chris!" the scrappy leather-skinned cracker woman says effusively. "Please tell me it's a Chris."

Dale wants to know if this is where we land to check in, if there is a grocery store, a courtesy car, and a place to get some lunch. I want an upwind moorage—being blown into a dock is better than being blown away from one. But the woman persists, "Is it a Chris?"

"Yes," I answer finally.

"I *knew* it. I *knew* it," she says, catching the oversized golf visor that slips off her head. "I knew it. Everyone in the place said, 'Naw, Ging,' it's an old Trojan.' Or, 'It's an old Owens.' Like I was crazy, y' know. But I knew."

She spits out an errant bit of tobacco and pulls another cigarette from the pocket of baggy white shorts. She throws back her head and exhales with the joy of being right.

"How'd you know?" I ask.

"The bow," she answers, watching the breeze snatch away the smoke.

"What about it?"

"It crowns both ways. Chris-Craft was the only builder to crown the bow fore to aft as well as side to side. Every other builder cut corners by crowning only in one direction." She jabs her cigarette at me for emphasis. "Every other bow rots, too."

"And that sound." Ginger cups her ears and hangs her head over the water behind the boat. "There's nothing like a Chris-Craft sound." She listens for a moment, then points to the transient dock and offers to shove us off. I look askance.

"Y' don't think I can do it, do y'?"

"No, ma'am."

"Well, I'll have y's to know that I was a river rat even before your Daddy came home to your Momma with liquor on his breath and loving in his eyes. I've launched more ships than Helen of Troy and never was even pretty. Why, the only reason I wasn't in the Navy was 'cause some snitch ratted me out as a girl."

"*Ladies*!" screams Dale—hot, hungry, and anticipating a difficult launch in this stiff wind.

He will have to throttle hard directly into a boathouse full of boats in order to clear the dock. We usually slam the aft flank against the pier when we try this maneuver.

"Go," she says, "y' get on that broken-down old tub of yours, and I'll show you. Go ahead. Go." She shoos me on to *Betty Jane* like a fly out of sugar and says to Dale, "All right, Cap'n, if anything happens to your boat, I'll buy you a new one just like it. Okay?"

"Fine," he says, in order to get going.

I climb on board.

"Okay, Cap'n," Ginger says around the cigarette clenched between her teeth. "Turn the wheel full to the port side. That means left."

Dale follows her instruction, which will push the bow directly into the dock.

"Is she full to port?" Ginger asks, all foolishness aside. "Sure?"

"Full to port, ma'am."

"Left?"

"Left."

"Okay. On my mark, drop her in ahead slow and bring up your engines steady and sure after that, okay? You falter; we're screwed. Y' hear," she asks and, receiving no answer, asks more insistently, "*Y' hear?*"

"Yes, ma'am," Dale answers.

Ginger slacks the bow line, unties the stern, and leans against the back of the boat. She walks, hand over hand, still leaning on the gunwales until the wind catches the stern.

"Not yet. Not yet. Not yet," she says to herself, paying out the bow line as the wind hits *Betty Jane* broadsides. When the keel is perpendicular to the dock, the woman throws the rope onto the bow and says, "Now, Cap'n. Now. Slowly. Slowly."

Unlike a car that steers by the front wheels, a boat steers from the rudders in back. The boat pivots on her nose; the stern comes around sharply.

"Now, now, now. Bring 'er up. Bring 'er up, Cap'n. An' straighten out," Ginger says. "Bring 'er up. Don't let that blow get y'."

Dale increases throttle and brings the wheel back to center. *Betty Jane* veers away from the gas dock and heads toward transient moorage. The boathouse in question is safely at our stern.

The river is nothing if not a place to learn.

When we are away, Ginger calls, "That's how stupid Florida cracker grandmammas launch when there's a gale blowing up they's asses." She doubles over laughing. "And welcome to Pebble Isle," she says, choking on her own smoke. "We're glad you're here. Oh, and"—between convulsions—"don't smack my damned dock when you land that wreck."

———◆———

New Johnsonville is as close as the Tennessee River gets to Nashville where Dale has relatives and where we can stow the car. We will go to the Grand Ol' Opry and visit Civil War sites. But, first, we need transport to Aqua Yacht Harbor to fetch the Cadillac.

"Wouldn't do you much good, anyway," the marina owner says of the courtesy car which *Adventure*'s crew has taken. Marjorie is too ill to continue. We will drop Ellen at the airport on our way to Opryland. Barney will stay behind to make arrangements for the boat. "We only lend the courtesy car for local errands, emergencies, and sightseeing. Mississippi ain't rightly considered local."

He is an efficient man, long in the hospitality business, therefore, short with guests. But he is also sympathetic to his competitor who has unavoidably been charged with keeping another man's stuff, our car.

"You're not planning to leave it *here*, are you?"

Dale begins a long-winded exposition about Uncle Larry and Aunt Marge who live in an exurb of Nashville called White Blu—

"I know White Bluff," the operator says dismissively as he leans back in his chair to consider our story.

"We'll park it there after we've spent some time in Nashville."

"You two go have your lunch. I'll see what I can do."

Lunch is miserable. The staff is surly, the kitchen is slow, the hamburgers are dry, the French fries are stale, and the Coca-Cola is flat; but our host brings good news. He has a friend in nearby Camden who owes him a favor.

"If you have a problem, just have 'em call me on my cell phone," he says dropping us off in front of a small-town car dealership where balloons droop in the heat, and "SALE" is painted everywhere in broad strokes. "But you won't have a problem."

A man in his late thirties, soft and prematurely balding, steps up and invites us to follow him behind a glass partition where a gallery of gap-toothed children line up on the credenza behind his desk. He asks how he can help.

"River trip, huh?" he says, unconsciously loosening his necktie while looking over our driver's licenses. "From Texas, huh?"

He does not believe a word.

"Well, I'm gonna have to have a credit card."

Dale and I produce one from each of our wallets.

"One will be fine," he says through an uncomfortable smile. "And you know, we really don't do this kind of thing. We're a au-to-mo-bile dealership, you know, we sell cars. Most of the vehicles you see on the roads around here come from this dealership. We sell cars, I mean, we're gonna have to charge you $35 plus fuel."

"Fine," we answer a bit too eagerly.

He stretches himself out in his chair like car salesman do when they mull over a deal. Sweat stains the pit of each sleeve; his shirttail is too short to stay tucked. Any other time, he would say, "No," out of hand. But he has his friend to consider. He looks past us at the heat radiating off the unsold cars and the sales floor empty of customers, and he thinks.

"Well, okay," he says, affirming a decision more than any belief in anything we have said. "I'll be right back. "

"God, Dale," I say after he leaves. "He acted like we were making this up."

"You have to admit, Alexander, that two unmarried men, dressed in clean shirts and slacks that smell like a boat, with some outlandish tale about wanting a car to go fetch a car out of state, all in the middle of a heat wave, can sound a little fishy."

"No pun intended."

"None. Besides, we are at the mercy of others. Consider it a character-building exercise for such a person as individual and bull-headed as yourself."

The manager returns.

"I'm having it washed," he says. "It'll be around presently."

This moment is awkward.

"So, you have a boat," he asks, bouncing a pencil eraser off his desk.

"Yes."

We've been through all of this.

"You're on the river?"

"Yes."

"Nice?"

"Yes."

My grandmother would call our behavior cruel, if not at least uncharitable; unbecoming, if not rude. She believed in the equality of all men and used travel to prove her point. She raised us grandsons to be ambassadors wherever they went, always cautioning, "Remember where you are," whether at the grocery store or the Louvre. But Granny, while never so conspicuous as a sidewinder on a rail fence, felt no qualms about sitting idly by and watching her old arthritic black Sally pour tea and pass scones to the Methodist Ladies' Wednesday Night Prayer Group. Granny was nothing if not a pragmatist.

She was nobody from nowhere Austin, Texas, in 1920 when she and Pap moved to Dallas. She was determined to work her way up the ladder until they were A-listers on Big D's social scene. She sent their only daughter, Vivian, to Highland Park High School and on to Randolph-Macon Women's College where she met my father, Mitchell Watson, at Virginia Military Institute. The Watsons were an old Dallas family; the Vinthers were rising stars. My parents' marriage was Granny's crowning achievement, but it ended badly.

In 1963, Dallas ladies wore hats, gloves, and divorce was indelibly scandalous. Watson women did not work, but Mother did, building a furniture business that was her only tie to the world of vacation homes and charity balls for which Granny had groomed her. It was Mother's mark on the world, always the priority, redemption for past failures, and vehemently defended whenever faulted. My selling it was so egregious to Granny that she exacted retribution in her will.

———— • ————

The car, a rat-gray Buick sedan with red velour interior, appears fresh from the wash.

"I bet this is his mother-in-law's car," I say to Dale.

"Hmm," he answers while adjusting the mirrors and checking the gauges.

The sales manager smiles and waves from his partitioned office.

"I bet he thinks he's never going to see this car again."

"Maybe," Dale says.

"He is going to have to go home and tell his wife that he gave her old dead mother's car to a couple of ho-mo-sex-u-als. I bet that, right now, behind that grin, he's planning the whole scene.

"After the kids are put to bed, he'll say, 'Honey, I lent your momma's car.' No, no. He'll say, 'I *rented* your mom-ma's car.' That'll sound better. Business, you know. 'To a cou-ple of sissies...pansies...I mean, queers.'"

"I doubt it," Dale says as we enter the highway. "She probably trusts him implicitly and believes that whatever happens at the office is none of her business."

"He'll probably say, 'Honey, I *had* to. They got a boat down at Pebble Isle and I didn't have no choice.' Then, he'll pull her close, kiss her on the back of the neck, and tell her, 'Honey, I love you.'"

"Does this shit go around and around in your head all the time?" Dale asks.

"Mostly."

The distance we covered one-way in a week by water, we cover round trip in under three hours by car. We return the car to Camden, drop Doris Faye at Uncle Larry's and Aunt Marge's, and continue on to the Opryland Hotel where the sheets are cool and showers are hot. Little Jimmy Dickens opens the night at the Grand Ol' Opry; Alison Krause closes; and Civil War sites abound in this part of the country.

When we return to the marina we find Ginger wiping down power pedestals. I confess that I am eager to get back on the water.

"'Course you are," Ginger says. "Yer a river rat. Muddy water got into your veins, and y' ain't nevah goin' to git it out."

It is our last night here, and Ginger is dying for a peek inside. She quietly opens and closes the drawers, carefully presses the locker doors closed. She notices the rainwater stains on our deckhouse ceiling and says, "All boats leak. The ones that don't, lie." Then she has her own confession to make.

"You know I met my first husband on a woodie. An Owens. I remember it like it was yesterday." Ginger smiles. "We worked on her all the time—stripping, sanding, varnishing. When she'd come out, I scraped the bottom and he'd paint." She looks off in space, relishing the memory. "Then, one day he walked through the kitchen door, home from work, and said, 'Ging, I've sold the boat.' Didn't ask me or nuthin'. You know what I did?"

She gets angry in the telling. "The next day I walked through the kitchen door and said, 'Jim, I've filed for divorce.' Didn't ask *him* or nuthin.' I had pluck, then. I was young. Thought things would always go my way." Her face goes slack. "Harold, he's my husband now, wouldn't have a woodie, no sir. We have a 'glass boat. It's all right, though. You have to make choices in life."

The next morning, the boat is strangely quiet—no coffee, no Dale, running from stem to stern and screaming, "Gonna be a scorcher. Gonna be a scorcher." Instead, I hear his hushed murmurings in the galley. I cannot think what it could be about, but it probably isn't good.

CHAPTER SIXTEEN
There is No Now

Sister has called from her office in a glass tower high above the streets of downtown Fort Worth and cannot know that there is no "Now" on the river. We cruise at eight knots, a hamburger and fries take an hour, and "Thirty minutes, Cap'n" is all afternoon at Toad Suck Ferry. We cannot hand the keys to the valet, hail a cab, and be in Dallas/Fort Worth in time for lunch. Even as Roy lies dying, there is a boat to consider.

Betty Jane needs shelter. Sun crazes her varnish, rain spoils her cabins, and she depends on electrical pumps to keep her afloat. Pebble Isle has nothing available. Cuba Landing has covered slips but not at the risk of electrical outages. We decide on Paris Landing, a state park on the way to a Travelift at Green Turtle Bay in case we have to abort the trip altogether.

"Fine," Dale says to me. "You take care of the breakfast dishes and walk the dog, I'll start the engines."

He has already paid for dockage and made a reservation for the last flight out of Nashville. Dock water and shore power are disconnected; electrical cords are wound on the deck; the water hose is drained and stowed in its locker. I load the dog and stand by to cast off when we hear, "Wait! Wait!" coming from down the dock.

It is Ginger. Her run becomes a trot after she sees that she has gotten our attention. The trot becomes a walk, then a stagger, until she arrives completely out of breath, bent over and gasping for air like a long-distance runner at the finish. She sticks out a skinny brown arm, the one that wears the tennis bracelet.

"Here," she says—*puff, puff, puff*—"take it."

Inside a white paper bag are an Eskimo Pie and a Nutty Buddy. Ginger remembers our standard four-o'clock-in-the-afternoon order. I take the cone and pass the pie up to Dale. We stand around holding our gifts like children posed on Christmas morning.

"Well, y' better eat 'em before they melt," she says, snatching the rope from my hand. "Now, git! Everyone 'round here is itchin' to git shed of the sight of you. Tired of your hifalutin' big-city ways. And I can't get anyone to tie up next to this leaky tub. Can't much say as I blame 'em. She's liable to blow up or sink at any moment." A bilge pump discharges. "See? She's sinkin' right now. Y'all better git outta here. Salvage don't come up this far."

Dale calls, "Cast all lines," followed by the requisite two toots of the horn.

Ginger leans into our bow, pulls a cigarette and a tissue out of her baggy white shorts.

"And I *better* see y'all down the river," she says, lighting her smoke.

Our last memory of Pebble Isle is of a hundred-pound cracker woman, hollering "YOU FAGS!" laughing through her tears and choking on her own smoke so violently that the transient dock shakes from one end to the other.

———◆———

We enter the river and cruise apart for the first time in our lives. Usually we are side by side on the bridge except at times when something on board needs attention; otherwise, one is at the helm and the other in the chair adjacent. At the moment, he is at the helm. I am on the sofa in the deckhouse.

A panorama passes in front of the deckhouse windows. Low, golden beaches rise out of a broad watery blue. Mother is on my mind. Her diagnosis came early in my relationship with Dale. Our honeymoon was in the first year; I sobered up in the second; her cancer came in the third. She chose not to fight and was dead in four months. It was an ugly death. The house of cards she called her business crumbled all around us; Dale supported me as I picked up the pieces. He sacrificed almost everything on a bet that we would stay together. Committed relationships had not even been named back then. Now it is my turn to support him. I'll go to Dallas.

"Cars on river right," he calls down from the helm.

Cars on the bank are sometimes parked in front of towns we cannot see. Towns sometimes have cell service. I climb on top of the deckhouse roof and scan the skies for a signal.

"One bar." We need at least three. "Two bars...three bars!"

"Right," Dale says, leaving the helm.

He bounces down the ladder and into the galley, collecting the wires needed to connect phone to the computer. I take the wheel and slow the boat to extend the window of connectivity. Three bars are not enough for voice conversations but can download data. Dale has asked Sister to e-mail rather than leave a voice message.

"It's like sucking concrete through a straw," he complains, but when the last message arrives, he throws his hands in the air like a rodeo roper and says, "Done."

The connection disappears just as fast.

"Fine," is all he will say about what he reads.

I move to the bridge where we can sit together, silent in each other's company until something unusual appears on the horizon.

"What's that?" Dale asks.

"Dunno," I say, training the binoculars on the spot. "Trees is my first guess."

"Shouldn't be any trees in the middle of the river."

He looks at the chart and discovers he has lost track of where we are. Dale is a conscientious captain. He knows our position, heading, and speed at any given time. He can rattle off temperature, oil pressure, and voltages without looking. He calculates how far we've come and how far we have yet to go based on the last mile marker we've passed, plus or minus time lapsed. But the distraction of Dad has broken his concentration. Confused and befuddled, he looks like a child who has lost its parent in a crowd.

"82.2," I read the marker posted on river left.

"What?" Dale asks distractedly.

"82.2," I repeat. "Mile mark 82.2."

"Oh," he says, recovering himself.

The charts make sense with that information. He counts down increments printed on the map.

"Not trees," he says, pointing to our position on the map.

"No, not trees," I say, adjusting the glasses. "Umbrellas, bistro umbrellas and if you give me a minute, I'll tell you whose."

"What?"

"Just a minute," I say, holding up my hand. "José Cuervo umbrellas. Probably blown off some riverside bar somewhere and salvaged from the river."

The silhouette against the hazy white sky looks like two oversized storybook toads sitting under fern fronds floating on a peapod. But they are people, big ones. She is dressed in a flower-print dress, looking worn and loved as an oversized down bolster on a four-poster bed somewhere in the English countryside. He, shirtless and busting out of overalls, could easily be a bull with a ring through his nose.

Fishing rods stick out on both sides of their boat. Languid lines drawn through wine corks settle on the water. Dream catchers and miniature wind chimes dangle from her umbrella. Lures and bobbers in monofilament hang under his. The one in the middle shades coolers within convenient reach of both. Our approach makes them uneasy. He is suspicious. She is self-conscious.

"What's biting?" I ask to break the ice.

"Ba-ass," she calls in two syllables.

"You selling?"

I imagine filet of river bass pan-seared with a tomato concassé for lunch.

"Yew buy'n?" the man grumbles.

Granny would call these two "simple, salt-of-the-earth" people who know that on the water and pretending to fish is the coolest place to be on a summer afternoon.

"How much for enough to feed two hungry sailors without a pole?"

"Some fer y' dawg, tew?" he spits brown tobacco juice over the side. "'At's a nice lookin' dawg. Ya's wont t' trade?"

"You don't want this dog, she's gun-shy."

"Yew'r raight. I d'n't won't that dawg." His thick tongue moves the chaw around his mouth to accommodate an extended conversation. "Tew bad, tew. Three bucks fer one. Fo-er fer two. Sho' 'em what y' got, woem'n."

Woem'n reaches with difficulty around her nest of bundles and bags in order to draw a string full of fish across her ample lap. The water off her catch washes down her skirt.

"Which 'uns yew wont?" she asks.

I point.

"This un? This un? Or this un?" she asks.

The two boats come alongside. I throw a line to the man while answering her next question, "No, I don't want the head."

She maintains a polite prattle while she cleans the fish, asking where we are from, how is our trip, and how far we're going. She sympathizes, "Aw, 'at's tew bad," when we say a family illness pulls us off the river and passes the severed heads to her man who throws them as far as he can towards shore saying, "No sinse callin' turtles when I got hooks t' bait." Then, finding a wad of newspaper scrounged around the bottom of their boat to wrap our lunch in, she passes the parcel between boats, saying, "Fer dollers, *please*."

We pay for the fish, and the man says, "Thank y'," as he pushes off. "Nice bowt. Really nice bowt, tew bad 'bout yer dawg, tho'."

———————◆———————

We continue downriver until the U.S. 79 viaduct draws a sharp black shadow across the water. We are near the Tennessee-Kentucky state line, the southern boundary of the Land-Between-the-Lakes, and the entrance to the marina. The LBL is the ridge that separates the Tennessee and Cumberland rivers. Both are dammed at Great Rivers, Kentucky—Kentucky Dam across the Tennessee backs up Kentucky Lake; Barkley Dam across the Cumberland backs up Lake Barkley—and both of them flow into the Ohio. The marina is part of Paris Landing State Park, which straddles the highway.

Dale picks up the radio to hail: "Paris Landing. Paris Landing. This is *Betty Jane*."

Landings were freight depots on the river built to service towns settled farther inland. They were shanty towns, disposable and cheap, sited on low gradual floodplains like the one here and at Cuba Landing. Cuba is gone, but Paris, "the Catfish Capital of the World," is high and dry, ten miles beyond the river's reach.

"Paris Landing. Paris Landing. This is *Betty Jane*. Over."

Marinas are not overloaded with customers at midday, in the middle of the week, in the middle of the summer. Staff members go to lunch often leaving the low man behind to attend the cash register, answer the phone, swab toilets, welcome visitors, pump gas, and man the radio.

"Paris Landing. Paris Landing. This is *Betty Jane*. Over."

"Hey, hey, *Betty Jane*," answers an out-of-breath female voice. "This is Paris Landing. We been lookin' for ya, Cap'n. Go to fourteen. How's yer dad?"

Dale retunes and answers, "We've got sunny skies. Both boilers holding a head o' steam. Dad's stabilized and getting stronger, and I got the 79 bridge rising over my bow."

"Well, that is fi-ine," the Southern voice draws out the final vowel, emphasizing the speaker's satisfaction. "Now, Cap'n, cut 'er hard t' port off the channel just below the bridge and follow the marina buoys home. Tie up at the transient dock. Welcome to Paris Landing. We're glad you're here."

Dale turns sharply per her instruction and asks me, "Which one is the transient dock?"

It's a nasty habit that assumes, because I am on the bow and fifteen feet ahead of him, I have somehow been here before. It started at Spadra.

"I have no idea."

A handsome woman in jeans and a tee-shirt, fit and blonde, hangs out of the harbormaster's door and yells, "There! There!" pointing to a ladder of open slips with one hand, stretching a telephone receiver to the length of its cord with the other. "Anywhere along there is fi-ine. You got a somebody there to help you land? I'm left short. Anywhere along there is fi-ine." She waves. "Come in when you're tied up. Welcome. We're glad you're here."

"My, what a pretty boat," she remarks to herself before jerking the phone to her ear. "No. NO! I did not say...I *did not* say..."

Her name is Vicki. She is unlike anyone we've met so far. A grandmother—they come young here—who, according to her stories, has worked all her life to get by. "With or without a man," she'll say, proud that she has learned not to take men's guff.

We land, and I suggest, "You and Doris Faye check in. I have to tidy these lines and sauté some fish for lunch. Do you want *concasée* or *almondine*?"

A huge weight has fallen off Dale's shoulders. We are here. *Betty Jane* is handled. His face is relaxed.

"Whatever," he says, smiling, for the first time today, at his dog.

They return with a slip assignment.

"We got a fifty-foot covered slip in A-dock right over there," he says, waving his arm across the lunch table. "There is no shuttle to Paris. There may be a rental agency there, but she doesn't know. The state park lodge is on the other side of the highway. They've got a dining room. She says the buffet is 'pretty good.' There's a swimming pool and camp sites and all that stuff they have at these state resorts. Dad's better, but I, or we, still have to—"

The phone rings. We've got cell service.

Dale answers, "Hello?"

It is Susan.

——————◆——————

Susan is a former tenant who has been following our trip via the e-mails we send from time to time. She is not in the habit of calling, has no reason to except that she is between appointments and thought she'd check in, miraculously at a time when we need help and the telephone works.

The cheerful lilt of her voice asks, "What's up?"

"Nothing."

Nothing?

Dale sees the surprise on my face.

"Well," he begins, "Dad's not well."

Not well? Your sister's not well. Your dad is dying.

My tacit commentary is not helpful. I excuse myself. I have things to do. Gear and equipment have to be put away. Food iced down. Clothes packed. Laundry collected. Trash taken out.

His *almondine* gets cold as the phone call continues, but he obviously needs to talk.

"...so, at any rate, the first thing we need to do is secure the boat and get the Cadillac. If Alexander stays, he'll need a way to get into Paris."

He doesn't know that I've decided to drive him to Texas.

He shoves the phone in my hand as I walk by. Susan is mid-sentence.

"...think you should call Rosemary. You remember Rosemary. She and Mark live somewhere around there. I've been forwarding your e-mails to them. They've been following your trip."

"Really?" I ask.

"Oh. Hi, Alexander," she says, unaware that she'd been passed to me.

"Hi, Susan. How are you?"

"Fine. Call Rosemary."

She begins to repeat the story about how "Rosemary and Mark have been—"

"Yeah, yeah. I heard all that."

"Well, you both sound pretty busy. I'm at my appointment. See you when you get here. 'Bye."

"She hung up," I mumble to Dale.

"What did she say?"

"She said, 'Call Rosemary.'"

"For what?"

"I don't know."

"She give you the number?"

"No."

The phone rings. It is Susan with the number and the instruction to "Call Rosemary."

Click.

"Then I bet you ought to call Rosemary," Dale says.

"Why don't you? I hate the phone."

"'Cause I'm eating lunch," he says, poking a slivered almond into his mouth. "It's delicious."

"It's cold."

"*Froid,*" Dale corrects. "Anyway, just because a person hates the phone does not mean that he or she cannot use the phone."

"And tell her what?"

"I don't know. You used to be a salesman. Made cold calls, didn't you? Ask her how she is. Remind her how we met. Ask her if Mark's got a big dick. I don't care."

"How *did* we meet?"

We met one night when Susan was our tenant. Rosemary came to Dallas to help cook for a huge annual croquet-on-the-lawn party, and the air conditioning went out.

"Okay, I give. I'll call her when I finish."

"No, I'll do it," I say, dialing the number. "It's ringing."

"Phones do that."

He protests the lack of dessert.

"You've had dessert."

"When?"

"Pebble Isle? A few hours ago?...Hello? Hello? Is this Rosemary?...This is Alexander Watson. You may not re-memb—"

"When?" Dale protests.

"Of course, I do," Rosemary exclaims. "How's Dale? How's the trip? Mark, Mom, and I have been following every word. Is Doris Faye surviving the heat? Where are you?"

"Can you hold on a moment?" I cup the phone to finish with Dale. "Skinny cracker woman waving a white bag full of ice cream at us on the dock this morning?"

"That was a good-bye amenity. That was not *dessert*."

"Right with you, Rosemary."

"Okay. Take your time," she says cheerfully.

"What was I supposed to do? Just let it melt in front of the woman?" Dale says.

"Okay. I am not arguing with you about it. If you want dessert, it's ice cream in the camp store. Take the dog. I want a Klondike bar and if Vicki doesn't have that I want—"

"A Nutty Buddy," Dale says, reaching for the leash. "C'mon, dog."

"And don't bring mine back melted."

"So," I say into the phone. "You have to get the children out of the house before you can have an adult conversation, don't you? Susan said she's been forwarding the e-mails about our trip. What's the last thing you read?…Uh-huh…Uh-huh… Yeah. We're out there in the middle of the night shuffling cruisers around in the dark because there's no electricity and that miserable woman at the desk says, 'Hava cuppa coffee.' No 'I'm sorry' or 'Let me take something off the bill.' Nothing like that's gonna do it…Well…Yeah, I know…Here's the deal. Dale's sister called this morning, and we need a ride to—"

"Mark and I will be right there," she says and hangs up.

Rosemary and Mark are retirees from Las Vegas, Nevada, who have relocated to Murray, Kentucky, and are still at loose ends in their new digs. Running rescue for a couple of almost-perfect strangers sounds like a fun escape from the solitude of being "not from around here."

Dale and the dog return with ice cream.

"A Klondike bar!" I say, greedily tearing open the silver and blue wrapper. "The chocolate hasn't even melted, and Mark and Rosemary are on their way."

"From?"

"I don't know."

"When will they get here?"

"See? I knew you should have made the call. Anyway, I'm driving you to Texas."

"I know."

"How?" I ask.

"The stack of folded clothes on the stripped bunk next to your kit was my first clue."

We move *Betty Jane* under cover. The boathouse is well built to government full-of-pork specifications. The slip is wide, long, and faces the rising sun.

"Better if she faced north," I complain.

"Better'n being out in the rain," Dale says. "You could be stuck up behind *Adventure's* ass without a car."

An SUV with Kentucky plates turns into the parking lot. A couple gets out. The woman looks vaguely familiar; the man I don't recognize.

Rosemary calls from the other side of the security gate, "Hi, Alexander. You remember my husband, Mark."

Not at all.

"Of course I do. How are you? It's so good to see you."

"Hottest June on record," Mark says.

"I know. We've lived it."

———◆———

Dale will talk to his sister several times while we are gone. She will be upset that he is not on his way, that logistics on the river have caused delay. His niece is already at the hospital; nephew will be there shortly. But there is plenty of time for them to talk.

There will be plenty of time while the patient's bones snap, his kidneys fail, his eyes cloud over, his lungs fill, his toes turn blue, and the rattle—that damn rattle—continues long, long into the wee hours until the fight is gone. The patient surrenders and the breathing gets shallower and the rattle quiets down. Death moves from wherever it has been waiting, takes what it came for, and leaves. I felt it when Mother died. Silence follows. The parent who has always been there is gone. What is left are remains. The shock of its happening—really happening— wards off any question of what happens now. Because there is no now.

Now we are with our new friends, road-weary and starved, at the only place open this late at night—a broken-down roadhouse on U.S. 79, five miles between Paris, Tennessee, and the river. Billy Ray Cyrus wails "Achy Breaky Heart" over the jukebox. The smell of hot grease mixes with that of spilt beer. Empty peanut shells crunch under foot. String lights in the shape of chilis blink among the posters of busty women selling whiskey. Our waitress wears a tee-shirt so tight that I can almost make out the tattoos on her breasts.

And this time tomorrow, I'll be hundreds of miles away, resting in another man's arms.

CHAPTER SEVENTEEN
The Sexuality of the Three People Involved

The contemplative silence we enjoy, sipping coffee and munching doughnuts along the bucolic byways out of Paris Landing, ends abruptly at Jackson, Tennessee. We enter the interstate where cellphone coverage begins in earnest. Calls from Sister, with updates, inquiries, objections, and entreaties to "Please hurry" riddle our cross-country trek. She is distraught. She has always been daddy's little girl and a dutiful daughter, and the man she has put above all others is dying while her brother lollygags around the mid-South, albeit at posted speeds.

At one minute before midnight, we arrive at the hospital where loved ones are huddled together. They stop to receive their own, their prodigal son, Dale, before entreating, with fervent prayer and faithful hearts, their Baptist god for deliverance. I have spiritual matters of my own to attend to. I have been too long in the country.

The gay bathhouse is where men go to have sex with other men. It is where promiscuity is encouraged, anonymity guarded, and anything consensual is possible. It is where the air smells of sweat and disinfectant, the lights are kept low, and a booming bass line covers up the sounds of bump and grind. It is also where sarcasm and a quick wit run free;

where things can be described as "fabulous" without turning heads; and where show tunes are considered common core.

I shower, shave, soak, and steam before retiring to the rooftop to enjoy the best nighttime view of Dallas the city has to offer. Shortly, a man approaches, allowing his towel to fall to the deck in order to present before me all that he has to offer, including the gold wedding band he has forgotten to remove. He asks if he can sit down.

Conversation is halting and cautious. He is unsure how to proceed and I am not helping. I am not here for sex. I have Dale who knows exactly how I like to be kissed and whose body fits mine precisely. Everything else is just a tug and a tumble, warranting a written apology from both sides. No, what I want is to be, if only for moment, with my people— the misfits and the outcasts, the perverts and the deviates— who, on the outside, look perfectly normal working jobs in commerce, finance, and law. But, in here, they want, like me, to let the mask fall.

He offers me a cigarette.

We sit side-by-side, watching the office towers blink on and off as janitorial crews move from floor to floor. The barflies stroll in after 2 a.m., the alcohol curfew. They don't see anything they want so they move on. I expect him to move on, too. Instead, he picks his towel off the floor and pulls it modestly across his lap. He asks about my day.

How was my day? I roll the question around in my head before answering.

He apologizes. He did not mean to intrude.

I wave him off and begin to answer, but I have trouble knowing where to start. I woke up this morning to drive the only man I have ever allowed myself to love six hundred miles in my grandmother's old Cadillac with my dog in the back in order to see about his father, dying in a hospital in Decatur, Texas.

"You see, we have this boat," I say, instigating a battery of questions about where we've been and what we've seen that makes me think he isn't here to have sex, either. He has probably had a hard day, too, and wants only to fall off the face of earth for a few hours, to unexist for a moment, to regroup.

When "—and here I am," comes out of my mouth and the caffeine high that I've been riding crashes, I get up to go to my bunk. He begs me not to go, offers to put his arms around me to keep me warm, says he has to be at work in an hour anyway. I fall dead asleep to the rise and fall of his breath.

If he had left me there, I would have been fine; most likely a towel boy would have kicked the soles of my feet and told me to go to my room. But he carried me, or had me carried, to my cell and laid me in my bunk like a weary foot soldier exhausted and collapsed from an extensive tour with the straight and narrow. I wake up to the final throes of climax next door, banging against the partition by my ear, and find myself neatly tucked into an unsullied bed. My clothes are undisturbed. Two unopened condoms lie next to a business card with "Sweet dreams, sweet man," scrawled on the back.

I dress and call Dale.

"Where the hell have you been?" he asks playfully. "It's three o'clock in the bloody afternoon."

"Bathhouse."

"Where's the dog."

"She's here. Panting quietly in the back seat. I gave a twenty to the security guards to keep an eye on her, but her breath smells decidedly like chicken tacos."

"Did you meet anyone cute?

"Actually yes. Married."

"To a girl?

"Who knows. We talked about you all night."

"Yeah, I bet. Did you do anything?"

"Don't think so. I fell asleep."

"Nobody'll believe that."

"Nobody believes that happy horseshit your family ban-
dies around about how 'Alexander's gay but Dale isn't,' how
'Dale's leading Alexander to the Lord,' and how we're nothing more than business partners, either; but we live with it.
Besides, we'll know when the baby comes and it doesn't look
a thing like you. How's Roy?"

"Getting stronger. We should be able to go back to the
boat by the end of the week."

CHAPTER EIGHTEEN
Aid and Succor

The lonely and quiet A-dock we left at Paris Landing is now a confab of Fourth of July preparation perpetrated by a crowd of people so genetically intertwined it could be a cast for some sci-fi thriller. Husbands teeter from ladders to hang decorations above wives distracted with gossip, fussing with ribbons, streamers, flags, and bows and rendering the boathouse a riot of red, white, and blue to such an extreme that Betsy Ross, if she had known the eventual effects, would have reconsidered her choices.

New arrivals of children, food, and gear thread through the "Happy Fowerth!" and "Gimme sum sugah," as they make their way to vessels that have been in the families for years. People we've never met stop what they are doing and address us, correctly assigning names from some description extracted from somewhere. They know Doris Faye, they know where we've been, and, with an unsettling sympathy and concern, ask, "How's yer daddy dewin'?" *Betty Jane* has made introductions.

"Ah fine wooden yacht doesn't just sayl in herah ev'ry day, y' know."

The ones that do not belong arrive without fanfare, pack their gear into the boats without ceremony, and slip into the harbor. *Calypso* pulls out, quietly leaving the ebullient mayhem at the dock. She is a mid-eighties thirty-five-foot Chris-Craft that looks like she could be the cruiser version of the Bartlett's *Enjoy Enjoy*. Her gel-coat needs buffing, spider poop stains her decks, multiple collisions have beaten her hardware into nubs. Most of her chrome is missing. Fishing tackle, stuffed wherever there is a space, peeks out behind cushions and from under hatches.

On deck are four carrot-topped little boys stair-stepped between ages six and twelve. Andrew, the next to youngest, is impatient and whines in protest of being too often told "in a minute." Their father, at the wheel, is a full head taller than the blonde woman who stands behind him and whose hand never leaves his shoulder. He may be the captain, but she is the admiral.

"Cast off," she says quietly.

The two older boys loosen the lines and push off.

"Easy forward," she says.

A baby, safely stowed below decks and out of the sun, cries. The woman, without raising her voice, says, "Aaron, see what your sister wants."

The child snaps to his mother's instruction and comforts the child.

Until the need for another instruction arises, she enjoys a moment of private reflection. She tilts her head back to finish a Diet Coke, her overly large sunglasses catch the sun. She considers her new sandals, bringing the left one to her knee to wipe off a smudge and calls, without looking up, "Boys, dress those lines."

Calypso, with a tattered U.S. Ensign fluttering over her wake, disappears beyond the bridge.

Merry-go-Ron belongs to Mary and Ron, who built her. She is a houseboat, a rectangular shelter atop a steel shallow vee-hull with little enough draft for easy beaching. Inside, braid rugs, paneled walls and hand-sewn curtains make her a Swiss chalet in homespun. Mary is happiest when preparing a meal for her family in the full-sized kitchen while holding a grandchild on her hip. The dinghy, also homebuilt by Ron, is a twenty-foot wooden runabout named *Pip*.

"Okay," says Ron, a nimble outdoorsman who owns the local lumberyard, to his son, Ronnie, "Your momma and I will be out a little later. You coming in for lunch?"

"We've got all that worked out, Papa," Mary says, passing her two granddaughters over the water to their mother waiting in *Pip*.

"Okay," Ron repeats. "Like I was going to say, your momma and I will come out later and set up a beachhead. You know, the usual spot."

"Yes, Daddy," answers Ronnie, whose hair is prematurely graying. He turns to his grinning pixie and says, "We're gonna see Ronnee up on skis today. Aren't we, honey?"

The tooth fairy's most recent and squirmiest client answers, "Yes, Daddy."

"I'm going tubing," her little sister asserts. "By myself."

"We'll see, honey," Mother says.

"Okay," Ron says, tossing *Pip's* bowline into the bottom of boat. "Be careful and please, please watch the weather."

"Yes, Daddy."

"*Yes, Daddy!*" mimic the two youngsters.

———— ◆ ————

Scenes like these unfold all around the marina with the bulk of the activity concentrated at the boat ramp. Trucks and trailers stack three abreast to launch. Picnics, sunblock and little children get transferred from car to boat. They complain about their PFDs being too tight and fidget until they get underway, but when their boat lunges forward to join the flotilla heading out to sea, they can hardly contain their excitement.

By ten o'clock, Dale and I are all alone. The boathouse is empty and the marina is quiet. Boaters asked if we are going to get a good place to see the fireworks shot from the state park tonight; they offered to let us raft up with them. But we can set sail anytime. The truth is that we'd rather not go out where a host of watercraft, from ski boats and cruisers, are roiling an otherwise calm river.

Cottony clouds dot the lazy afternoon sky. A barge creeps along, periodically blowing its throaty horn as admonishment for being too close or in the way.

"Dale?"

"Yeah."

"Hand me the glasses, please."

"What do you see?"

Merry-go-Ron is coming in.

"So?"

"They were going to beach somewhere on the river so they could see the fireworks."

"Changed their minds, I guess."

"I guess," I say, casting my eye across the sky for signs of trouble but seeing none. "Coming in kinda hot."

"Mmm."

Dale's not interested.

I walk down and stand by her slip, more as a courtesy than a necessity. Boats that are liable to ram the dock are best left to ram the dock. However, if a little nudge will save a repair, it is neighborly to be on hand to provide it. It is another way boaters look out for each other.

Ron lands as if his vessel were on a tractor beam. Mary exits the kitchen to tie lines.

"What's your hurry, Captain?" I ask.

"Storm blowin' in. Gonna be bad, too," Ron says, grimacing at partly cloudy skies and a fresh breeze. "Comin' in fast, too."

NOAA predicts the changes in weather; river men sense them.

"And it's going to be bad, too," he repeats flatly.

He calls his son on the radio, "Ronnie? Ronnie, tune into NOAA. Your momma and me are landed, but you don't be too long, hear?"

"Yes, Daddy," comes over the airwaves.

"You gonna be around a while?" he asks me.

I nod.

"Good, 'cause we're gonna to be busy pullin' in boats."

With binoculars and radio in hand, he paces the dock as the sky thickens. The sun is gone.

"Blink your lights," Ron orders his son and looks through the glasses. "Yeah, I see ya. Now, c'mon in before your mother gets too worried."

Mary is calm. She lays out towels, blankets, and dry clothes. Fresh coffee is in the pot; hot chocolate is on the stove.

———— ◆ ————

Across the cove, the Coast Guard gets ready to deploy. They pull their PFDs tight across their chests, board their boats, and head to the river. Raindrops, like crocodile tears, splish-splash the surface. Wind topples tables and tears at holiday decorations. Dale has come out to look at the sky.

"Ever run rescue in a squall, boys?" Ron asks. "Our first job is to secure anything that is not tied down." He looks around and points randomly at blown debris. A balloon can clog an intake or foul a prop. "The boats are the least of our problems. Captains get addled in a blow. If some jerk wants to argue, you don't have time. Push 'em off and let them think about it while you help the next guy."

He nods to emphasize what he has just said. "Keep your commands simple. And, for Heaven's sake, don't use boat talk. Back, Forward, Right, Left is all you need. They can't hear you anyway and most of 'em would not know what you're talking if they could. And you will repeat 'Throw me a line' until you're hoarse. Isn't that right, Ronnie?"

Ron's son, daughter-in-law, and grandchildren landed safely in the slip next to *Merry-Go-Ron*. Mary is seeing to the girls.

"Yes, Daddy. Man, it is moving fast."

The father checks to see that his son is wet but okay.

"Foul weather just does things to people," Ron says, looking at the landscape shrouded in gray. "You...you must stay calm. And, whatever you do, do not, do not go in the water. Is that clear?"

"Yes, Daddy."

"Perfectly," Dale and I say together.

"Here they come," Ron says.

A wall of boats advances on the harbor mouth, as if to attack. Red and green navigation lights hover over black and choppy waves; white mast lights whip around in the air above their decks. Rain begins to strafe.

Ron stands at the end of the boathouse to direct the onslaught. Dale takes one side; I take the other. We pack small craft into empty slips, the space around *Betty Jane*, tying the larger boats broadside, rafting the second tier next to those.

Sailboats, aimed at the ladder of uncovered slips, fly in at full sail, dropping their rags at the last minute. Their crews line up to send ropes out like tentacles in hopes of snagging a hook, a cleat, a piling. Hands on the dock withstand the wind and the rain to help pull them in.

"Throw me a line!" we hear echoed all over the marina.

Thunderclaps rattle the steel roof overhead as the boathouse itself pitches and rolls.

Boat after boat, full of bawling children and terrorized mothers, file in under cover and lash themselves to whatever. The children, indiscriminate of whose, get passed to safety, swaddled in a towel, pointed where to stand and warned to stay out of the way. Some watch in awe. Others, desperate to escape the chaos, scream to drive away the terror until their faces are beet-red. "We'll find Momma later" is all the comfort they will get for a while.

Momma is pulling in boats. The rescued become the rescuers.

"Throw me a line!"

"Pull her in!"

"Everyone all right?"

"Not that slip. Not that slip," Ron says, keeping one of the largest berths empty for the better part of an hour.

"She's comin' in," he insists. "*She's coming in,* I said. I've got 'er on the radio and she's comin' in. Dammit."

The boat he is expecting is a floating lakehouse, one hundred feet long and twenty feet wide, designed to be run up on a beach somewhere for weeks at a time. She is nothing but a box on a raft, a sail in the wind essentially, and underpowered to outmaneuver weather like this. She is caught in the blow and could smash to bits against the bridge pilings. She has to turn.

"Hard rudder. Hard rudder," Ron whispers to himself.

Her lights flash and her horns squawk in panic, but there is nothing anyone can do but watch as she gets blown into the rocks. The Coasties will get her if she sends up a flare or calls MayDay, but her crew is too proud for that.

For a moment, a mere trice, the wind abates long enough for her captain to bring her nose around. The twin engines on her stern swing perilously close to the riprap. By this time everyone who is coming in, has. No sign of *Calypso*.

A crowd pushes in to watch.

"Here she comes and if she makes it," Ron yells, "it's gonna take every one of us to land her. If we can't, we'll have to let her go."

Apprehension grows as the behemoth pushes slowly across the white caps. Her captain fights for every inch. Her crew stands by in the deluge.

"Full reverse! Full reverse, Cap'n!" the man on her bow calls back to the helm.

"Throw a line!"

"Throw a line!"

She has to get her nose into the boathouse so she can get some leverage against the wind dogging her stern. Until she does, a rope is just going to pull a man overboard. She gets her bow into the slip. The crunch of metal. The tear of fiberglass.

"Hard port rudder! Punch it!"

Her heft, like an elephant scratching at a tree, shifts the boathouse, causing everyone inside to find a handhold.

"Grab that line! Grab that line!"

Teams of men duke it out against Mother Nature herself. If we let go, she takes out the opposite dock and every boat in it. If we hold on, she swings around and crushes her length in vessels we just tied.

"Straighten 'er out, Cap'n…That's it…Now, power, power. Goddammit, POWER!… NO. NO. NO. FULL REVERSE!"

"Slack those lines…Slack those lines before somebody goes in."

Between the mayhem on the dock and the confusion on board, the captain manages to center his craft in her slip just long enough for Ron to call, "Okay, men, pull! Pull, you bastards. PULL!"

She's in. A cheer goes up in the boathouse.

My hands are bloody.

"Shut 'er down, Cap'n. You're here. Welcome home," Ron says, as if the landing were under sunny skies and light winds, adding, "Nice work," his scant acknowledgment of the ordeal.

———◆———

The sky ruptures one last time before the storm heads off to the southeast, leaving behind a boathouse in shambles. The decorations are tattered and torn. The spangles are blown away, The sparklies have all been trod under muddy foot. But the celebration will not be daunted. Coolers and baskets pop open as people who haven't known each other but for a moment spontaneously ask each other "Wanna beer?" "Y' hung-ree?"

We're all starving from the stress, if not the exertion.

Wet, half-naked people—uprighting blown-over chairs, leaning on decks, sitting on coolers—find a place on the dock. Camp stools, cushions and air mattresses come out of boats. A company of men head into the lingering drizzle and to shore where they light portable grills. The hot dogs and sausages will follow as soon as they can be found. Families, separated by too many people and too much gear, decide to wave furiously from across slips, calling, "Y'okay?" and "Man, did you see that?"

See it? We lived it in a way that is real, visceral, and raw. Every boater weathers a storm, but few weather one where there is as much at stake. Not all these people belong to this boathouse or even know these people. Urgency brought them together.

The last drops fall into the water. We are fed and the excitement has worn off. A park ranger announces that the weather has officially passed, there will still be fireworks, and "If y' hurry, y'll still get a good spot." Like passengers at the boarding call of a long-delayed flight, the mob gets up slowly, stretches, and begins to claim its belongings. All mommas have been found.

They return to their boats. Untangling the mess takes as much as the tying in. Boats start up and cast off as soon as they are released from those around them. Their passengers wave, saying, "See y'. Nice to have met y'," and "Thanks," as they speed away.

Dale and I walk across the highway to the campground where those who spent the afternoon chasing tents have assessed the damages and made repairs. Fireworks explode behind a gauzy cloud deck like psychedelic lightning, a radio blasts the popular post-9/11 anthems, and I recall another Fourth of July, on a levee, standing in front of a steam-driven Ferris wheel loaded with squealing girls in Fort Smith, Arkansas, one year ago.

Gosh, what if we'd scuttled the trip.

If we had scuttled the trip we would not be here today to witness Americans—fiercely individual, independent, and selfish at times—come together in a crisis. It is that ethos, the one with the gumption to set sail for the New World and teamwork to settle the West, that is especially apparent from the pace and perspective of a boat.

The next morning, we shove off before the holiday traffic wakes up. Dale checks his gauges. I cast off lines. *Betty Jane* pushes into the rising sun even as *Calypso* is still not back, and the phone rings.

It is Sister.

*F*unerals are those social occasions where everyone loses any sense of propriety. Weddings are the same thing but dressed up as happily-ever-after. It was when my great-uncle Eddie died that I met my great-Aunt Ann for the first time.

She had always been a name rarely used; a single photograph propped up on a guest room dresser somewhere, of a young woman under a large straw hat. On the day of Eddie's funeral, she was an inconsolable sixty-year-old woman, head-to-toe in widow's weeds. I marveled at the stamina and discipline she must have had to drag around that much angst and grief. But I'd been to a show. Any minute now she was going to throw herself on the floor. Maybe even writhe.

The next morning, Eddie's dead and intestate body was in the ground. That afternoon, Aunt Ann went to see the probate judge. By that evening, having gotten what she came for, she was on a flight back to her home in Salt Lake City.

"At weddings and funerals, Alexander," Pap said at the time, "don't pull any shit. Someone will do it for you."

Roy was dead before August first. Preparations for his funeral ensued over the next four weeks. The body was prepared for shipment to Milton, Wisconsin; the deceased wished to be buried next to his in-laws. The funeral party gathered from around the country, new clothes were ordered and packed, airline tickets were bought. Dioramas— commemorating the life of the high school football star, the WWII veteran, the dutiful husband, loving father and grandfather—filled the church hall. A eulogist was flown in.

Flowers banked the walls of the church, refreshments were served at the visitation, and banquet after banquet were hosted for both local and out-of-town mourners alike. There were also incidentals: nail polish, lip gloss, cigarettes, and candy for the great grandson. Absolutely no one bore any of the expense at this time of bereavement. Then the gratuities came due and the invoices payable. Then Sister pressed her brother to underwrite the entirety of the extravaganza on her oral promise of complete reimbursement after probate. I was not surprised. When Dale agreed without asking me, I remembered my Pap's advice about wedding and funerals and I chose to do nothing about it at the time. But I was livid.

Sister had promised before.

CHAPTER NINETEEN
Crossing the Line

We return to the river in the second half of August. The trip is beginning to get stale—too long, too many interruptions—except we are cruising to Green Turtle Bay, the last marina before we enter the Ohio, where yet another river culture will take over.

Green Turtle Bay is Aqua Yacht Harbor, but rather than being in the middle of the Tenn-Tom, Green Turtle Bay is the first to receive or launch Loopers from or to the wilds of the Ohio, the Mississippi, and the Great Lakes. It is Aqua plus a couple more swimming pools, a day spa, condos for sale, cabins for rent and a members-only dining room.

We tie up behind the fuel dock on a pier accessible by a single flight of unmarked stairs, convenient to all services and personnel but separated from the rest of the boathouses. Our slip, number six, exactly at the bottom of the stairs, is our account number, our table number in the brass and leather Admirals Club, and our hooch locker number behind the bar for which we've been given a key marked with a discreet brass numeral. A rock cliff shades the dock and cools the breeze so that an impromptu *paseo* can take place there every afternoon.

Our neighbors are yachts so huge with decks so high and bows reaching so far into the future that *Betty Jane* looks like a runabout. Their captains have command centers; their owners have offices; their wives have boudoirs; their passengers live-in suites. Live-aboard crews spit and polish everything from stem to stern daily. Their fiberglass is blinding and their chrome gleams even as I've got spider poop on my windows. Still, *Betty Jane* works her magic, calling the beautiful people off their boats, behind which stewards have placed trays of hors d'œuvres and aperitifs, to gather around what they cannot have. A wooden boat takes time, money, and skill; and though these men and women are at the top of their fields, at the top of their game, they have only two out of three.

They are slow to warm up, polite but reserved. Our offering of Triscuit and Velveeta on a paper plate does little to impress them. Overalls are not standard dress. But as the days go on and our tableware improves, we ease into the group. The invitation to join them for supper comes. Everyone in the restaurant knows that we are number six.

We are waiting for news of the river, now the Cumberland, below the dam. Running five knots and full of debris is all the uniformed gas attendant can tell us, and he is not sure because, like Pickwick, below the dam is a mystery.

"It's called The Leap," John Bartlett explained from his imaginary helm at Applegate. "It's the jump over the bottomland between up top on Lake Barkley and up top above Smithland lock. You gotta git out of Barkley, down th' Cumberland an' back up th' Uh-hi-yuh above Smithland to Golconda before you can rest." He uncurled the cigarette from his lips and shook it for emphasis. "You'll be pushin' up the Uh-hi-yuh now an' don' chew forgit it. Iff'n that master's water lettin' out, you just gotta punch it and crawl all th' way to the lock wall." He shoved the cigarette back in his mouth before adding, "An' y's gotta do it all before dark 'cause they ain't no anchoring out in The Leap."

Overnight anchorages are ill-advised because what is hooked deep and sticky at dusk can be high and dry or on its way to Baton Rouge by morning. Pool levels fluctuate in the bottomland around Smithland, Kentucky, where outflow of three major rivers—Tennessee, Cumberland, and Ohio—combine into the one and only Big Muddy.

"Iff'n you don't make it to Golconda," John said, "you'll have to drop down to Paducah, 'cause all that turb'lence keeps the Corps from markin' the channel. Which means, you lost your fifty-mile head start on the Uh-hi-yuh by going down the Cumb'land in the first place. Fuckin' hard day's work is what it is. An' that's if nuthin' goes wrong."

Current river conditions would be helpful in knowing what to expect. I suggest we drive down to Smithland Lock and look. Dale suggests that we call.

"And say what?" I ask, and in an effeminate falsetto, add, "We're two faggots in a fabulous wooden yacht and we want to go to Cincinnati but we're too scared of the water and what lies beneath and what might happen to us. What if we crash on the rocks? What if we run aground? Then, then, then, what would we do? Whatever would we do?"

Dale sits patiently on the other side of the table. When I finish, he smiles, and says patronizingly, "That may do. But I was thinking of something more along the lines of 'How fast?' and 'How much debris?'"

He dials the number and introduces himself to the curt business-like manner we will come to expect from the lock-masters on the Ohio.

"I'm letting out thirty-six feet and it's fairly clean," says the Smithland lockmaster.

"What's 'fairly clean'?" I ask. "And what does thirty-six feet mean?"

"He wasn't taking interviews," Dale answers as a matter of fact. "He just waited a minute and said, 'That all you want to know? Okay? 'Bye,' and hung up."

"What do you want to do?"

"I dunno, what do *you* want to do?" I answer.

The great joy of *Betty Jane* has always been that when neither of us has an idea of how to proceed, we talk out the problem. In this case, we decide to throw caution to the winds and shove off, come what may. Dale hails the lock.

"Barkley Lock. Barkley Lock. This is *Betty Jane,* over."

"Go to fourteen, *Betty Jane.*"

"*Betty Jane* to fourteen."

"I bet you want to lock down, don't you, *Betty Jane?*" answers a cheery and playful voice, like the ones we heard on the Arkansas. "I knew'd you was coming. I seen you last night in slip six. I've been waitin' fer yew."

"Thanks, we're on our way."

"Well, yer just gonna have to wait," he says. "Yer outta bed too late. Early Bird. Early Bird. I jist drained the chamber...but I'll get it ready for yew just as soon as I ken. C'mon, lemme get a look atcha."

———— ♦ ————

Below the lock, the dam's whitewater tail lashes against our stern and pushes us down the channel at twelve knots going to fifteen. *Betty Jane*'s prow crests and dives into the waves like a porpoise, forcing me to hit the deck more than once to avoid being thrown overboard. Dale hollers, "WEEE, WEEE," as the scenery flies by.

The riverbed comes up sharply over the delta; the river slows and widens dramatically. Cumberland's sandy beige tendrils melt into the Ohio's deep blue. The propellers kick plumes of silt into our wake. Navigation buoys are rare. We keep our eyes peeled for any obstacle above or below the surface. Dale wants to change pilots.

"Here?" I ask in disbelief. "Now?"

He has remembered that he forgot to clear the bilge pump screens before casting off—the bow planks are certainly dry, which will cause us to take on water as we go against the Ohio's current—leaving me to plot the upstream course. Our speed plummets to 5.5 knots, the engines growl under the strain. We are at 302 feet above sea level, the bottom of the trip—Applegate was 459 feet, Pickwick was 414, Cincinnati is 455—but we are in high spirits. We've made excellent time. When he returns, I sweep the heavens for connectivity and type a brief e-mail to our friends—"Me-OH, My-OH, We're on the Ohio." Dale entertains himself with a fantasy about rough miserable crew chained to their oars and pulling in the swelter of a sweaty bilge.

"Harder. HARDER, you lazy scum. I need more power. MORE POWER, do you hear?" he says, cracking an imaginary whip over his head before assuming a more radio-proper persona and pressing the call button on the microphone.

"Smithland Lock. Smithland Lock. This is *Betty Jane*. Over."

"Go to thirteen, Cap'n."

No longer is channel fourteen the go-to frequency. It is now thirteen.

"*Betty Jane* to lock up."

"ETA?"

"Mile 921 opposite Hametsburg Island at six knots."

"Ready?"

"Ready," Dale repeats.

"Copy."

"Not very chatty, this lot, are they?" I ask.

"Mmm," Dale grunts, waiting for instruction.

"Northbound small craft. Northbound small craft. Smithland, over."

No longer do we lock up; we are northbound.

"Copy, northbound small craft," Dale answers.

No longer are we *Betty Jane,* we are small craft.

"Copy. In visual."

Locking through is no longer a spot of sociability that interrupts the monotony of eight knots an hour. It is a business of monosyllabic blips.

"Illinois chamber, small craft. Over."

"Copy."

No longer are chambers inside or outside; they take their designations from their adjacent states.

The signal light on the lock wall blinks green. We slip into the looming shadow of cast concrete where the lockmaster, hanging over the parapet, offers only, "Barkley said she was pretty," before returning to his work.

Locking up is more than a passage; it is a resurrection. Unlike locking down, which is a passive letting out of water, of being lowered into a vault with no apparent way out, like burial. Locking up is a fight against gravity, against water rushing in from the bottom of the chamber causing a fizzy effervescence at first, growing to a turbulence that threatens to scrape *Betty Jane* against the aggregate chamber walls, and rising past the mossy green depths to arrive at the top in the fresh air of a clear blue sky. The upper doors open up on *Betty Jane*'s new home; mine, too.

———◆———

It is said that a true river man searches the earth until he finds his very own river. A search that is as personal as it is for a mate. Dale and I have whitewater rafted extensively. Each river had its distinctive personality. All had aspects I could fall in love with, but even my first river, the South San Gabriel, which I splashed through with the unbridled exuberance of youth, could not contain my ambition. As I take in the Ohio from the bridge of my boat, I know that this is my river.

It is old and patient and knows that Time is on its side. That any development within its banks is temporary and remains there only by its pleasure and permission. The bluffs are green, the water is blue, and its course moves slowly across the countryside, like seduction itself. It was here long before I was. Will be here long after I'm gone. There is something calming in the knowledge that my existence does not matter in the least. Two hours ahead, with plenty of daylight to get there, is Golconda.

The depth sounder goes into a frenzy the moment we are off the river. Charts and harbor specs indicate ten feet of depth, but the alarm squeals and "Shallow...Water...Shallow...Water..." marches across its display. Dale pulses our propellers, dropping them in gear in short bursts so that we glide over rather than power through any submerged obstacles. We shouldn't have a problem; but fewer than twenty-five miles from Green Turtle Bay as the crow flies and over an hour by car, Golconda is no place to need a repair. Fate does not favor this tiny town.

In the eighteenth century, it was a ferry crossing where General Lusk transported pioneers and settlers from Kentucky to the Illinois Territory, landing his boats in the tributary that still bears his name, Lusk Creek. It became a county seat when Illinois became a state. Ancient trees shade the square in front of a red-brick-white-trim courthouse. Explorers Lewis and Clark stopped here on their way west.

But trains carry more freight than packet boats. Bridges put ferries out of business. The United States Congress sanctioned the surrounding countryside as the Shawnee National Forest, further isolating the outpost. A secondary state road, 146, is the only way in or out, a four-way stop marks downtown. The marina was an attempt at revitalization.

Golconda Marina State Recreation Area was sited on the excavation that supplied the material for the flood wall in 1937, opened in 1988, and was proclaimed the most modern facility built on the Ohio. In complete compliance of the ADA and with the potential to be a gateway on a par with Green Turtle Bay—except that Loopers don't go up the Ohio—it promised to bring recreation to all Illini and economic prosperity to Golconda. However, budgetary constraints cut back on the plantings in the flower boxes, the fountains are dry, saplings grow in the cracked masonry that makes crossing Lusk Creek ironically wheelchair inaccessible. And there is no one standing on the gas dock to say, "Welcome to Golconda! We're glad you're here!"

Inside, two teenagers wait for their summer jobs to end. Tweedle-Dee drapes himself over a picnic table under a beer sign. Tweedle-Dum loiters next to the register. They daydream about football camp, the start of school, and girls until our clattering through ill-fitting steel doors announces our arrival.

"Hey," I say while Dale grumbles about the shallows.

"Yeah, it's supposed to be ten feet," Tweedle-Dum explains, "but the state won't afford a dredge."

"What do you think it is really?" Dale asks. "My sounder says two-point-seven feet."

"That's about right. We're supposed to say three 'cause most cruisers draft shallower than that."

Dum assigns us to a slip while Dee worries a toothpick into a knot hole. I ask about the ladder of small craft slips whose decking is warped and waterlogged. Dum answers.

"We have a lot of fishing tournaments. Used to be that fishermen would slip overnight to get a fresh start early the next morning, but mostly everyone trailers in their boats these days to save money. Business is bad."

"Budget cuts," Dee mumbles, shrugging his shoulders without looking up from his toothpick. "We close at five. Town shuts down at eight."

A seemingly endless game of twenty-questions drags from the teens the information that there is no cell service. The library where we can check our e-mail closes at five, so that will wait until tomorrow. The library, the restaurant, and the post office are at the four-way stop. The bar stays open until two. There is a grocer, and a farmer's market sets up on the square every Saturday, the day after tomorrow. We plan to be gone by then.

"We got a thirty-inch draft," Dale explains before leaving the counter. "Will we make it to Boathouse C?"

"You might scrape bottom, but you'll be all right."

———— ◆ ————

It is the end of the longest day, the day John Bartlett had promised. *Betty Jane* is a mess and her crew is collapsed on bunks. Doris Faye makes her own dinner out of kibble she has scattered across the galley and water she drinks out of a glass on the floor by my bunk before lying down, as is her custom, with her back pressed against my side. She has probably gotten up in the night, walked around in circles as dogs do before lying down, snuggled and fussed, noted that it is dawn and that neither Dale nor I have stirred. Finally, unable to wait any longer, she wakes me up with an urgent and sincere face-licking.

"Hey, girl," I ask, looking around. "'Sup?"

Dale is dead where he landed. His eyeglasses still hang in his hand.

"You wanna go outside?" I ask a dog, wagging frantically from muzzle to tail.

I fumble at getting her quivering legs onto the dock where she pees immediately. She is ashamed and expects to get beaten—Doris Faye was a rescue and severely abused before being dumped—but I tell her it's no big deal. While looking for a hose to rinse off the dock, I note that the sun is in the east, unless I've gotten myself turned around and confused. Doris Faye leads me out of the boathouse where we encounter some fishermen launching their boats. It is awfully late in the day for fishermen to be launching boats.

"'Morning," the broad figure dressed head to toe in green camouflage bids me.

"'Morning," I answer reflexively, but *Is it morning?*

I look around again.

"We slept through the night," I announce to Dale, waiting beside *Betty Jane* when Doris Faye and I return.

"Naw, we dozed off."

"We slept through. Look at the sun. Which way is east?"

He prepares to make coffee as NOAA predicts rain. We don't care. *Betty Jane* is under cover, we are wiped out, and the local boys say there is nothing doing in town. We climb into his bunk and spoon while Doris Faye bathes herself on mine. I put my arm under his and pull him close to my chest to whisper, "We made it. We goddam made it."

Dale breathes a sigh of relief before instantly falling back to sleep.

The following morning, being Saturday, we avail ourselves of the fresh produce displayed under the shade of the village green. I am particularly interested in the assortment of peppers a woman is pulling out of the back of her car.

"Did they ever find the head?" she asks the man presiding over his mobile five & dime under the next marquee. "I knew she cut his head off, but did they ever find the head?"

She sizes and sorts her merchandise into a variety of containers—cut-off milk jugs, plastic fish-'n'-chips baskets, shoe boxes—keeping her back to her customers until she has summarized all her suspicions while he searches all four pages of the local paper for a continuation of the story.

"I'm not surprised. That woman was mean as a snake," she says.

Crinkly gray hair pokes out from under the brim of her broad straw hat. She stoops, is round-shouldered from decades of sorting peppers, and ties her apron sloppily. "I'm not surprised she did it. And I'm not surprised they haven't found his head yet, neither."

The customer behind me pushes into the conversation.

"You talking about that woman who cut off her husband's head?"

"Yeah," the pepper lady says. "Have they found the head, yet? D'y'know?"

Characterizations of the suspect in custody supplant any interest she has in my making a purchase until I interrupt, saying, "I'd like to buy some peppers."

"Come to the right place," she answers.

She fiddles with her stock waiting for me to make my selections and then suddenly barks to no one in particular, "WELL...You KNOW she did it!"

"With you in a minute," the five & dime man says, putting off his customer in favor of scanning the newspaper. "Here, here it is!" he reaches out in excitement. "I found it! It says, 'Authorities are still collecting evidence and mounting their case.' That means they *found the head*!"

"That means no such thing," the pepper woman snaps back. "It means they've fussed around so long the trail is cold and she's gonna get away with it. That's what *that* means."

I repeat, "We'd like some peppers."

"Y' said that...looking for anything in particular? I got hot peppers, bell peppers, stuffin' peppers, roastin' peppers, serranos, jalepenos, and bell."

At this, the first chance I get to look her in the face, I see that we have crossed a line somewhere. Gone are the pampered women in stylish clothes, the sun-tanned captains aboard gleaming yachts, the gas dock hunks and beer hotties; the riparian estates tiered with putting greens, private docks and airy gazebos; all of that is of the Great Loop, the Tennessee and the Cumberland. This is the Midwest, populated by work-hardened people accustomed to long-abiding trials. This is the Ohio, a transportation artery, where the thing that shuttles barges between depots—pushboats everywhere else we've been—are now called tows.

CHAPTER TWENTY
The River's Business

We depart Golconda in a muddy froth stirred up from the bottom by our own props. Rosiclare, Illinois, appears around the bend, on river right. Cave-in-the-Rock farther up was the one-time hideout for the Mason Gang and the Harpe Brothers, then a tourist attraction in the steamboating days, now a state park covered up with visitors.

Civic ballparks, high school stadiums, playgrounds, and picnic pavilions dot the riverside lowlands. In-town apartments, looking out through tiny windows, take the river for granted. Their suburban counterparts survey every inch of what there is to see through sweeping walls of glass. They herald our approach to any town. Between them, stairs from out of nowhere dangle over the water, floating docks surrounded by nothing bob next to shore, and tarpaper fishing shacks perch in the trees. The Ohio is an extension of everyone's backyard.

The segment between tie-ups—Golconda and the next port, Mount Vernon, Indiana—is seventy-eight miles, one long, hard day. An overnight on the river will split the distance into two shorter, easier days. However, anchorages on the Ohio are not the placid pool of Ozark, Arkansas, where the town is on one side, a campground is on the other, and conscientious masters in the lock warn the occasional tow-boat that our mast light is out.

Anchorages on the Ohio are subject to sudden weather changes, pool fluctuations, heavy current, and, worst of all, barge wakes so severe as to rip our anchor out of the riverbed and send flying anything on board not tacked down. Deep enough inlets are rare and unreliable. Tributaries are full of stumps, mosquitoes, and made inaccessible by their deltas. The surest shelter is behind some island; the Ohio is full of them, and they, too, are called tows. Some are the size of farms; others are no more than low piles of sand dropped by the last flood. The good ones have a stand of trees for shade. The better ones have a beach where Doris Faye can run. The best ones have chutes deep enough to pull straight through, something only the locals can know. Regardless, we must put something between us and wakes as constant as surf.

"What about that?" Dale says, pointing upstream.

"Let's look."

I train my binoculars on a stand of trees.

It is an island with a suitable beach for walking the dog. The secondary channel is wide enough and allegedly deep enough for our draft, but charts are approximations, not certainties. The map also shows an exceedingly long tow, the name also given to a submerged shoal that trails far below where the dry land stops. Without sonar to scan the bottom, Dale has to tack back and forth, keeping his eye on the depth sounder, to find the channel between the shallows.

"There she is," he calls out, turning the boat back to shore and away from the mainstream. "There's the secondary channel, the chute."

We continue feeling our way along. I'm watching the water. Dale's watching the depth sounder.

Suddenly, *Betty Jane* runs aground and will stick unless Dale immediately spins the wheel to starboard which he does, punching the engines to break her free. We change course and head back to shore.

"What's your depth?" I ask.

The shoreline is getting uncomfortably close.

"Thirty feet...Twenty-nine feet...Twenty-eight feet... Thirty feet..."

"You're awfully close."

"Thirty-three feet...Thirty-five feet...Twenty-nine feet... Twenty-five feet."

"You can come about any time you want," I say. "I ain't got no swing this close to shore."

Swing is the distance *Betty Jane* can move on a length of rope, called scope, tied to the anchor. A good scope is three times longer than anchor depth, but it needs more room to swing.

"It don't mean a thing if it ain't got that swing," Dale singsongs.

"Seriously?"

"Doo wah, doo wah, doo wah, doo wah...Twenty-four feet...Twenty-three feet...Twenty-six feet." He asks where to drop anchor: "How far up?"

"Not too far I don't know that we can get out the other end."

"Me, neither."

"So how far back do you want to have to drift when we leave in the morning?"

"Just tell me where."

"I'm concerned about swing," I call back.

"You ain't gonna hafta worry 'bout no swing," Dale says. "Not in dis current."

Dale treads water while I decide.

"What's my depth?"

"Here? Twenty."

"Okay, push up another sixty feet. I'll throw anchor, pay out that much rope, and fall back. That should put us back here again."

"Copy that," Dale says, acknowledging that his is not the only control on the boat.

"Back up. Back up."

I wave with my right hand, paying out the anchor rode with my left. *Betty Jane* falls back.

"Back," I say, looking for landmarks against which to judge any slippage. "Back." I whip the rode around the mooring post in the middle of the foredeck. The line goes taut.

"There," I call to the helm. "Cut prop."

The line tightens. It groans as it strains. The hull, now held fast, can no longer yield to the river. The current deflects off the keel, snapping the boat in line with the channel. Dale picks his landmarks. I pick mine.

"Pull!" I instruct Dale to reverse prop and set anchor. "Stop!"

Betty Jane springs back on the stretched line, then relaxes. Dale checks his marks. I check mine.

"Pull!" I call back, testing the anchorage and setting the hook deeper in the mud. I want to sleep tonight.

Dale checks his marks. I check mine.

"Pull. Pull. Pull. That's it...and STOP!"

———◆———

Satisfied that we are well hooked, I bend down to secure the rode. *Betty Jane* goes silent. She sways slowly and gently back and forth in the current. I check my marks. Dale checks his. The sounds drowned out by the engines take over. The wind ruffles the leaves like rain. Cornfields extend as far as the eye can see. The rain-cooled morning has turned into a humid August afternoon. Our exercises have made us sweaty.

We tie PFDs to the ends of ropes secured to the back of the boat. These will be our lifelines in fast-moving water—that's what the master at Smithland must have meant when he said, "letting out thirty-six feet." We strip down and jump in, believing we are alone. Our sunburned skin tingles in the cool silt-ladened river. We slide down with lifelines in hand, holding tight so at the end we can bob up and down like dolphins. We pull ourselves back to the boat and hang on to whatever we can find to rest. We really should be wearing PFDs.

Suddenly, we hear, "Ahoy! Ahoy, the big boat. Ahoy, the men overboard. Ahoy!"

It is a pontoon boat as neat as a pin with a burgundy surrey top trimmed in yellow fringe rippling in the breeze. On board are men in ties and women in starched cotton dresses, out for an afternoon ride. As they float towards us, Dale grabs the swim ladder and I hang onto the props. Visiting is why boaters boat.

"Hey," Dale says.

Their first question is the inevitable: "This your boat?"

These are elderly people trying to be friendly. My sarcasm has no place here, but I am thirty-five miles above Golconda and twenty miles below the Illinois-Indiana state line. I cannot imagine whose boat it may be if not ours.

"You from around here?" is their second question despite the Dallas, TX, emblazoned on her stern in two-inch letters. Fortunately, Dale is here to answer.

"*Betty Jane*," reads the woman in white framed sunglasses and an Aubrey Hepburn hat, saying "Lovely," with a song in her voice.

She reminds me of my father's mother. She was a Victorian by her own admission, a Reconstruction Democrat who wore white gloves, except to funerals, all the way through the '70s until she once saw Nancy Reagan with a pair. I never saw her even handle another glove again.

They pass pleasant conversation in the way I remember overhearing my grands do all the time—saying little about nothing, talking just the same.

"Is that your dog?" coos the second woman. She ties a blue and lavender scarf over her platinum hair.

Those polite inquiries, those gracious and ephemeral exchanges, make my generation's demands for information blunt and grotesque.

"Isn't she just precious?"

"Does she hunt, I wonder?" asks the second man who we will learn is Lucius. His undergarments must be soaking up the sweat because his pants are creased; his shirt is immaculate.

Each time the river pushes their boat back, their captain powers back within earshot. The current that was so invigorating is getting annoying. My arms are tired. Normally, I would have no compunction about climbing out of the river. We're all family, right? But this is not the no-shirt-no-shoes-no-problem gang. These are my elders. They don't sweat, they blot. They don't argue; they discuss. They don't drink; they imbibe—out of real glasses, not plastic shots liquor-stuck to the table. The gentlemen have standing in their communities. The ladies serve on charitable boards and committees. They have probably never taken the Lord's name in vain, even in life's most climactic moments, but they are candid.

"Honey," says the woman in the scarf, drawing a long periwinkle blue cigarette holder out of her purse. "I have seen a naked man. My first husband was naked once and I am living proof that I did not die from the sight."

"Go on. Go on. Let's not have a drowning on ceremony," she says, then, to the captain. "Percy, Percy, turn this jitney around and give these guys some privacy"—rhymes with Hennessy—"You just let us know when you're decent."

Dale and I climb out, dry off and pull up our shorts. I drag in the rescue lines and hang up the towels. As they motor back, Dale asks, "You wanna tie up? Throw me a line."

"Thanks ya, kindly," Percy says. "Lucius, look under that hatch and throw that man a line. Now tie it off to that cleat. There, that's it. Thanks ya."

Before going forward to get our own refreshments I ask, "Y'all want anything?"

"Here, we've got plenty of lemonade," the lady in the broad hat says, pointing to a pitcher full of ice and dripping with condensate. "You just get yourselves some glasses and share ours."

"Sure? Thanks."

I return with two plastic glasses, a salad bowl, also plastic, for serving the pretzels that I bought at the grocery in Golconda against Dale's protestations.

"What do we want those for?" he asked at the time.

"I just don't sleep well at night knowing there's no pretzels on board."

"Since when?"

"Since forever," I answered back. "I don't mention it because I don't want to burden you with my personal problems, but I've always harbored a fear of having no pretzels in the cupboard…always."

"Ha," Dale answered.

We pass refreshments back and forth over the water and settle into chairs Dale has set up on the aft cockpit.

"Now let's just talk," says the woman while tucking her sunglasses next to her white gloves under her skirt.

"We keep a camp just up ahead here," Percy says. The waning sunlight gives him permission to loosen his necktie. "Ya're pushing up so ya wouldn't have seen it, but just above this island, there's a creek. Doesn't look like anything from the river, but it's deep enough to tie this and his Bass boat up out of the mainstream."

Lucius nods at the mention of his fishing boat.

"We keep a couple of fifth wheels up there. It's our summer camp. Lucius got his and I got mine."

Percy unspools the facts leisurely; each one contains a story.

"We grew up together...These girls are my cousins...On my mother's side, of course."

Of course.

Pearl and Ethel nod and smile as Percy introduces them.

"They're both widows."

Pearl pulls the cigarette holder away from her face, leans forward and mouths, "Cancer," with a mischievous smile.

"Anyway, like I said, we like to spend time on the water. It can get lonesome with just Lucius and me. The girls come by for a visit time t' time."

I doubt the true nature of our relationship enters their minds. They probably think we are brothers. If not, Grandmother would say, "Bachelor-types," dismissing the matter entirely. They want to hear about *Betty Jane*. She is of their period. They used to frolic on her sister ships when they were young.

"That's what caught our attention," Percy says. "We saw ya all come up, watched ya anchor, saw ya with ya dog and

I said to Pearl, 'There's some sailors, and there's a boat. We oughtta go look up those people.'"

"I told him, 'No,'" Pearl says, "That you were probably hot and tired and did not want any company. But they insisted."

Percy turns on his navigation lights. Dale turns on our mast light.

"You pulling out tomorrow?" Lucius asks, stooping over to untie their boat.

"Yeah. We want to get to Mount Vernon," Dale answers.

Percy points up the channel and says, "Ya can pull right straight through here if ya want to. It's deep enough."

"Thanks, but I'd rather go out how I came in," I say.

"I understand. Don't blame ya'. Just remember that tow goes well down below this island."

"They know that," Lucius waves Percy down. "They got all the way from *Texas*, didn't they?

"If you want breakfast, I ring the bell in the morning," Ethel announces, stubbing out her cigarette and removing the butt from the holder. "These boys," pointing to Lucius and Percy, "get on the rivah and forget what time it is. We have a big ol' dinner bell hanging in a tree. Pearl and I just ring and ring, and they never come, but they don't complain about eating cold supper, either. So..."

She shrugs.

"Probably just get underway," I say.

"Don't blame ya," Percy says, starting his outboard engine. "Youngsters, ya know," he says to his company.

"'Bye."

"'Bye."

"Pleasure talking with you," each says, followed by, "See you down the river."

I watch them go. Dale closes screens and hatches against the bugs. The party barge with the fringed surrey top cuts blithely across the tow we so scrupulously avoided and disappears.

The Ohio is like that.

———————•———————

The whine of barges plowing the fifty-five mile length of Smithland pool at balls-out speeds run over the night noises. Frogs croak, fins slap, crickets chirp. The sandy water sounds fizzy, brushing against our hull. Searchlights, filtered through the trees, flash into the cabin. Wakes wash onto the island like ocean to shore. Dawn comes early, much too early.

"Push up," I call from my position on the bow.

Dale engages the engines until there is enough slack to wrap the anchor rode around the windlass. The electric winch purrs happily at first, but as the slack becomes taut and the anchor does not budge, the electric motor bears down hard, setting gear against sprocket—*clink, clink, clink*—pulling *Betty Jane's* bow into the river. The line gets as tight as cat gut before the anchor suddenly pops loose. The bow lurches up and I call to the helm, "You're adrift," a signal to Dale that he is in control.

I wash the anchor of its accumulated mud. *Splash. Splash.* Twist and turn. *Splash. Splash. Betty Jane* slips from behind her overnight anchorage and into a now negligible current.

We see the break in the trees on the opposite bank and the small creek, their boats, their two trailers oriented to catch the prevailing breezes. A fine wisp of smoke from first fire drifts through low-hanging branches. Dale hails the bucolic setting.

BLOAT! BLOAT! BLOOOOOOOOAT! Our air-horns trumpet up the valley, *BLOAT! BLOAT! BLOOO-OOOOOAT!*

CLANG! CLANG! CLANG! CLANG! CLANG! the campers answer on the triangle hung from a branch. *CLANG! CLANG! CLANG! CLANG! CLANG!*

They are Ethel, Pearl, Percy, and Lucius, dressed like the cast of *I Love Lucy* in bathrobes over pajamas waving their good-byes from the middle of a cornfield, thirty-five miles above Golconda and twenty miles below John T. Myers.

CHAPTER TWENTY-ONE
Swimming with Whales

John T. Myers is the lock and dam across the Ohio where the river bends and bows on an almost level floodplain. Below are the mouth of the Wabash river, the state line, and a formidable delta—high and broad enough to be plowed, splitting the larger river almost evenly down the middle. The Army Corps of Engineers has created a mainstream by shunting water out of one channel and dredging the other. And there has been a disaster.

Heavy rains and extreme flooding have blown out the Wabash's mouth with explosive force. Dirt, debris, and clean-up crews all but close the shipping lane. Acreage is lost. Cornstalks cling to the topsoil by their roots as their tassels drown in the receded floodwaters. We passed other floating vegetation as we came upon the scene that is stymied by a bottleneck. Three commercial southbounds on the other side of dam wait to lock down. The northbound commercial ahead of us makes four. We and the northbound commercial coming up our stern make five and six. In addition, the small Indiana chamber is closed for repair. Dale tunes the radio to hail the lock, which lets loose a barrage of radio transmissions.

"... John T. Myers, John T. Myers, Commercial northbound. John T. Myers. John T. Myers, Northbound." "South-

bound tow, Southbound tow, ETA." "This is Myers, ov—."
"Southbound, this is John T. Myers." "John T. Myers. John
T. Myers… Com—… —bound…" "Myers, Myers, South-
bound Commercial." "Southbound, Stand-by." "Copy."
"Copy." "John T. Myers. John T. Myers…"

"Sounds like traffic," Dale says as he grabs the microphone and waits for the air to clear.

"John T. Myers. John T. Myers. Northbound Commercial in visual."

He points to the towboat ahead of us and says, "That's
that barge," and waits.

"John T. Myers, John T. Myers, Commercial Traffic
Southbound. Myers, Myers, Southbound."

"Stand by, Southbound."

Then, there's a break. Dale presses the call button, and
hails, "John T. Myers. John T. Myers. This is *Betty Jane* locking up," momentarily forgetting that we are small craft and
northbound on the Ohio.

Masters, dispatchers, captains and mates work out protocols and priorities according to number of containers, cargo, lock cycles, and wait times. "Stand by" punctuates every
transmission. "Stand by." "Stand by." "Stand by." We wait
quietly until it is our turn. Patience greases the wheel.

"Northbound pleasure. Northbound pleasure. What's
your ETA? Over."

Dale answers, "John T. Myers. John T. Myers. This is
northbound pleasure. We're right behind Northbound Commercial. Over."

The master says, "Roger, northbound pleasure. Stand by."

"Northbound pleasure standing by. Over."

Tow captains call in from above the lock. Somewhere
behind us come still others.

"John T. Myers. John T. Myers. Northbound Commercial. Northbound, Myers." "Northbound, Roger. This is John T. Myers. What's your twenty?" "Northbound to John T. Myers. Below Wabash tow." "Copy, Northbound. John T. Myers. Out."

"What do you want to do?" I ask.

We can either tread water or throw the hook. There is nowhere to tie off while these guys work this thing out.

Dale listens to the radio for clues. We have no status. Commercial pays; we don't.

"The barge ahead has a green," he says. "The southbound will probably ride down the drain in time for the northbound behind us to ride up the fill—"

I finish his sentence: "—which puts the next southbound on the drain before we get a turn on the following fill, provided that other commercial doesn't show up in the meantime. It'll have priority."

"Exactly."

On the one hand, we patted our foot all afternoon at Toad Suck Ferry. On the other hand, an afternoon of reading and napping would do us good. Dale looks like he got no sleep last night.

"Right," he says, "Let's pull out of the channel and throw anchor. You mind?"

"No. I'd rather that than being in the way and burning gas."

———◆———

I suggest that I walk the dog. It is an ordeal but we cannot know when the next opportunity for Doris Faye to go ashore will be, and the sandy shallows sparkling with sunlight beg for a barefoot wade. Dale suggests that I stay on board while he makes sandwiches. A chance to lock may come up. I settle into the banquette on the bridge and the sunlight reflected off the water hypnotizes me.

"Northbound small craft. Northbound small craft," comes over the radio. "Northbound small craft. Northbound small craft."

I ignore the call, dismissing it as more gibberish between the big boys.

"Small craft. Small craft. Come in. This is John T. Myers," the voice repeats patiently. "Small craft, do you copy?"

I jump with a start when I understand they are hailing *us*.

"Dale! Dale!" I scream into the galley. "He's on the radio. He's on the radio," pointing to the instrument as if it were on fire.

"Pick it up," Dale says, nonchalantly assessing mold colonies collected on the bread slices.

"What'll I say? What'll I do?"

He stops. Looks. Enunciates with exaggerated deliberation: "John. T. Myers. John. T. Myers. This. Is. Small. Craft. Oh-Ver."

I stand like he does with hand on hip, eyes set forward, and mimic his example.

"Go to thirteen, small craft."

"Small craft to thirteen. Copy," I repeat, bending down to carefully retune the radio three channels down. "One. Two. Three," I count out loud and confirm, "That's thirteen," before depressing the call button purposefully and speaking into the microphone, "Small craft on thirteen."

"Small craft, you are going through as soon as I can release this northbound, copy?"

"Dale! Dale! We're pushed through! We're pushed through!"

"Copy?" repeats the master. "Small craft. Small craft. Copy, small craft."

"This is small craft," I fumble.

"I need you at the gates ASAP. I'ma gonna drop the chamber, there's gonna be some outrush. Then, I'ma gonna run you up. Copy? That means, 'Do you understand, small craft?'"

"Yessir," I answer eagerly. "Yessir. I...We...I certainly do...I mean 'copy'. Roger. Thanks. 'Bye. I mean, OVER!"

Dale recognizes that he has left an idiot on his radio. He climbs up the ladder.

"Gimme that." He grabs the mike out of my hand playfully and says into it, "Small craft copies, John T. Myers. Over."

"Copy, small cra—,"

Dale turns to me and says, "These are instructions from a federal agent, not some Junior Leaguer inviting you to a style show at the Women's Club."

"I wouldn't know. I've never been invited to a style show at the Women's Club by a Junior Leaguer. But who cares? It means we're not stuck here for the rest of our lives; it means we may make Mount Vernon by nightfall. Forget lunch. Let's go."

We wait against the lock wall, which is rusticated stone wall of medieval proportions. The siren warns fishermen downstream of the turbulence, attendant to draining chambers. The steel doors crack open just enough for us to slip in and snap closed behind us when we do. My tie-up is hasty and ill-suited. The rumble of *Betty Jane's* engines falls away and the klaxon sounds an ominous warning just as the waters rush in. The ride is an express to the top.

"THE STERN! THE STERN!" I yell down the length of the boat.

Roiling like a cauldron, the inrush causes *Betty Jane* to writhe against her moorings as if possessed. But soon we are easing to the top of the lift and a voice from overhead says, "Start your engines, untie, move toward the doors, and clear the AP ASAP. Nice boat, fellas."

Betty Jane exits like a queen. Waiting on us are two monster three-by-fives, one behind the other. From their pilot houses, captains prepare their loads for lockage ahead while cooks grill lunch on enormous barbecues behind. Everyone is busy, even in waiting, yet they all have time to smile and wave and say, "Be safe," "Nice day," and, "Like yer boat."

CHAPTER TWENTY-TWO
Burden Unbound

M ount Vernon, Indiana, is a port—the seventh busiest port in the nation—transhipping grain, grain products, fertilizer, cement, and minerals by river and rail to worldwide distribution. Its infrastructure clings to a ninety-degree bend of open river, around an island, and to the tiniest strip of Kentucky on the opposite bank. Despite there being no shelter at all, the guidebook suggests overnight moorage. The number listed answers, "Mayor's office."

The city clerk takes the particulars so as to alert the police of our allowed presence. She asks that we try not to take up the entire length and bids us welcome on behalf of the mayor and the city. The fire chief comes, with sirens blaring and several of his best in blue, to ogle *Betty Jane.* Police cruise by to keep an eye on us and close the city park to the loitering hoodlums who suggest that we "Go back to San Francisco!"

The dock is three steel plates hinged in two places with a simple handrail down the center. It is in the middle of the curve where the water is deepest, the current is fastest, and in direct line with barges turning the corner in two directions. *Clank, clank, clank, clank, clank,* like blades spinning in a blender full of ice, *clank, clank, clank, clank, clank,* all night long. *Clank, clank, clank, clank, clank*. We are gone by dawn.

Henderson, Kentucky, is a suburban utopia of child-rearing, shopping, and dining. We walk into town and find freshly painted traffic signals, lampposts festooned for the Labor Day celebration, and the town mascot—a simple man named Joe whom the good citizens have kept employed in some capacity all his life. He promises to look after our boat while we have some lunch.

Before we can get away, a group of naval veterans, bent on sharing their enthusiasm for *Betty Jane*, come down to the dock to welcome us. They are on busman's holiday from moving the WWII LST landing craft, moored at Evansville, to an exhibition in Louisville.

A local lawyer who had seen us on the river, swings into the parking lot to say "My wife's not going to believe this" and asks if he can come back and get a couple of pictures. Hunger and fatigue weighs on my patience until, finally, lunch is meatloaf, mashed potatoes with brown gravy, and collard greens with lots of sweet vinegar and fresh Georgia peach pie for dessert. But true relief from two hard days on the river comes from a 5' 2" tall twenty-something named Katie who knows that river men respond well to simple commands, constant praise, and untiring repetition.

"OK, Captain," Katie says, applying lip gloss, "I want you to spin her around, put your bow facing the river, and back your stern up to this other boat. Pull alongside and tie up right here."

She shows with her hands exactly the piece of gas dock that will be our moorage for the next few days. The canal is not very wide nor very deep, according to the depth sounder. Dale is sleep-deprived and hesitant.

Pulling her bug-eye sunglasses from the brim of her hat and placing them over her eyes, she says, "It's all right, Captain. You can do it, you've got plenty of room."

Dale is not so sure.

"There's plenty of water, too. Tell you what. If you run aground, I'll buy you a new boat. How's that? Now, you can do it. Just spin her around her like I said and bring her alongside right here. Ready? Go."

She has the confidence of having heard her father give this instruction thousands of times.

"That's it. Nice and easy. You're doing a great job, Captain. Now, ease her back." "Throw us a line!" she says to me. "Good. Now, go up to the bow. That's it. Throw us a line," which she catches intuitively from practice. "Good. Keep it coming, Captain. You're doing a fine job."

"Farther?" Dale asks.

"Cut your prop, Captain. We'll pull you in."

She casually winds the line around the dock cleat.

Betty Jane is tied to a salvaged barge reimagined as a gas dock, moored in the middle of a short canal. The river is off her bow. An embayment full of boats floating in slips is at her stern. Dale asks about tying up directly in front of her gas pumps.

"Let *me* worry about *my* gas pumps," she says. "And Welcome to Evansville, Indiana. Shut 'er down. You're here."

Dale jumps off the boat and fires off our needs onto Katie like a Gatling gun.

"We need a grocery, a drug store, a laundry and haircuts, movie would be a nice, and," he says, looking back at me for affirmation, "a sit-down restaurant with tablecloths, chandeliers, and does not smell like baby poop, preferably not in a mall. We like to hold menus in our hands."

She answers like a young woman who is used to receiving sunburnt river-weary guests.

"Unfortunately, everything is on the other side of town. I'll show you where. The roads are torn up with construction. You can use the marina truck after hours. Keys are in the ignition. Don't mess with the radios. Toilets are at the end of the booth. Showers are beyond that. We set up hot dogs, burgers and fries at the snack bar overlooking the river. Ain't bad if you're hungry. There's a convenience store in the LST parking lot up top."

An overhead stair lands on the gas dock.

"They've got beer and some wine, I think. I got quarters for the laundry in town. Movies are at the mall. There's a Walmart. Kroger is next to that. I'll get you a reservation for dinner. When do you want to go? Steak? Italian? Country club or no? Tonight or tomorrow? Or, oh, when are you leaving."

"Steak," I say. "No country club. Tomorrow night."

"Do you have jackets and ties?"

"Absolutely."

"Of course you do. Anything else. No? Great. Let us know if you need anything. That guy down there taking down umbrellas is Ron, he's my dad, he owns the place. Welcome to Inland Marina."

She walks away, taking the cellphone out of her pocket, jabbing at the keypad, and saying, "Hello?...Hey, whatcha doin'?" It is one of her girlfriends. Someone is getting married. "Oh, my God!"

———◆———

Dale and I are exhausted. We have survived The Leap, the first anchor out on the Ohio, and pushing up the second largest river in the United States. We have become confident in our abilities and our vessel, no longer needing to investigate every odd plink or yaw; we have learned the abbreviated shorthand of lockmasters; and that one field of corn looks pretty much like the next. In short, there is no going back, and barring any circumstance beyond our control like an engine blowing up, Cincinnati is attainable; setting my mind free to stray from its discipline of river, boat, and trip. I have a score to settle.

If Dale and I were actually married, the conundrum of his immediate family could be dismissed and universally understood as "in-laws." We are not. In fact, the exact nature of our relationship has no name in Roy's fundamental Christian lexicon. Nevertheless, Roy finds irksome the half-hidden smiles of his brothers, sisters, nieces, nephews, and cousins, as well as the awkward silences whenever the subject comes up. Dale and I need to be explained in the context of "Alexander's gay; Dale isn't," a tall order but not insurmountable. Roy's "Dale is leading Alexander to the Lord," casts Dale as the saint, me as the sinner, and frames the relationship in an acceptable way without besmirching him or his.

In practice, each Harris pays his or her own portion whenever the family gathers; when I am present, Dale and I pay the entirety. It is an inequitable arrangement, but as it excuses me from petty and innocuous celebrations of life, I do not mind. However, when it is an extravaganza of death and mourning as was Roy's funeral, and we are asked to pay, without prior arrangement and on short notice, I take exception.

I have held my tongue up to now on Pap's advice: *At weddings and funerals, don't pull any shit. Someone will do it for you*; but I have no confidence in Sister's promise to reimburse. The uncertainty gnaws at my gut as we spend down our nest egg in the middle of the Great Recession. A call from Dallas sets me off.

A fellow director of the homeowners' association which governs our condominium tries to dissuade me from casting a contrary vote against a trifling matter. We usually agree, but this time, he complains more about my proposed action rather than my rationale. The longer we talk the pettier it gets until I am blind with rage. I see nothing except Dale, in complete horror, cowering at his place. I end the call.

We sit across from each other at the galley table where we've solved any number of problems—about the boat, about our pasts, about our relationship, our future. Silence. When I calm down, I can hear the *drip, drip* of a fine mist falling into the canal. A morbid gray gloom squeezes through the portholes.

"You are not the man I fell in love with twenty years ago," he says calmly.

"And I cannot take this anymore," I answer.

It is pure soap opera, so cliché as to be comic, but it is not.

Of course we've talked about it all before, any number of times, but I can never understand why we are always solvent, and they always aren't.

"It is always like this," I shriek, hurling breakfast dishes into the sink. Doris Faye slinks into the stateroom. "When your family needs, we buy. When they want, we buy. Do you get a party on your birthday?" I pace the five feet of galley floor, back, forth. "When did you *ever* get a party on your birthday?" My eyes dare him to answer. "When was the last time I got a Christmas gift that had not been opened and used?"

Dale waits.

"And what's so Jesus about sponging off other people?"

His silence is aggravating.

"Answer me!" I scream like my drunken mother used to do.

"But you don't go to those parties," Dale defends, pounding his fists on the table.

"Do you want to know why? Because when I go, Dale and Alexander foot the whole bill. When just Dale goes, everyone pays his own."

Back and forth.

The slights, the gaffes, the hurt feelings and the remember-that-time-whens, all the bile from all the years of my being the hare-lipped hunchback, the beneficiary of Harris family Christian charity.

The excuse that his parents were raised in the Depression.

"They aren't frugal. They aren't careful. They're CHEAP."

I stomp and wail.

Sister's divorces, the nasty niece and nephew who call me Aunt Alexander while they greedily stuff down the chicken fingers we pay for.

"Oh, and suffer the little children whose fathers are losers. Tell me what is so godly about failed marriages. I'll wait. It stumped Henry XVIII for a while, too…Yes, my mother was married twice, and everyone in my family drinks…yes, yes, to excess…and the abuse, and the dysfunction, agreed… BUT my family has never held themselves up as the paragon of Christian virtue."

I cannot breathe anymore. I cannot think anymore. No pain that I can inflict on him can compare to that which I feel. I am caught in a rage that is going to destroy us. As I grasp for the next barb that will hit its mark, I suddenly recognize.

It is not the money.

It is that I am afraid to move to a city where neither of us knows anyone with someone I do not trust. Dale does not want to make the same mistake with me, who exhibits all the symptoms of complete insanity.

I slump over at the waist. I am going to pass out. Then, an eerie calm comes over me. I regain my composure and stand upright.

"It is that I have always thought of us as a team," I begin quietly. "Making decisions together and enjoying the rewards together. But when it comes to your family, you *obviously*," I make that word sting, "get to decide."

"It is *not* for me to decide," Dale says. "It *is* our money— mostly *your* money, if we have to start naming names."

"Then, why, why, why, goddammit, why did you not ask me?"

Enraged almost to tears again, I shake the bulkhead terrified of hearing what I suspect is the truth.

I've been duped. He was never mine. He will always be theirs.

The moment can only be described as divine. Dale does not answer. Instead, he gets up from his place, reaches for the pen and notebook kept on the top of the refrigerator for making lists, resumes his seat, and calmly asks, "Okay. What do you want?

I have to think.

We'll have to find a place to haul out the boat, put it up for sale, or give it to somebody. We'll have to drive back to Dallas, split the sheets, and begin again just like we planned except apart, which is not how we planned. Worst of all, Mother will be right.

Lowest common denominator, she said.

It'll end up badly, she said.

"NO, IT WON'T!" I scream, causing the dog to come back into the galley and investigate the commotion. Her tail

quivers; her ears droop around her chin. In twelve years, she
has never seen us fight. "We will *not* give up."

"Fine," Dale says, cracking a smile and petting Doris Faye.
"It's all right. It's just your daddies were fixin' to kill each other, but they've thought better of it. Go lie down on your sofa."

"But I want full reimbursement for Roy's funeral. Everything for everyone from typing the obit to the last very last
after-dinner mint."

"Got it."

"I want all expenses from driving your wayward niece
and her crap from Wisconsin to Texas."

"Got it."

"I want all expenses for my trip to the Wisconsin Dells
while waiting for Niece to get her shit together. Especially my
birthday dinner, which I had to eat alone."

"Got it."

"And I want Sister to pay for the car she bought."

"Got it."

He scribbles down the last item and asks, "Anything else?"

"No."

"Fine."

He examines the list.

"Do you want to collect or do you trust me?"

That is a problem, isn't it? Dale has always handled the
money and will know where all those records are kept and
the amounts owed.

"You collect. It's your family. I'm gay; you're not."

In the meantime, late summer storms have rolled in over
the fine mist. Thunder and lightning crackle both overhead

and in Dale's bunk. Between rounds of lovemaking, we climb the stairs to sit in the parking lot and recall the embarrassing moments at the visitation—widows of long-dead farmers confused as to why they were there, Betty's dementia asking where Roy was, complaining that all these people had come to see him and that he has disappeared.

The next band of rain sends us back to bed where Dale pulls me close and whispers in my ear, "Look at it this way, few victors get to bury their own nemeses," adding, "and have the grace to pay for the funeral."

"Very cute," I shoot back. "But I still want the money."

The next morning, Katie is in her enormous bug-eye glasses and ponytail slipped out in back of her floppy straw hat.

"Okay, Cap'n! The river is running downstream today. All the way to the Gulf. So if you're meaning to go upstream you'll want to get outta here and bear to port. That would be your left. Show me your left hand. Good. Now, keep her off my banks and breakwaters, mind my buoys, and I'll see you down the river!" she calls like an amusement park barker at the end of a long hot summer, and, with a bright orange tennis shoe, she kicks *Betty Jane*'s bow away from the dock. She walks down the pier to help Ron get the snack bar open for lunch and says, "Remember us to the guys at Rocky Point!"

"You'll love the oxbow region."

"Prettiest part of the river!"

Thank-yous pass from ship to shore until at last we hear, "And, don't FIGHT!" amidst a barrage of poorly muffled giggles.

CHAPTER TWENTY-THREE
Temporary Quarters

We cannot land at Owensboro, Kentucky, the latest comer in the trend of beautifying a city by developing its waterfront. Unlike Henderson, Owensboro is in the pile driver-bulldozer-hard hat stage. We push on to Mike's Marina, listed in Rockport on the Indiana side and a few miles upstream. We hail but get no answer. We call and leave a message. We arrive at the spot and find the shipwreck shown on the map. We see the Highway 231 bridge spanning the river; its cables draw a dark tracery on the water. The town must be on top of that cliff, but we do not see Mike's.

We would resolve to keep going and find anchorage on the river, except that the lone ski-boat tearing up the water had to have come from somewhere. Its captain sees us idling, plots an intercept course, and pulls alongside. His name is Luke. He works for the local water company. He points to the boat ramp at the bottom of the cliff and draws a line to where, floating on the water, there is a hut no bigger than a toll booth. A single tee-dock stretches one hundred feet in two directions. There is shore power and gasoline but no dock water. Stairs scale the cliff in one continuous flight. At the bottom, half-drowned concrete mermaids splash among suncatchers. At the top of forty steps, a chain drawn between the handrails provides the only security. Off-street parking is a gravel lot where a portable toilet and a fuel tank stand side-by-side.

Luke takes us into town, running by Mike's house to see if his truck's in the drive. It's not. He shows us the old Victorian house that some big city doctor has bought to renovate. Metropolitan Owensboro is creeping into this small used-to-be ferry crossing. He drops us at the grocery from which we can walk back, passing two- and three-story houses with wrap-around porches looking out on the river. Hanging baskets swing gently in the late afternoon breeze.

After a while, a man comes down the stairs. He is tall, muscular, with a Buddha belly. He wears his Hawaiian shirt untucked into khaki shorts, sandals, and pulls his thick brown hair back in a ponytail. Mike smells of shampoo and aftershave. He opens up the hut, pulls out a chair and joins our sitting on the dock after dinner. He is slow to talk, but a sliver of moon, its light shimmering on the water, loosens the man's tongue.

"The dock is about twenty-two years old," he says softly.

Dale and I turn and nod, but Mike relates more to the river than to us.

"Before that it belonged to Ike," he says.

Doris Faye gets up, walks around in a circle, and lies back down on top of Mike's sandals. He reaches down to pet her, then sits back in his chair.

"Ike lived in that house up there, downstream from where the stairs are now. He used to live there, and he'd have the dock."

Mike's talk, like everything else about Mike, is simple and forthright.

"Ike died."

Traffic goes over the U.S. 231 bridge. When we close our eyes, we hear the trucks especially.

"I bought the dock."

It is dark now. Mike gets up.

"Right up there where the picnic area and the recycle cans are, that used to be the landing for Miller's Ferry."

He checks to make sure the beacons on both ends of the dock are burning brightly.

"They used to drag ferryboats across the river between here and the other side. That road used to be the highway."

Moving headlights still sparkle between the trees.

"Eventually, they rerouted U.S. 231. They just finished that bridge a couple of years back."

The bridge is a Calatrava-esque suspension.

Before sitting down, he turns on the string of chili pepper lights that crisscross the ceiling of his hut. Small bags of chips and cookies, the refreshments noted in the guidebook, are clipped to clotheslines with clothespins. The two radios that were alive earlier today with our unanswered hails—"*Betty Jane* to Mike's Marina...*Betty Jane* to Mike's Marina... Come in Mike's Marina"—are turned off and wiped clean. Their curly cords hang undisturbed.

"When they built the bridge the first time, there was no need for a ferry, but Captain Miller kept the land. Now his daughter owns it. For twenty years, she let me use it for just mowing and keeping the place clean. Now, she asks me to pay insurance."

Towboats loaded with barges pass in both directions. Their wakes rock *Betty Jane* only slightly. The river is straighter, wider, deeper here.

"Used to sell about five thousand gallons of gas a season...but business has dropped off...bad."

Mike's is not a business. It is the sanctuary where Mike spends his evenings in the summertime.

"We have to haul the whole kit out of the water before winter. Everything is made to come apart and fold away. Me and some buddies, we come down in late October or early November depending on the river. We take this marina apart and float it onto trailers and haul it out on that boat ramp over there. The city parks department keeps that up. We stack it up on the shore out of the river's way. When she floods, she takes everything that is not out of the water with her."

He points toward the city boat ramp, invisible in the moonlight. Being nice, Dale and I say we can see it.

"Last year, we got a cold snap real early. It was getting time to haul out but the weather was turning bad. My wife, she usually makes a batch of chili and gets a lot of beer and everyone comes down and helps in order to have some of her chili...and beer. Last year, we hauled out late, after my buddies went hunting."

We look out at the river.

"Folks don't want to work in cold water. My wife and I, we didn't have so much help. We ate a lot of chili last year. It's good chili, but...and beer keeps...Anyway, we just stack it all up there until the spring floods are over, then we haul it all back down, re-run the gas lines and the electrical, and start tying up boats."

Mike's departure is as unobtrusive as a monk from prayers. He lowers the glass panels on his hut, turns off the chili pepper lights, and stows his chair. I watch as his Hawaiian shirt climbs the steps and disappears into the darkness. He carefully clips the chain to its place. A car door slams, an engine starts. Second gear grinds in the gearbox as Mike's

truck passes slowly by the houses where the baskets of flowers swing on the porches.

"Good night," Mike calls to his river.

————————•————————

No less temporary than Mike's but with a more frenetic
atmosphere is Rocky Point, Indiana. Dale tunes the radio.
The ensuing jibber-jabber is as overwhelming as at John T.
Myers, but this traffic is all pleasure craft.

"Yeah, we're here down below the dam... *static*... catching some go... *static*..."

"...last time I saw 'em they were in the baby's mouth."

"I can't underst—," whines the first voice.

"What? ...—peat," comes back.

"...'bout five o'clock..." trails in and out.

We cannot possibly break in, but it does not matter. The
chamber is busy transferring small craft from above and
below the lock as families enjoy the last bit of fun out of
summer before the leaves turn. *Betty Jane* crowds in like an
overlarge schoolmarm among her pupils. The doors open at
the top, and *Betty Jane* waits until the lock empties of small
craft before entering the fray.

Rocky Point is the confluence of Deer Creek and the
Ohio River. Boats tie up to docks that are little more than
rafts on both sides of the bridge that vaults the creek. Indiana
66 runs in front of gas pumps in front of the gift shop-*cum*-
camp store where the main road turns inland and its spur,
Spur 166, runs parallel to the shore.

Travel trailers uniform in size and color park cheek-by-
jowl with only a utility pole and electrical drop to separate
one from the other. The ersatz Maginot Wall in white steel

separates vehicular traffic from teams of children playing, kicking, jumping, running, and swinging on the lawn. All of which is presided over by grandmas and grandpas, sitting in lawn chairs in the shade of their trailers, to whom all maleficences are reported and from whom all restitutions are prescribed.

We look for a place to land. A tangle of ice-beaten, flood-driven steel trusses loom out of the water like a monster, but we see no dock.

"Rocky Point. Rocky Point. This is *Betty Jane*. Over."

"I cannot understand you," the voice complains. "What? *What?*"

"Let go of the button...Let go of the button...Darn it wom..."

"Cannelton Lock. Cannelton L—"

"What?"

Dale tries again: "Rocky Point. Rocky Point...Oh, forget it. I cannot get through this."

I suggest we telephone.

"Called this morning. No answer."

"Did you leave a message?"

"Yeah," Dale answers before picking up the mike again.

"Rocky Point. Rocky Point. This is *Betty Jane*. Over."

"*Betty Jane. Betty Jane.* This is Rocky Point. Come in, *Betty Jane*," pushes through the confusion on the radio. We cannot get an answer through the interference.

The caller tries again.

"*Betty Jane. Betty Jane.* This is Rocky Point. Come in, *Betty Jane*."

"*Betty Jane* to Rocky Point."

"Has anyone answered your hails?"

"Not until you."

"All right," says a woman's voice, which sounds inconvenienced but not distressed.

"All right, *Betty Jane*...Are you there? *Betty Jane?*... Come in, *Betty Jane*..."

"*Betty Jane* to Rocky Point. Go ahead, Rocky Point."

"I'm sending—*static*—get you."

"Repeat, *Rocky Point.*"

"....Jim...you."

"Garbled, Rocky Point."

"*Betty Jane, Betty Jane*...is coming...you...Over."

A lime green golf cart with bright orange wheels and matching top emerges from the shadow of a lean-to, first in fits and starts, then by lurches and finally in a full bore down the incline, scattering the children and pulling up sharply just short of a splash.

"Jim," I say.

"Jim," Dale agrees, while replacing the microphone to its cradle.

———•———

Jim is in his late sixties, slight and spry enough to jump out of the cart, leap over a trace of water, and land onto a hastily built raft.

"Really?" I call across the water.

"Sure," Jim insists.

It is a dock of sorts, pressure-treated pine plank nailed to Styrofoam flotation, longer and wider than the ones that separate the runabouts on Deer Creek. A single spud pole sticks one corner to the riverbed, leaving the balance to drift in the current. It is less than Mike's but serves the purpose of landing *Betty Jane*.

Jim ties us up and says, "You're here, Cap'n. Welcome. My name's Jim...That used to be my gas dock," pointing to the steel wreckage. "The river took it last winter. This here,"—he jumps on the raft—"this here is just temporary. Not built real good, but I don't care; I don't own it."

Instead of rebuilding, Jim and his wife, Gail—"She's the one on the radio"—decided to sell to the man who runs the small engine repair shop on the other side of Deer Creek.

"Tried to get her move to Florida, but she won't...won't leave the grandkids. Anyway, I'm off to town. Need anything?"

I ask for a melon.

"A case of straight forty-weight motor oil," Dale adds.

"See what I can do."

Meanwhile, the grandpas who had been napping in the chairs, took notice of our pending arrival when we were out in the river. They know exactly what has landed and while Jim was making welcome, they pulled themselves to their feet and staggered, two and three abreast, like the crippled to Lourdes. They ford the gap of water that Jim so easily jumped across. The raft tilts and rocks, forcing them to shuffle bent-kneed in order to grab on to *Betty Jane*'s gunwales. They don't say anything at first, but their eyes sparkle and their dentures shine. *Betty Jane* conjures up memories they thought were long forgotten. Dale and I are invisible while they pat her decks and caress her stanchions.

"Nice rig," says one of them.

"Thanks," I reply.

"Yours?" another asks skeptically.

We are dressed more like hired ferrymen than yacht owners.

"Yes," Dale answers.

"Lot of work."

Dale: "Yes."

"You do it?"

Dale: "Both did."

"Partners?"

Dale: "Yes."

Having covered the preliminaries in monosyllabic brev-
ity, which Dale later explains is conversation to a Midwest-
erner, they begin to talk all at once.

"My uncle

"Father

"Brother

"Cousin

"In-laws had a boat like this…"

More yarns than a knit shop and too many to count.

"We used to take her out all the time, and…"

———————— • ————————

The longer the story goes on, the more corrections are
interjected. These men have known each other all their lives.
Each remembers a detail slightly differently than the other.
They are more than acquaintances; they are related. Some
more closely, some more distantly, a chromosome or two
may have strayed in from the outside. They don't all look
exactly alike, but everyone at Rocky Point shares a lift of the
brow or a curve of the nose except the little brown-skinned
girl with the straight black hair; she is obviously, never mind,
but suffice it to say, the resemblance is there.

Eventually the truth wins out. The boats they remembered weren't like *Betty Jane* at all.

"She wasn't quite this long

"High

"Beautiful."

"She wasn't a

"Cruiser

"Chris-Craft."

"It was in

"Michigan

"Florida.

"…and besides, no one in your family ever owned a boat like this; it was your father's boss's

"Wife's brother's

"boat."

But they could agree that

"It

"She

"They

 did

"sink."

They turn and wade through the water holding on to each other for support, and go—much like Barney, Morgan, and Owen at Applegate—to women who are waiting for a report and arrive after they have laid their families' supper on the counter. Dale and Doris Faye are ashore on some made up errand involving the staff and ice cream.

"Helloooo," says the head of the herd as she teeters on the raft. "Yoo-hooo!"

They've changed out of their housecoats into "something presentable," applied a spot of blush and a dash of lipstick.

"Hey," I call out loudly enough to be heard from the bilge where I am clearing pump screens and swabbing out an oil leak.

"Hellooo," repeats the spokeswoman. "Got time to visit?"

"Sure."

I unfold myself and climb up to the gunwales where a pie is laid into my greasy hands.

Each gather around with daughters and granddaughters and excuse their interruption by saying, "Our husbands said we ought to come look at your boat."

"How many can sleep on board?" they ask. "Who does the cooking?"

I complain about a micro-fridge and two-burner hot plate.

They try not to peek in the windows. They try to engage me in conversation, but what do they know to say to a man smeared with muck other than, "Get washed up. Dinner's about ready." Their leader breaks the awkward silence.

"What do you do?" she asks.

"Retired."

"From what?"

"Real estate."

"Oh?" with an approving nod passed all around.

"Married?"

"No."

"Been married?"

"Never."

"So…you probably don't have children."

"No."

The announcement of water to the damned would not be better received.

"What about your friend?"

"Never."

If I were to broadcast the exact nature of my relationship with Dale, inclusive of who likes to do what to whom between the sheets, I doubt it would make any difference. "Boys will be boys" excuses a lot. We are unencumbered able-bodied men on the face of it, which is all they want to know. They waddle to the edge of the raft, jump onto the bank like ducks where they meet Dale and Doris Faye's return.

"When are you leaving?" their leader asks abruptly.

"Day after tomorrow," answers Dale, startled by the question.

"Good."

Each disappears into her trailer, closes the door—*slam. slam. slam. slam. slam*—and hatches a plan.

"What was that all about?" Dale asks.

"All I will say is, 'You'll see'."

The next day, our habit of napping and reading in the warmth of the afternoon is interrupted by a female assembly.

"Don't bother. Don't bother," the elder of the group insists, waving off our attempts to pull on a shirt and snap shoulder straps onto an overall bib. "We just wanted to get another look at your fine boat."

Dale and I climb out of the deckhouse.

"This is my granddaughter," begins the introduction of a circle of unmarried women.

They are lovely women, all. They have been washed, pressed, and curled in order to be foisted off on a couple of fags on the river's edge of Indiana. It would be flattering if it weren't so embarrassing for them *and* us. I know a million permutations of "What a pretty dress." They know to say, "Pleased to meet you." Doris Faye keeps things polite while I look across the river and concoct a fantasy for myself until this awkwardness passes.

Across a river of blue, the barn and the silo are red in fields of green; the farmhouse is white. Its shutters are black. Picking corn looks really attractive at the moment. I can imagine myself cleaning the barn, working up a sweat, and dousing myself with cool well water or taking a dip in the river. There must be cows on a farm like that. They need milking. Afterwards, I'll change the spark harness on the old tractor, whitewash the garden fence, and pick fresh tomatoes for tonight's supper. I'm sure the bailer needs oiling and the dog need worming...

"Oh? Really?" I hear myself say, "No, we really don't have much shade to sit in, do we, out here on the water... Well, that's too bad...Thanks for coming by. 'Bye. And thanks for the pie. It was real good. 'Bye."

Introductions have been made, they have nothing left to do but let nature take its course. We are invited to coffee "at any time."

I return to my bunk as Dale sees the last woman across the water. When he comes into the stateroom, I ask, "Are we married?"

"Not yet."

We pull away from the make-shift dock early the next morning. Gail's store, Jim's restaurant, the line of camp trailers, and monosyllabic conversations are familiar comfort to Dale, who remembers similar camps in Wisconsin. The respite I felt at Mike's, he feels here.

But Rocky Point, like Mike's, will be gone in a few weeks. The camp trailers will be hauled away and stored. The docks will be pulled out and stacked on high ground. Jim's kitchen will be cold. The gas pumps will be locked. Gail's store, boarded up. The only thing in operation will be the small engine repair shop, advertising snowblower tune-ups and personal watercraft winterizations. The line of power poles along Spur 166 will stand like a giant fence whose pickets have blown down. The wreckage of the gas dock will again suffer the brunt of winter on the wild and angry Ohio River.

CHAPTER TWENTY-FOUR
The "Most Beautiful Part of the Ohio"

Between Rocky Point and Leavenworth, Indiana, the river folds itself around curves named Switchback Bend, Horseshoe Bend, and Backwards Bend. High bluffs guide the sun down into slot canyons where radio is useless and access to the water is impossible by road. These forty miles, "the most beautiful part of the Ohio," are primitive and remote.

Home is what can be brought in by boat. Tarps shade a propane stove, a cistern, and beds made out of old quilts over plastic crates. Ladders, leaned against the bank and half-buried by sand, reach down to the beach below. The campers are men and boys. The figure—wearing a skirt, stirring the pot, and with a child on its hip—is more likely a guy in a dress than a woman with a pipe. It's *Lord of the Flies* for all ages.

Betty Jane's engines announce our intrusion. The adults look up from their fishing, the teenagers stop fussing with their boats, and the youngsters grin. No one is menacing or unfriendly. They just don't know what to think about a motor yacht passing through. More typical is the craft coming towards us.

The deck's a slab of board fence tied to a couple of canoes. Stacked around the edges are ice chests wrapped in blankets, hand tools, rifles, rods, reels, tool and tackle boxes of all descriptions. Their ladder hangs just over the water. One man suckles a peach at the front while the other crouches by the motor at the back. Their dog barks, causing them to stand. We exchange hails.

"Hey."

"Hey."

They come alongside.

I marvel at how magnificent they look—red-headed, tall, and fit. Their sun-kissed bodies remind me of June 1979.

My friends and I had just finished high school careers of being tops in our class, national merit scholars, and advanced placement candidates. We were bound for snotty east coast liberal arts colleges where we would learn to lead overachieving lives. I remember being overwhelmed by congratulation and advice: "Plastics," Mr. Robinson said to Ben Braddock in *The Graduate*. We escaped to the ranch and we went to the river, the South San Gabriel River.

Driving our Jeeps from the trailer, barely more than a bunkhouse that my Pap had installed on the opposite side of the lake from my great-uncle Eddie's ranch house, we slipped through the gate that kept the livestock away from the water. We lit out across the limestone riverbed. We ate out of coolers and army-surplus ammo boxes which bounced around our feet; we lolled under leafy sycamore trees; we explored what felt good to male bodies.

Some of it we liked instantly, other parts would take practice, and still some of it a few thought was "just plain *gross.*" We were smart, uninhibited, and the prides of our families until we got back to Dallas where Pap was waiting with an interrogation ready. I evaded his questions.

His invective ran its usual course—"How could you be so careless?" "What were you thinking?" "What if someone had gotten hurt?"—*Hurt?*—except its practiced and measured delivery, this time, was shrill and erratic; the outrage more explosive; and the pounding—I'd never seen grandmother's Spode jump quite so high off the table before.

My offer to make reparations was refused; instead, I was forbidden from operating any motor vehicle anywhere on the ranch—a stiff sentence and peculiar because it applied also to my brother, five years older, the golden boy, and not party to the incident in question. But the punishment was not for the petty mischief boys-not-quite-men do. The real punishment was for that which was unspeakable, therefore unsaid. Our behavior on the river had been seen by my Uncle Eddie--a man who never married, lived alone on fifteen hundred acres, and hung out with his boyhood chums.

It did not matter.

Six months later, Eddie was found in his bedroom—facedown, naked, and dead. Hours after his burial, my Aunt Ann had the deed to all he owned tucked securely in her purse. I never saw the South San Gabriel River again.

The two men on the Ohio are naked as well. Freckles everywhere and tufts of bright orange hair in the usual places. They invite us to go with them.

"Sure. It'll be awright. C'mon," says one.

"We know a place," says the other.

"Sum'un'll bring us beer."

The disparity is too acute. They are twenty-year-olds on a floating campsite; we are middle-aged men in a classic motor yacht. We cannot accept. Instead, we explain that, in these blind switchbacks, *Betty Jane* would be run over by any oncoming barge. We'll anchor in the straight-away above Leavenworth.

We watch them float away.

Louisville, Kentucky, is a city with municipal docks located below the Great Lawn, part of a lush green space called Waterfront Park. Bridges fly across the river to the Indiana shore. Buildings—higher than anything we've seen since Nashville—reach for the Kentucky sky. We need groceries and a case of forty-weight motor oil, so decide to walk to the NAPA auto parts store on the other side of downtown and do the rest of our shopping somewhere on the way back.

We stumble onto the Actor's Theatre and buy tickets to *Lookingglass Alice,* our first live show since the Grand Ole Opry, eat lunch at the first Panera we have ever found near the river, and stroll down Fourth Street Live—an entertainment district where not much happens until after dark. Return takes us by gay bars and tattoo parlors, Jewish Hospital, and the Louisville Slugger Stadium, home of minor league baseball's Louisville Bats. The evening is dinner and the show.

The next morning, Waterfront Park and the Great Lawn are a frenzy of preparation. Local public radio station WFPK hosts its Waterfront Wednesday which tonight will feature music artists Cracker, Will Hoge, and Great Lake Swimmers. By lunchtime, cables are strung. By afternoon, lights and sound jacks are patched in and "Test, Test" comes booming across the river. Shortly before dusk, grandparents stake out territory for their young families, followed by the urban pioneers and the hip-and-cool who straggle in halfway through the first set.

Attendees look over the rail during the performance and see *Betty Jane* among the other boats. Her green vinyl top, stained mahogany decks, and planked hull stand out from the assemblage of white plastic vessels strung nose-to-stern along the docks. Between sets, they come down to make inquiries. And after the concert, they bring their families and friends to gather around and ask about our travels. It is the only celebration of the journey we will have.

The next morning, we are awakened by the police.

"Prepare to be boarded," a voice blares though a bull horn. "Prepared to be boarded."

Dale sets the coffee measure on the counter with a clink and looks out the deckhouse window.

"We've got company," he says, on his way to collect *Betty Jane's* documents. "You better get up. You may want to pull on some overalls, too. They're men, but I doubt they'll be interested."

"What's up?" I ask vaguely.

"It's the cops. We're busted."

A patrol boat lands across from *Betty Jane*. It is one of those aluminum jobs built to be off-putting, with three super-powered turbocharged outboards and a light bar that can blink and flash a message to alien species. An intimidating crew of six, straight out of Central Casting, Louisville's finest—trussed, snapped, and kitted up with PFDs over Kevlar—stand on her decks; their hands rest on their holsters. The leader looks like Tommy Lee Jones in *U.S. Marshals*. I scramble out of bed and report to the dock where Dale and Doris Faye are already waiting.

"This your boat?" asks the ranking officer in front of his company.

"Yessir," we answer nervously.

He shuffles through our papers, walks to the stern to see that the name, number, and hailing port are in order, ambles forward to inspect her bow, and hands back our documents, raising the black Ray-Bans to betray the ruse of his stern demeanor.

"Well, she's a mighty fine one. She sure the hell is," he says, after introducing himself as Ed.

"That's not the name on your badge," is the first thing I say.

He points to his name badge and says, "I know that it says Lockhead, but you can call me Ed."

He rattles off, "Buzz...Alvin...Steve...," the names of his men.

"So, what's the problem," I ask.

"No problem," Ed admits. "We just wanted to see your boat. Alvin here hasn't stopped talking about it since he got to the precinct this morning. He saw y'all last night. We've just been waiting out in the water for one of you to get up. Saw you moving through the cabins."

The boys in blue fan out to take in their own interests. Some are familiar with woodworking: "My daddy's got a shop in the basement." Others want to know about power, speed, and range.

"Dallas, Texas, huh?" Ed asks. "What're you doing way up here."

Doris Faye and I leave Dale to it, and when we return, they've all got tiny styrofoam cups of *Betty Jane* coffee in the hands. Ed is holding court.

"—yeah, we're here to keep the swimmers safe. Iron Man starts tomorrow and the swimmers want to get some training in. They've closed the river to barge traffic but not all the pleasure boaters get the message. Some forget. We remind them. Anyway, we're on patrol and thought we'd drop in.

"Well, it was nice to meet you. Nice to see your boat," Ed says, the signal to his men to return to their vessel. Each does his manners to us and tightens his vest.

But as they turn, I ask plaintively, "You're not going to board?"

Ed stops.

"I mean, you said, 'Prepare to be boarded.' And now you're not going to get on? Don't you suspect us of contraband or conspiracy or something? Isn't something in our documents out of order? Shouldn't you at least check or radio in or something? How am I going to tell our friends back home that we were peaceably minding our own business of a Thursday morning when suddenly the Fuzz was all over us, flashing lights and brandishing *pistolas*, and y'all just walk away?"

Ed considers.

"You heard 'im, fellas. Don't come out 'til you find something."

"Deep step," Dale warns. "Deep step just inside."

The men tiptoe around the deckhouse while Ed detains us on the dock.

"What are your names?" he asks in his officer-of-the-law fashion. "Where are you from?" His deadpan does not falter. "Where are you going? What's your business here? How long are you staying?"

He takes make-believe notes with the pencil and pad he has taken from his pocket.

"Don't forget to lift the hatches," Dale calls into the deckhouse. "The engines are under there."

"No, no, now, don't pay them any attention. They know their jobs, you just keep your eyes on me," Ed says.

Behind our backs, we hear lockers open and close, drawers slide gingerly out and back. The officers comment to each other about what they see and take turns standing at the wheel and pretending that they are cruising down the river.

"You build this?" Alvin asks about *Pramela*.

"Never mind that," Ed says sternly. "What d'you find?"

"Nothing, sir."

"Too bad," Ed acts disappointed. "I'd sure love to impound me a boat like this someday. Sure would. Umph."

They jump aboard their vessel and call, "Safe trip," over throbbing outboards before cutting a trench across the river.

Dale and I prepare to leave in a couple of hours. There is no hurry. In fact, as I am about to cast the last line and push us off into the mainstream, I catch Dale on the bridge, staring at the skyline. I know what he is thinking because I've thought it, too. *Louisville's a nice town.*

"Not in a northern state," I call up from the dock to disturb his daydream.

"What?"

"It's not in a northern state. Cincinnati's in a northern state. Let's go."

CHAPTER TWENTY-FIVE
The Home Stretch

We stop in Madison, Indiana, for a few days to get groceries and haircuts. Madison is America's Main Street, the model small-town for 1950s television. It is our glimpse of what life will be like in the Midwest. We do as we have done since Ozark.

"Well...," the woman says, regaining her composure. She is not used to being approached by people she does not know. She is flustered. "Well," she says again, primping her hair nervously, "Let's see, the grocery is over there, a bite of lunch is around the corner, and the barber shop is across the street." She waits, obviously hoping that we have no more questions, then says, "They'll be glad to help you with anything else you might need," and briskly beats a retreat. She was not kind, hospitable, or generous, as most everyone else we had met on the river had been.

At once I understand why: river charts show detail only close to the river. Somewhere beyond the shoreline there is an invisible but very real line. Beyond that lies the America of us versus them—the reds against the blues, the rights and the wrongs, the ins and the outs, the true patriots, the true believers, the true Americans. It is called the real world. Applegate Cove and the people we met there shepherded our departure from it. My heart breaks knowing that there will be no one to gently bring us back. Re-entry, alone, will be turbulent, fast, and hard.

The barber shop is the single barber's chair facing a line of chrome and vinyl seats layout where men talk about local politics and the kids nowadays. It smells of hair tonic and aftershave with a lingering hint of tobacco from long ago.

"Yeah, this is a nice town," the barber says. "Now, o-cca-sionally, we get some city people in here. Folks what drive down from Indian-a-polis or up from Lou-ee-ville. Don't get many from Cincinnatah, do we, Bill?"

"No, not too many from Cincinnatah."

"They come down on a Sunday drive. Eat in the restaurant, buy their kids something at the soda fountain. They stroll up and down Main Street and they think to themselves, 'This is a nice town.' They think they might want to move to this town, raise their kids here and all. Some of them do, don't they, Bill."

"Some of them do."

"They buy themselves a house, fix up all nice inside and paint the outside all pretty and bright. Keeps our contractors busy in these hard times, don't it, Bill?"

"It do. Mighty obligin'."

"Did you want me to do your eyebrows, too? They plant their gardens and ask for things we don't have. And all that's all right, isn't it, Bill?"

"All right by me."

"Once they get their houses like they want it and invited all their big-city friends down to see how nice it is to live in a small town, they get bored. They start looking around. They start getting ideas. Now I'm not saying that a new idea is a bad thing. It's just that some of us have lived here a long time and have a few ideas of our own."

"Uh-huh," Bill says.

"Ideas that make big-city boys drive down and look around and say, 'This is a nice town.' Then we townsfolks have to get together and remind them that it was our town long before it was their town and we like it just fine the way it is. Hard to do. Painful to watch. Some get disgusted. Others get mad promising that 'This one-horse town isn't ever going to be anything more than a one-horse town.' Still, others quietly move back to where they come from. They sell their fine pretty house and we wish 'em well. And that's fine, isn't it, Bill?"

"Fine by me."

"There, now you're done."

He proudly holds a hand mirror behind my head so I can see that a buzz cut in Indiana is almost identical to a buzz cut in Oklahoma.

———◆———

At Vevay—rhymes with TV—Indiana, we stop for lunch at the annual wine festival and meet boaters who insist that we berth with them at Craig's Creek. Craig's Creek—located immediately above the next lock, Markland, and convenient to the small town of Warsaw, Kentucky— is well off the river, the boathouses are new, and the slipholders speak highly of its management. We will be hard pressed to find any place more ideal, even though it is sixty miles downstream of Cincinnati. The next few days are a blur.

We scour the greater Indiana-Kentucky-Ohio area for a covered slip closer to the city but find none; we rent an apartment at The Belvedere, an old Cincinnati address where everyone we meet has lived or known someone who has; we drive to Mark and Rosemary who will keep Doris Faye in Murray, Kentucky, while we pack up and ready our condominium for sale. We fly to Dallas. Dale sees about his mother.

As we are about to leave in a van packed with most of our belongings, Sister calls. Betty has had a stroke; we will not know the full extent of her injuries for three days—time enough for us get to Cincinnati, unpack, and catch a flight back to Dallas. We drive to Murray.

I have not seen Doris Faye for a month and she does not look good. She does not run up to greet me, has never had a bowel accident before, and rarely refuses food. I am not concerned. Mark and Rosemary live on five acres in the country. She could have gotten into anything, but I mention it to the veterinary assistant when I drop her off for boarding. When I return, the assistant says, "You need to speak to the doctor."

I load my black and white spotted dog in the truck. Dale calls.

"I don't know. I don't know," I wail in the grocery store vestibule. Tears well up. "Something about...about...," I hang over the cart and bawl. "You'll have to call the vet. I really didn't listen. I...I..." I hang up.

Doris Faye is a more constant companion than Dale. She and I did everything together. We prospected properties, chased squirrels, fixed houses, played ball, welcomed new tenants, and bid old ones farewell. We ate together, slept together, bathed together. She dried my tears, licked my wounds, and listened to my tantrums. Impromptu kisses were her solution to everything. She was never consulted, never complained. For Doris Faye, sticking together was the only thing that mattered. Now, she is gravely ill.

She suffers from neurological and cardiac disease, consequences of age. Medication will treat the symptoms, but the dog I will have is not the dog I remember. She is not in any discomfort, nor is she going to get any better.

The doctor says, "Whenever you're ready."

Dale's mother is in the ground next to Roy at the end of September. Doris Faye is dead on Halloween. I watch the black serum go into her veins.

On my way back to the car, my heart jumps out of my chest, my knees buckle, and I collapse on the asphalt. My body writhes against the grief that threatens to suck me into the darkness. Dale's hands press against my back.

"You have to get up," he says.

"Fuck you. I just murdered my dog."

The hole in my chest expands. I cannot breathe. I drown in the teary landscape.

"You have to. You are in the middle of the parking lot and other people cannot get around you."

Night—bouts of convulsion separated by bouts of exhausted sleep separated by wails so piercing that Dale clamps a down feather over my head ostensibly to muffle the screams but equally wishing I'd suffocate and end the pain.

Morning—We are at the bus stop as the first city bus of the day rattles down Reading Road into town and lets us out at the Greyhound station. We arrive in Chicago in time for lunch at Lou Mitchell's and a leisurely flight to Boston-Logan Airport. We have tickets for the afternoon departure to Frankfurt with a connecting flight to Istanbul where we will board a repositioning cruise from Turkey to Miami, Florida. We booked this trip when we thought we would be one-year established in Cincinnati.

Hagia Sofia, the Blue Mosque, Jerusalem and the Holy Lands, Alexandria, Giza, Cairo, Malta, and Tunis are distracting enough. The unvarying constancy of life on board is comforting, a welcomed respite from the catch-as-catch-can we have lived for the last fifteen months. But on the morning between sighting the Queen at Bermuda and landing at Miami, I make the daily run to the top deck to fetch morning coffee and croissants. Then when I slide in bed next to Dale, the inescapable truth returns.

It starts as a twinge at first; then, a tiny convulsion which Dale dismisses as a hiccup or a cough I've tried to suppress; but soon, it blossoms into the soulful wail delivered forcefully between pillow and mattress. What could be the matter after such a glorious trip?

"Doris Faye," I answer between convulsions.

CHAPTER TWENTY-SIX
Cincinnati

B*etty Jane* is the priority when we get home. The marina operator called twice while we were gone—the first time to say we needed to winterize our boat and the second time to ask "When?"

December is late. The marina is abandoned, deserted of all life except the telltale blue glow of television flickering in the office. Dale and I unload our buckets, pails, and gallons of anti-freeze and board the boat. We close the portholes and hatches, take off our gloves, and go to work.

Starters spin slowly and the lights dim before engine discharge ricochets across the cove; warm, moist heat fills the cabins. We take off one layer of clothes. I go up to the bridge as Dale drips oil into the carburetor shouting, "OFF!" just before the engine chokes. He does the same thing to the second engine. It's called fogging. He takes the caps off both distributors and removes the rotors as a precaution; these engines won't start again until they are put back.

We stand side by side in the engine room as we have so many times before. Dale works at the back of one engine; I work on the front of the other. We unscrew the drain plugs, disconnect the hoses, and open all the pet cocks, remarking it would be more difficult except we did it only a year ago at

Applegate. That time we were looking for leaks and the source of steam coming out our exhaust. The mention of Applegate reminds us of the people we met all the length of the entire trip.

Kenn: "You're gonna want white."

Debbie: "But I am telling y'all menopause makes a pretty girl hot so if you don't mind."

Adventure's Dale: "You'd do that for me?"

The Pepper Lady at Golconda: "Did they ever find the head?"

Mike: "It's good chili, but…"

The two red-headed river men: "Sum'un'll bring us beer."

And Ed: "Prepare to be boarded."

When the water has drained out, we reattach the hoses and close the valves; refill the voids with antifreeze; snatch up our buckets, pails, and empty anti-freeze jugs. *Betty Jane* floats quietly in her slip where plenty of people will keep an eye on her until we come back. She's the marina mascot.

———◆———

The rest of December is an opportunity to investigate our new hometown. Cincinnati was a center of culture and commerce, steeped in German tradition, when Ohio was the Silicon Valley of its time. Today, the natives defend that heritage almost to a fault. But we flatlanders must first adjust to the topography. Cincinnati is built on seven hills, like ancient Rome, and is said to have a street plan, laid after a torrential rainstorm, which paved over where the water went.

Dale and I go everywhere together. One drives while the other navigates, saying, "Nope. Missed it. You'll have to make a U-turn," because among these gullies and ravines, "around the block" does not necessary put us back where we started. Less challenging is the local cuisine, a pleasant surprise after the privation we suffered on the river.

Chili—made of pork and served over spaghetti instead of my accustomed beef in a bowl—comes from the city's Mediterranean immigrants. Slaughtering pigs used to be the industry, predominate enough to earn the city its nickname, Porkopolis. Natives split their allegiances between two area franchises, Skyline Chili and Gold Star Chili. Graeter's, Aglamesis, and UDF keep residents supplied with ice cream. Servatii's and Busken's are the bakers. The local obsession is the tea cookie—a tiny butter biscuit topped with a dollop of colored icing or a sprinkle of nonpareils—which appear wherever two or more Cincinnatians are gathered. IPA breweries pop up all over. And at Christmas time, the Cincideutsch Christkindlmarkt sets up in the center of town to sell traditional gifts items, decorations, holiday treats, and gluhwein.

We do not go home for the holidays. All the deaths and burials over the last several months have given us too much opportunity for family togetherness. Instead, we celebrate Christmas at Christ Church Cathedral, a venerable Episcopal congregation graciously endowed by industry and community leaders from when Cincinnati was the cutting edge of innovation, technology, and politics. Lunch and a movie are across the river in Newport, Kentucky.

New Year's Eve finds us surrounded by *bürgermeisters* and their entourages in the front room of Jeff Ruby's iconic downtown steak house. Dale raises his glass as if to toast Auld Lang Syne but says, instead, "Helluva year, Watson, helluva year."

"*A* boat is a hole in the water you throw money into,"
is one of thousands of sayings that denies the truth
which every sailor respects: a boat is conduct into a hostile
environment. Water is a hostile environment. Seafarers are
so afraid of it that we make jokes about running aground,
catching fire, and blowing up; accidents happen. But that
danger is the bond that holds together otherwise free-spirited
individuals into one cohesive lot.

In between ports of call and chance encounters on the
water, Dale and I are alert to our surroundings. At first it
was nervous oversensitivity; then as the days strung together, it became more of a practice, then a habit, then a sort of
communion which we shared. On a boat in the middle of the
river is a great place to get to know someone. We knew each
other's moods, concerns, and blood sugar levels almost, from
tone of voice, facial expression, and even where each placed
the hat on his head. Hunger, fatigue, and dehydration were
concerns, particularly with Doris Faye who really did not
like the constant drone of the engines. She lay on the bridge;
her red tongue sending a trail of slobber to find its way into
the river. Until we shut Betty Jane down, for the moment or
the night, she ate nothing and drank little.

Fatigue was the culprit between Dale and me. Being underway seemed an idle endeavor, but we lost track of how
many times we scaled a ladder, shinnied down the side decks,
threw and retrieved a line, weighed anchor. Our eyes were
peeled and our ears sharpened to the first sign of trouble. It
became subconscious work but work nonetheless. Fortunate-

ly we had so much experience with near-crises in boatyards that we were practiced in calmly asking, "I dunno. What do you want to do?"

When we did land, I believe that we would have gotten the same reception should we have been dressed in ballgowns and tiaras with burly chest hair popping out of our bodices and sweat staining our white gloves. Betty Jane and Doris Faye were responsible for that. One was a testament to our skill and prowess as boaters. The other made us approachable—whatever else we were, we had a good-looking dog. We also had money to spend at a time when cash was scarce. Whatever it was, we were well received which was good; the river is a hostile place. Without the kindness and generosity of people completely unknown to us, we would not have gotten much beyond Lock Fifteen below Applegate Cove, Sallisaw, Oklahoma.

They were the simplest courtesies, too, extended almost without thinking. "Welcome" "How's your trip?" "Need anything?" made the end of some of the longest, hardest days bearable. A bottle of ice water anonymously pressed into our hot hands; fresh produce left on our decks; convivial conversations anyone can step into; no matter who he is; and that uncanny ability to remember our names as well as those of Betty Jane, Pramela, and Doris Faye. We were part of a very large family.

It was a trip, taken in the prime of our lives when we could truly enjoy the challenge, when we could afford to live nowhere in particular, and when we were prepared to toss off the familiar in exchange for the adventure. As a result, we got to see our country and our countrymen as they are rarely seen. The America we saw was not the angst, anger, and fear we see on broadcast and social media. It was the America *that explored the New World and settled the West; and gath-ered its great diversity into one united force whenever the homeland was threatened.*

It was the America from which we hope to never fully return.

GLOSSARY

AP—Arrival Point. A pair of dolphins—one above the lock, one below the lock—where barges can tie up and wait for lockage; demarcation points which define the lock zone.

aft—towards the stern.

amidships—the middle of the vessel.

anchorage—place suitable for securing vessel by the anchor.

astern—backwards.

anchor rode—the line that connects the anchor to the vessel; a chain, rope, or a combination thereof.

barge—in strict usage, the individual rafts which carry cargo, also called gondolas; commonly, the name given to the entire consist of gondolas including the tow.

beam—overall width of the vessel; a wide boat is said to be "beamy."

berth—slips for boats; beds for people.

bit—hardware to prevent the anchor rode from chafing the deck.

boathook—hook and prod mounted at the end of pole for retrieving lines and maneuvering the vessel.

bollard—a knob or ring suitable for tying off.

bow—front when facing in the direction of normal forward operation of the vessel; nose.

bow rail—raised molding on each side of bit to fend anchor rode from the deck.

breakwater—an obstacle placed in the water, usually behind the harbor mouth, to prevent wakes from entering the marina.

bridge—the area of the boat where is the helm.

bulkhead—partitions between cabins.

chart—map.

chamber—the part of a lock that fills and drains.

chine—edge where the side of the hull and the bottom of the hull meet; also the framing member that secures the side and bottom planks that form said edge.

cleat—hardware on deck or dock for tying off.

companion way—passage between cabins.

deckhouse—the cabin, a gathering place, also called salon and saloon.

dolphin—large pylon which provides moorage for barges awaiting lockage.

fender—bumper, cushion deployed to separate two vessels or vessel from dock to prevent and/or minimize damage to either.

finger—narrow deck or catwalk that defines the sides of a slip.

fore—front when facing in the direction of normal forward operation of the vessel.

gates—the doors on a lock that hold back the river.

gondolas—the vessels that hold cargo in a barge and pushed by a tow.

gunwales—side decks.

hard—dry land.

hatch—door or access panel.

head—the porcelain receptacle to receive human waste elimination, also the cabin in which said receptacle is found.

helm—the controls, the driver's seat.

hook—anchor.

jack stands—adjustable height jacks which stabilize the vessel when on dry land.

klaxon—siren posted on lock wall for signaling.

lifeline—tightly drawn cable to form a deck rail.

line—rope.

lock zone—the stretch of river above and below the lock itself, under federal jurisdiction, marked by AP.

lockage—passage through a lock.

lock down—passage from higher river pool to lower river pool.

lock up—passage from lower river pool to higher river pool.

moorage—place to secure vessel by tying onto a stationary object

mooring post—the post in the forward deck used for tying off.

NOAA—National Oceanic & Atmospheric Administration, providing updates on local water and weather conditions and forecasts.

PFD—Personal Flotation Device, "life vest."

port—left when facing in the direction of normal forward operation of the vessel.

port light—window.

pram—a small craft, dinghy, or tender distinctive in its wide beam and snubbed nose.

pushboat—the vessel that pushes barges, also called tows.

quarters—private cabin for crew.

raft-up—the lashing up of several gondolas or pleasure craft into a raft.

rip-rap—aggregate rubble used to control shoreline erosion.

salon/saloon—deckhouse.

scope—the length of rode paid out between anchor and the vessel at anchor.

slip—parking place for a boat.

slippage—slip.

stanchion—deck post for holding up lifeline.

starboard—right when facing in the direction of the normal forward operation of the vessel.

stateroom—private cabin for owners and guests.

stern—back when facing in the direction of the normal forward operation of the vessel.

swing—the arc a vessel can be moved by wind and current when at anchor, a function of scope as its radius.

toe rail—the raised molding that prevents slipping off gunwales, that which forms the gutter which drains water from the decks to the transom and overboard.

tow—island; the submerged continuations above and below and island; the boat which pushes the gondolas that make up a barge; to pull.

transom—the curved panel that comprises the stern.

MEET THE CREW

DALE HARRIS

The same skills that made Dale Harris the Director of Music, indispensable to several of Dallas's important Episcopal congregations, also made him able to build a real estate portfolio with little cash in hand. He haggled interest rates, collected delinquent rents, and argued with inspectors as Alexander prospected purchases and renovated acquisitions. The two were affectionately referred to as "value-investors." The dynamics of their relationship are a key ingredient in *River Queens*.

DORIS FAYE

Doris Faye was a rescue. She was a Christmas present to a child who adored the 101 Dalmatians puppy but had no use for the dog. Forty pounds, ten pounds underweight, with kennel cough, and recovering from spaying surgery; she adopted us. She was the envy of everyone we met in *River Queens*.

ALEXANDER WATSON

Alexander's grandparents are responsible for his writing ability. His grandfather was a pioneering air-conditioning engineer, taming the summer heat from the Sonora, across the Caribbean, to the Negev Desert and beyond. His Pap journaled obsessively. His Nan sent postcards and letters. But to get, he had to give. Alexander learned to write. Alexander still sends postcards, letters, and emails to friends whenever away from home.